Consulting for Real People

A client-centred approach for change agents and leaders

Second edition

Consulting for Real People

A client-centred approach for change agents and leaders

Second edition

Peter Cockman
Bill Evans
and
Peter Reynolds

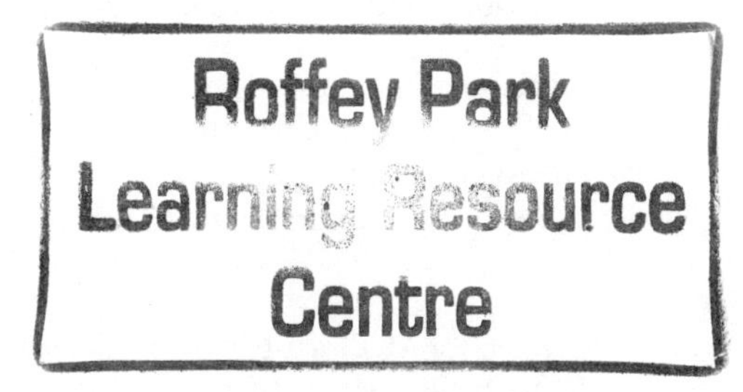

McGraw-Hill Publishing Company

London · Chicago · New York · St Louis · San Francisco · Auckland · Bogotá
Caracas · Lisbon · Madrid · Mexico · Milan · Montreal · New Delhi · Panama
Paris · San Juan · São Paulo · Singapore · Sydney · Tokyo · Toronto

Published by
McGRAW-HILL Publishing Company
Shoppenhangers Road, Maidenhead, Berkshire, SL6 2QL, England.
Telephone +44 (0) 1628 502500
Fax +44 (0) 1628 770224
Web address http://www.mcgraw-hill.co.uk

British Library Cataloguing in Publication Data
A catalogue record for this book is available from the British Library

ISBN 0-07-709334-8

Publisher: Alfred Waller
Development Editor: Elizabeth Robinson

Created for McGraw-Hill by the independent production company
Steven Gardiner Ltd TEL +44 (0)1223 364868 FAX +44 (0)1223 364875

McGraw-Hill

A Division of The ***McGraw-Hill*** *Companies*

4 5 BB 3 2 1

Printed and bound in Great Britain by Bell & Bain Ltd., Glasgow

Contents

About the Authors

Peter Cockman has been both an internal and external consultant specializing in the development of people and organizations for over 30 years. During this time he has been facilitating development and change initiatives to enable people to contribute to the effectiveness of their organizations in whichever way they wish. He has experience in industry, commerce, national and local government, education and the voluntary sector. He still believes that organizations could be more effective and better places in which to work if only their leaders and managers paid greater attention to the people issues in their desperate dash for efficiency and profit via the 'quick fix'.

Bill Evans founded Oxford Management Consultants in 1982, committed to the principles of client-centredness. This means helping organizations to become more effective while supporting, developing and empowering their people. He has considerable expertise in experiential approaches to training and is involved in helping other trainers to develop similar skills. In addition to undertaking organizational change and team development projects he has worked on the training and development of internal consultants and managers in Africa, India, the Middle East and the Far East as well as the UK. He has written training materials for sales people and sales managers which are used throughout the world.

Peter Reynolds has over 25 years' experience as both an internal and external consultant. During this time he has worked with many leading organizations in the industrial, commercial and financial sectors as well as local authorities and voluntary organizations. He now consults with one of the world's leading oil companies in the Middle East. He holds a Bachelor's degree from the Open University and an MBA from Bradford University Management School. He has had four books and many articles published on a variety of training and development topics. His particular specialism involves working with the human implications of organizational change.

The authors, together with other associates, have run public and in-house Client-centred Consulting Skills programmes for many years. Participants have come from a wide range of professional disciplines and client organizations;

manufacturing industry, IT, telecommunications, banking, education, national and local government and religious communities. The workshops travel well to other parts of the world and have been run in Ireland, Europe, Finland, America, Africa, India and the Far East.

If you would like more information on our approach or a meeting to discuss your particular problems please write to or telephone:

Oxford Management Consultants
29 Western Road
Henley on Thames
Oxon RG9 1JN

Tel & Fax 01491 579949

Preface

We are not alone in recognizing that the challenge of change is one facing every human endeavour, large or small, national or multi-national, private or public, and the challenge will not decrease in the new millennium. Neither are we the only ones who believe that organizations can be successful while providing a challenging, supportive and rewarding climate for their people as long as leaders grasp the challenge. You will see from the following quotes from eminent consultants and authors on both sides of the Atlantic, that such a view is becoming increasingly popular.

> There is a quiet revolution taking place in many organizations. The source of the revolution is the growing realization that tighter controls, greater pressure, more clearly defined jobs, and tighter supervision have, in the last fifty years, run their course in their ability to give us the productivity gains we require to compete effectively in the world marketplace. Attention is shifting to the need for employees to personally take responsibility for the success of our businesses if we hope to survive and prosper.
>
> Peter Block, **The Empowered Manager**, Jossey-Bass (1987)

> As we approach the end of the millennium, will life somehow quieten down? Will the business, social, political and economic environments become more or less turbulent? I think the answer will be 'more turbulent'. You probably feel likewise. Certainly we would want very long odds to bet on the answer being 'less'. More turbulence, more complexity, more change. More change in the rate of change. It's frightening. Organizations are the crucial interface between the micro and the macro. If we fail at an organizational level then we fail at every level. This is such an appalling prospect that we dare not even contemplate it. We must make organizations work.
>
> Michael Ward, **Why Your Corporate Culture Change Isn't Working . . . And What to Do About It**, Gower Publishing Ltd (1994)

> The responsibility for change, whether he likes it or not, rests with each and every individual to take action to confront the company politics that detract from the productivity of the organization. Whilst much has been said about instilling a 'Passion for Excellence' in organizations by creating a culture of shared values and goals in a safe climate, little has been said to mobilize passion and action on a

personal level. This is one of the main reasons why conventional culture change programmes have been so ineffective in the long term.

Beverley Stone, **Confronting Company Politics**, Macmillan Press Ltd (1997)

Credibility is at a premium these days. Leaders are being scrutinized as never before. Fifty years ago this was not the case. The public sector has grown more voracious and vociferous since the Depression. Attention to welfare, social services, health, education and environment has spawned a mass of advocacy groups, government regulations, organized consumers and unions to whom the media is ever more responsive. All are questioning and challenging authority, and powerful people must move with the caution of alley cats negotiating minefields.

Warren Bennis and Burt Nanus, **Leaders – The Strategies for Taking Charge**, Harper and Row (1985)

Most of us know and experience daily the limitation of command and control. Part of the reason we continue to operate this way is that we are unsure of the alternative. This is partly because we have never experienced it. The situation brings to mind Bertrand Russell's statement: 'The problem with Christianity is that it has never been tried.' The same goes for the alternative to patriarchy. We are even unsure what to call what we are seeking. Entrepreneurship, intrapreneurship, empowerment, partnership, employee involvement, total quality management, continuous improvement. All have in common the wish to minimize bureaucracy, cut costs, and better serve clients and customers . . . If the issue of real power, control, and choice are not addressed and renegotiated, then our efforts to change organizations become exercises in cosmetics.

Peter Block, **Stewardship**, Berrett-Koehler Publishers (1993)

Humanity has walked on the moon, has hurled a satellite 600 million miles into space to send back telephotos of Jupiter, has conquered disease and ignorance, and has raised a remarkable number of people to a standard of living that by medieval standards is truly regal. Individuals have produced brilliant works of art that inspire and instruct us. We have, it would seem, advanced to a degree that our ancestors could not even have imagined. But they probably could not have imagined our foolishness either – our profligate waste of the Earth's resources, our continuing devotion to war as a means of settling disputes, our investing billions in weapons we claim we won't use, our apparent inability to educate our young people and care humanely for the poor, the sick, and the elderly, our addiction to drugs, and perhaps most of all, our appalling ignorance of ourselves.

Warren Bennis, **Why Leaders Can't Lead**, Jossey-Bass (1989)

We often think of change and improvement coming from the outside in rather than from the inside out. Even if we recognize the need for change within, we usually think in terms of learning new skills, rather than showing more integrity to basic principles. But significant breakthroughs often represent internal breaks with traditional ways of thinking. I refer to these as paradigm shifts.

Stephen R. Covey, **Principle-centred Leadership**, Summit Books (1990)

> When managers begin to think about empowering their organization or department, they also begin to think about the nature of power itself, and how this relates to or differs from authority. They may start to wonder about the consequences for themselves of empowering others. Does empowering others mean giving up one's own power? Does it mean that managers no longer have authority over their staff? The most urgent concern which managers have related to power and authority is the fear that empowering others will weaken their own position and their ability to ensure that targets are met and standards maintained. Accustomed to rule-based systems they worry that if the rules are whittled away then efficiency will dwindle too.
>
> Aileen Mitchell Stewart, **Empowering People**, Pitman Publishing (1994)

> The field of consultation is in many respects unlimited, ranging as wide as there are knowledge to be used and problems to be solved. The varieties of consultation are so great that the person wishing to become competent faces a bewildering array of possibilities. Within each particular intervention, however, there are underlying uniformities. Once the uniformities are identified, it becomes possible to recognize that the field of consultation is premised on relatively few basic assumptions as to how a client can best be helped to solve a problem.
>
> Robert R. Blake and Jane Srygley Mouton, **Consultation, A Handbook for Individual and Organization Development**, 2nd Edition, Addison-Wesley (1983)

Others have also recognized that successful organizations will increasingly depend upon the skills of effective change agents, be they consultants, managers or leaders. We set out in this book to describe some practical, down-to-earth techniques which will help you to bring the high ideals and common sense ideas in the above quotations to life. Wherever you work, with whom ever you work or whenever you work to help as an agent of change, we believe passionately that to achieve real change you have to work in a client-centred way. Lasting change only happens when the people affected feel themselves to be involved and empowered participants in the decision-making process and are committed to the new order of things.

Peter Cockman Bill Evans Peter Reynolds
August 1998

Acknowledgements

This second edition owes much to the many highly successful and enlightened managers and consultants with whom we have worked to improve the competence of consulting departments. It may seem naive to suggest that we have learned as much from working with them as they have learned from us, but we believe it to be true for all consultants especially those who try to work in a client-centred way. The main impetus for this edition came from working with managers who demonstrated that by working collaboratively with their staff they achieved impressive results and massively reduced their stress levels at the same time.

So we would like to pay tribute to the people who have practised what they preach, turned themselves into very powerful consultative managers and consultants and along the way taught us a lot about what it means to be truly client-centred. Indeed some of them have been so successful that they have moved on to be powerful senior managers or consultants in other organizations.

Peter Brooks, Roy McAuley and Beth Carruthers at Bairdwear Ltd
Chris Hildyard and Iain Thomson at the Bank of England
Brian Fries and Bill Imeson at Chase Manhattan Bank
Nigel Lower at Eastern Electricity
Lynn Williams and Carole Grimwood at Hertfordshire County Council
John Springford and Perry Bayani at Johnson & Johnson (Asia Pacific)
Juliette Sibson and Sue Bament at McDonnell Information Systems
Karl Brown, Brenda Wroe and Tricia Hamilton at NatWest UK
Fiona Tordoff and Thera Tollner at the Rover Group
Bob Bateman at SmithKline Beecham

In addition we would like to offer our thanks to the many hundreds of consultants and managers we have helped to be more client-centred and who contributed to the examples of good practice which we have quoted in this book. The following organizations have adopted and adapted our ideas for their own particular circumstances and cultures:

Abbey National, Aer Lingus, Allied Irish Banks, Bank of Ireland, British Airways, British Council, British Gas, British Telecom, BUPA, Devonport Management Ltd, Prudential Assurance Company, Royal Mail, Thorn Europe, Tyneside TEC, Ulster Bank, Woolwich Building Society.

We would also like to acknowledge the tremendous help and support we have had from our associates, especially Gill Thomas and Geraldine Grindley, in the continuous development of the Client-centred programmes which have been and continue to be so successful in helping clients develop their knowledge, skills and attitudes to consulting.

Finally to Alfred Waller and Elizabeth Robinson of McGraw-Hill go our appreciation for their continued belief in the book and their patience throughout the painful process of revision and rewriting.

Peter Cockman Bill Evans Peter Reynolds

Introduction

The late 20th Century has seen hundreds, if not thousands, of quick-fix solutions to organizational problems. Few of them have made a real difference in the long term. Perhaps this is because most of them failed to take account of the complex nature of organizations which are a mixture of culture and history, goals and objectives, systems and procedures, tasks and technology and *real human beings*. Maybe it is this last factor that is the most important, yet often the most difficult to deal with. After all is said and done, any change initiative affecting any part of the organization will always affect the people in one way or another. It is these real people who must ultimately implement these changes, whatever they are.

When we wrote the first edition of this book we focused entirely on the needs of the internal consultant, the man or woman who is responsible for initiating and facilitating change or for helping their colleagues solve problems, and who does so without formal power or authority. Since then we have encountered many line managers and leaders who are themselves in the front line of progress and find that their formal authority is much more illusory than real. When writing this edition, therefore, we have set out to make it relevant to everyone involved in influencing or helping others and managing change.

More and more people need new skills to help them take a more dynamic role in managing or coping with change and filling the new roles being created. The people already in organizations need help to embrace and accept the new skills and styles. Effective organizations seem to be those that help people understand and positively and productively deal with change and learn new skills. This means that managers at all levels need to adopt a range of skills and styles which will enable them to coach and mentor their staff and facilitate change. They are now expected to use consultative and collaborative styles rather than prescription and telling people what to do. They are urged to relinquish some of their power and control, to empower their staff to take initiatives, to think for themselves and to make decisions which managers have hitherto reserved for themselves. They are being exhorted to use people's strengths and allow them to solve their own problems rather than solving them for them. They are being forced away from the knee-jerk reaction and the quick-fix with its emphasis on short-term gains, into taking a longer-term, more strategic view. It follows that the people in organizations who are hired to advise, counsel, persuade, influence or sell new ideas to these managers, must work in the same way. To do this they have to understand how an organization works and what effect its culture has on its ability or readiness to change. They must know why quick fixes don't work in the long term. In addition they need a set of styles and skills which will enable them to help their clients solve their own problems so that they stay solved.

So it would seem that managers and their consultants are all change agents in some way or another. The most successful seem to be those who work in a client-centred way; managers with their staff and consultants with their clients. This means always starting where the clients are and not where you think they are. It means remembering that nobody has to change – they always have a choice. They will only change willingly if they are committed to the change. Faced with the consequences of not changing they may decide to accept them and not change.

We believe that people who are genuinely client-centred work hard to empower their clients and support them right through the change process to the point where the new behaviour replaces the old. However, being client-centred doesn't necessarily mean giving the clients what they want. It may mean working quite hard to help the clients see what they want isn't what they need.

You may not be called in to deal with problems which focus on the development needs of the whole organization, but we believe it is possible for you to extend your influence far beyond the narrow limits of the task you are often called upon to improve. You can extend your boundaries by always looking to see how the problem is being managed in terms of the systems, procedures and processes, collecting data about technical and task aspects, and always looking at how people feel about the problem and everything surrounding it.

In the quest for continuing improvements, the problem-solving process has become particularly important. Going through the stages – gathering data; analysing the data; generating solutions; selecting the solution; planning for implementation; implementing and then continuing to improve – has become an essential part of continued organizational success.

Our aim is to offer you a holistic approach, encompassing all aspects of change management. This is best described by use of the holistic model of change agent development described in detail in Chapter 17.

Developing client-centred consulting or leadership skills is rather like building a multi-layered pyramid supported by three pillars. We assume that you already have a significant level of skill and expertise firmly rooted in your own professional or technical discipline (see Pillar 1). We hope this book will help you with every other layer of the pyramid and Pillar 2 (Management and Organizational Support) and Pillar 3 (Self Awareness etc.):

- Facilitating Organizational Change, *Chapter 3*
- Using a Range of Intervention Styles, *Chapters 4–7*
- The Consulting Cycle, *Chapters 8–14*
- Personal and Interpersonal Skills, *Chapter 15*
- Self Awareness, Self-Esteem, Clear Values and Attitudes, *Chapter 16*
- Management and Organizational Support, *Chapter 17.*

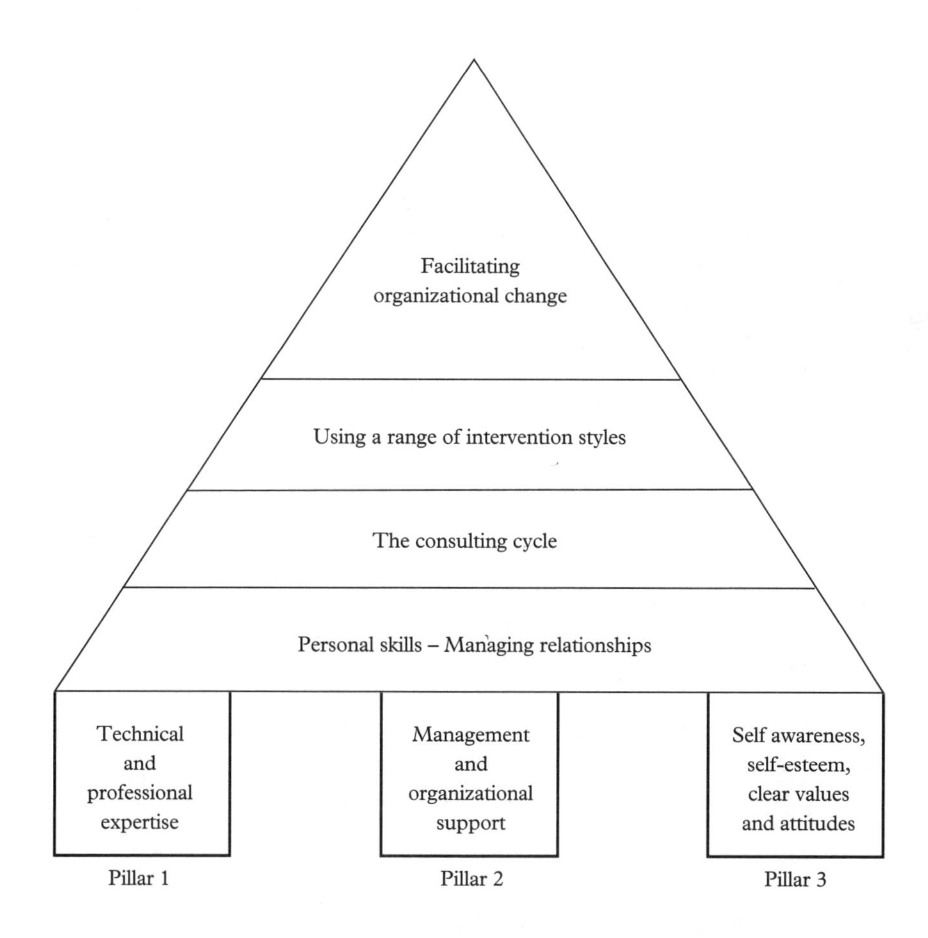

Figure i.1 A holistic model of change agent development

We have divided the book into four sections, each section examining specific aspects of this holistic model. Section I serves as an overview for the rest of the book. It aims to give a context for the intervention styles and the consulting cycle outlined in Sections II and III, as well as looking at the dynamics of organizational change. To be a successful change agent you need a wide range of skills. Being client-centred, however, means going beyond skills. You also need a high level of self-esteem, an acute awareness of the image you present to others, and a deep understanding of your values and attitudes. Being client-centred is about being different, not just about doing things differently and this is a theme we expand in Section IV.

We have tried to produce a 'how to do it' book on the assumption that most managers and consultants develop their skills by trying them out in practice. We hope our readers will use this book as a guide and try out the ideas with their own clients rather than as a book of instructions.

Throughout the book we refer to facilitators of change as consultants, change agents, managers or leaders. These are generally interchangeable but we decided to use all four terms as appropriate in order to include rather than exclude anyone responsible for change within organizations. We hope it does more to clarify than to confuse.

We hope that our contribution will appeal to experienced practitioners as well as to those who are just starting. We have had great fun writing it and it has helped us to clarify our thoughts and integrate many of the ideas we have collected and developed over the years. We hope you will get as much from reading it as we have from writing it.

Section I

Going Beyond the Quick Fix – How to Really Change the Organization

Introduction to Section I

Successful change agents, consultants, leaders and managers are all in the business of solving organizational problems so that they stay solved. This means that the people factor is crucial. No solution will work if the people involved are not committed to making it work. Facilitating change then, is largely a matter of managing relationships – not only managing your own relationships with your clients but also helping them to manage their relationships with each other, more effectively. Getting people to work together effectively is still a significant challenge – perhaps a growing challenge as organizations themselves expand and become more and more impersonal.

Chapter 1 provides a broad look at the role of the internal consultant who takes on the difficult task of facilitating organizational change without any formal authority. We look at the consultant–client relationship, how to manage it and what it means to work in a way that is truly client-centred. It introduces you to the models, issues and dilemmas which will be dealt with more fully in later chapters.

Chapter 2 introduces the book to the client-centred leader – the line manager who sees change as potentially a positive force and wants to manage it in a way that empowers people, involves them in the change process and leaves them with a high degree of ownership and commitment to making the new system work. If you are a manager it will show you why you too need skills akin to those of the client-centred consultant, how mastery of the range of intervention styles outlined in Section II will help, and how you can use the consulting cycle outlined in Section III as a change management process.

Chapter 3 takes you beyond the quick-fix and describes all the factors which need to be taken into account whenever you engage in any organizational change initiative. As a change agent you are intervening in a complex web of inter-related systems. At first sight introducing a new training and development strategy, performance related pay, updating an IT security system, modifying a financial control system or introducing continuous improvement might all appear to have clear boundaries around them. In reality all of these interventions are likely to have wider implications and repercussions for the whole organization. If you are working as an agent of change, with or without formal power and authority, you need to understand what is likely to happen in the wider organization whenever you try to change something.

Consultants, Clients and the Consulting Process

1

What is Consulting?

If you are reading this book you are likely to be someone who has been hired to facilitate change in an organization. You could be a consultant, adviser or member of a staff department, a project manager employed to see a particular project through to a successful conclusion or a line manager with responsibility for the day-to-day running of the business.

In some way or another you will be an agent of change. It will be at least part of your job to advise, persuade, influence or help people to do things differently. You could be helping them adapt to changes in technology, in organizational structure or market conditions. You could be helping them to work in entirely new ways that require new attitudes or new skills. If you are successful, people will not just behave differently they could well be different. Helping to make these sorts of changes to individuals or organizations is difficult even when you have the power to say what changes are to be made as well as the power to punish non-compliance. If you have limited formal authority or perhaps none at all then life can be extremely stressful and frustrating. If you have the formal power and authority but do not wish to resort to using it, life can be almost as difficult.

The purpose of this book is to help you explore ideas that will help you become more personally powerful in facilitating change by being more client-centred.

History has a way of dealing with people who exert tremendous political or military power over others. It cannot be denied that, in their day, Roman emperors, feudal kings, Indian maharajas and Russian tsars exerted such power. Napoleon, Hitler, Mussolini, Franco and Stalin all wielded such power and had a huge impact upon the lives of the people that they ruled. Their place in our collective memory is assured but their power and influence was eventually undermined and rejected, sometimes within their own lifetime. The recent collapse of communism and the rejection of ruling tyrants have proved the point about the corrupting influence of absolute power. It is perhaps open to discussion that Margaret Thatcher's reign might have been a good deal longer had she been less dictatorial and prescriptive with her cabinet. However, at the other end of the scale we have had people with a great deal of charisma and personal power whose influence has lasted well after their death. Socrates, Plato and Confucius still affect our lives by what they wrote. Jesus Christ and Mohammed have touched the lives of millions across countless generations by their teachings and ways of being. Within our own time we can think of people such as Mahatma Ghandi, Martin Luther King, Mother Theresa, Albert Schweitzer and Nelson Mandela who have influenced the world without exercising power over other people.

So from where do these great 'consultants', change agents of history, derive their power? Firstly it seems that they have the power to capture peoples' imagination so that others take their ideas on board and make them their own. They are all people-centred with a vision and a mission to empower others rather than control them. They are sensitive to the needs of others and are not afraid, on occasion, to confront those in authority. They have a passion for what they are doing. In addition, they have ultimately sufficient personal power to accept their own vulnerability and death. In short, they are truly client-centred.

The dictionary provides some fascinating meanings for the act of consultation. To consult is 'to ask advice of', 'to decide or act in favour of', 'to look up for information or advice', 'to consider jointly, to take counsel'. A consultation we are told is a 'meeting for conspiracy or intrigue'. Consulting is what you do to a physician or lawyer or anyone who is prepared to give professional advice to others in the same field.

For the purposes of this book we believe that consulting should be what happens when someone with a problem or difficulty seeks help to solve that problem or resolve that difficulty from someone who has special skill.

How is Consulting Different from Counselling?

From our point of view a counsellor is someone who specializes in working with a single client or maybe a couple to help them with personal difficulties which they are experiencing in their lives. Counsellors may be part of an organization set up specifically to do this kind of work – Samaritans or Relate – or they may be people at work who happen to be good at listening to others. There are also many commercial organizations which have taken this problem seriously and appointed counsellors to work on such problems either full or part time. Counselling – in the sense of helping people resolve problems in their personal life which affect or may affect their work – is often part of the job description of managers and supervisors. Where it is, they should receive special training to help them do it well.

For us counselling is a specialized form of consultancy which tends to be used with people who have personal problems which they find difficult or impossible to solve on their own. Consultants, especially client-centred consultants, sometimes find themselves in the role of counsellor during the course of their work in organizations. Indeed, we would argue that counselling skills should be part of the stock in trade of every effective client-centred consultant.

Who Needs Consulting Skills?

By definition, a consultant is someone who takes part in a consultation and can be the person seeking help or the person providing it. Common usage, however, has the consultant as the person providing help. Although there is still some reluctance among the helping professions generally to accept the title of consultant, more and more people in advisory roles are beginning to perceive that this is what they are.

In addition to the classical consulting areas such as medicine and law the field has expanded enormously to include:

accounting and audit
business process re-engineering
computing and information management
continuous improvement
corporate planning
industrial relations
occupational health
operational research
organization development
personnel services
process improvement
productivity services
quality control
research and development
health and safety
training and development
vocational guidance

This means that anyone who is in a role where the main emphasis is on helping individuals, departments or organizations to be more effective in whatever they do can be fairly considered to be a consultant. Line managers are finding that they have more than enough to do keeping abreast of their current jobs and they need the help of a large number of specialists with the knowledge and skill to work with them to solve problems so that their department can be more effective in meeting its objectives. Also, as a result of increasing specialization in many walks of life, people in many specialist jobs find themselves being consultants for some of their time. For example:

accounting
communications
design
development
inspection
marketing
new systems
programming
public relations
sales

Furthermore, changes in organizations are still taking place to reduce the number of managerial posts with the consequent difficulty or impossibility of close supervision. There is, hopefully, a realization that the exercise of control and authority over people at work, and the use of prescription as the only way of helping people be more effective is no longer a sensible option. Collaboration, involvement and the empowerment of people at work has to be the way forward if organizations as we know them today are to survive. Commitment to change has to be gained if it is to be sustained in the long term.

So, for our purposes, consultants are:

People who find themselves having to influence other people, or advise them about possible courses of action to improve the effectiveness of any aspect of their operations, without formal authority over them or choosing not to use what authority they have.

This can be described as a consultant/client relationship. It is present whether you find yourself helping people to be more effective, helping teams work better together or launching a major initiative to improve quality throughout an organization be it commercial, industrial or educational and in the private or public sector. Whether you are someone stopped in the workplace by a colleague saying 'Can I have a word with you?' or the Secretary General of the United Nations jetting across the world in an effort to avert global war – you are a consultant. Managers themselves are beginning to act as consultants to their staff whenever possible without giving up their ultimate responsibility and authority. They therefore need the same skills as the consultants who are hired to help them. In addition such consultants need to understand the new way of working and adopt a similar style when helping them.

From our point of view, if you are involved for even part of your time in providing help to someone else, in whatever manner you do it you need consulting skills. We will offer you an opportunity to consider these skills and assess the degree to which you have acquired them. Throughout this book whenever we refer to consultants we include managers who are intent upon working in similar ways with their staff whenever possible.

What is Client-centred Consulting?

Until comparatively recently the term 'consultant' conjured up the idea of enormous expertise and experience based on impressive academic qualifications. Most people aspiring to be consultants had to demonstrate their unusual competence for solving problems and their personal and career success. This gave rise to the idea that consultants were people who diagnosed your problem and gave you a prescription to follow which in their opinion would solve your problem. Nowadays, effective consultants still have expertise and experience in solving problems; however, it is impossible to identify a consultant's qualifications by looking merely at academic success.

While many consultants seem to be in the business of dispensing small amounts of professional advice for very large fees (and in the process ensuring dependency) that is not our view of a healthy relationship with a client. That is not to say that there aren't times when the client wants and needs professional advice to solve a problem. If a piece of machinery breaks down what most people want is an expert to fix it so that it stays fixed. But, and we believe it is a big but, for each one of those there are hundreds of situations and problems which the client could solve with a little judicious help from a client-centred consultant who is not interested in fostering dependency but wants the client to be able to solve similar problems in future without recourse to the consultant.

This book is about consultants who are client-centred. They are presumed to have sufficient expertise in their own technical discipline, accounting, social science, health and safety, training and development, systems analysis, learning methods or teaching. What they have in addition is an extra competence in the process of consultation. They are also likely to have:

- a high level of self-awareness;
- a thorough understanding of the ways in which clients are likely to behave as individuals and in groups;
- a wide range of professional and interpersonal skills;
- sufficient flexibility of style to deal with a variety of clients and situations;
- a real understanding of the helping process within the context of their professional discipline.

We believe that all consultants are more effective if they have a feeling of self-confidence which stems from adequate knowledge, skill and ability and consequently a positive self-image. We also believe that the majority of people called upon to be consultants are competent in the technical content of their own jobs and are usually familiar with the technical aspects of the jobs done by the people they are called upon to help. However, the effective use of that technical knowledge depends to a large extent upon the personal style of the consultant. The most effective consultants seem to be those who have worked on their personal styles to make them appropriate to the circumstances, particularly in the way they build relationships, identify problems and arrange implementation of solutions.

The ways of influencing and generally being sensitive and responsive to the needs and feelings of clients are at least as important and probably more important than technical expertise. It is our experience that when consultants and clients treat each other with mutual respect then the outcome is usually successful.

In summary, client-centred consulting is about:

- starting where the clients are, not where you think they are;
- helping clients decide what data or information to collect;
- allowing clients to diagnose their problem for themselves;
- helping clients make sense of the data rather than doing it yourself;
- providing theory to help clients make sense of the data or make decisions about courses of action;
- helping clients gain commitment to the plan of action;
- assisting clients to implement the decisions and arranging follow-up if appropriate;
- disengaging responsibly as soon as possible;
- ensuring that clients retain ownership of the problem and the solution and don't become dependent on you.

How Do I Stay Client-centred?

Consultation is an intervention designed to bring about change in an existing unsatisfactory set of circumstances to effect improvement. While many consultants take it upon themselves to decide what is right for the client and therefore get involved in influencing, persuading or directing the client into changed behaviour, the client-centred consultant does not operate this way. It is always possible for the client to terminate the consultation; the consultant, while having an opinion, leaves the client with the option to change or not. Thus the client-centred consultant is less likely to be manipulative in helping the client come to a decision about how to solve the problem. The client always has freedom of choice. This is not to say that the consultant shouldn't work very hard to ensure the client assesses the implications of not changing and considers the advantages and disadvantages of all the options for solving the problem. But the final decision about action or inaction should remain with the client. Particular circumstances in which the consultant might choose to impose a solution will be discussed in Section II on intervention styles.

Most behaviour, whether of an individual, members of a team or people in a larger organization or social system, follows standard patterns and is repetitive or cyclical in nature. In other words, behaviour repeats itself within specific situations and time-scales. Much of the time such standard patterns are useful: who would want people to experiment with driving on the opposite side of the road to everyone else just to see what it was like to change the cyclical nature of their behaviour pattern? But sometimes such behavioural patterns are not functional. What happens to the children who have been well schooled in how to cross the road in Britain when they go on a school trip to France? With any luck there will be feedback immediately they step off the kerb in the shape of screaming tyres and the gendarme's whistle. But this is not always the case with ineffective or cyclical behaviour in other circumstances, especially in organizations. Often ineffective behaviour patterns do not get challenged by the people working in the department or company. How many times have you heard the answer 'We've always done it that way' to the naive question' Why do you do that?'.

The consultant's function is to challenge ineffective patterns of behaviour which are seen to be inhibiting effectiveness or change. When you come across operators continually making the same mistake, when you see a management group constantly ending meetings in uproar, when you witness the same breakdown in communication time after time, it is up to you, the consultant, to point out the incidence and implications of such cyclical behaviour and help the client replace it with more effective behaviour. The consultant's function is to help the client identify and break out of such damaging cycles of behaviour.

Another function of the consultant is to point out and challenge examples of company culture inhibiting change. You will almost certainly come across instances where people say they are committed to new behaviour but when they return to work they go back to their old ways of doing things. Beverley Stone makes the point for us in *Confronting Company Politics* (1997) when she writes:

> Some people sabotage the system either openly and aggressively or secretly and manipulatively in an attempt to score points. Others perpetuate the status quo by attempting to do their job in spite of the saboteurs. They say nothing to the saboteurs or management for fear of getting it wrong, being a misfit, making waves, being disliked, losing the chance of promotion, disapproval, the discomfort of an argument and so on. They hide their imperfections by trying to be what they imagine others expect them to be. Superficially, they keep their heads down, do what they are told and suppress their views, ideas and opinions. Yet bubbling underneath and surfacing at every 'safe' opportunity – at the coffee machine, in workshops, in the pub at lunchtime – are the frustrations, anger, stresses, disappointments, feelings of impotence and depression of those who see a better way of doing things yet are too scared to say.

This is possibly an extreme example of where the decision to be client-centred or consultant-centred is a difficult one to make. How you decide to deal with this issue will depend, to a large extent, upon your relationship with the client, your own personal style and your ability to deal with the anxiety such an intervention might invoke. It may be easier said than done to suggest that managers and internal consultants should confront such ineffectual behaviour. It may well be easier to collude with it and avoid the issue altogether rather than take the risk of doing something and have it go wrong. But if you don't deal with it you will have to live with the guilt of not doing what you know you should. The external consultants who avoid the issue and do nothing about such behaviour must surely have to ask themselves whose needs they are meeting and whether or not they consider themselves worth their fees.

Dilemmas for the client-centred consultant

There seem to be two important dilemmas for the client-centred consultant. The first is 'How do I use my technical expertise and know-how without appearing to tell the client what to do?'. The second is 'How do I avoid being the "expert" who tells the client what to do, when the role is such a seductive one?'.

To address the first dilemma, the consultant should never withhold expertise and know-how from the client if, by withholding it, the problem doesn't get solved. However, we believe that the consultant is well advised to help the client see the consultant as a source of information which the client can use. If the client cannot see this then the consultant may have to 'bite the bullet' and be prescriptive. This is especially so if the client is in a desperate situation and has no idea what to do to solve the problem. But there are implications and you will have to decide whether the advantages outweigh the disadvantages in the particular situation at the time. However, giving advice early in the relationship may set up dependency and give rise to poor problem solving. Giving advice when the relationship has developed may be acceptable.

The second dilemma concerns how you feel about yourself and your client. If your personal power comes from being seen as an expert then you are likely to be very attracted to giving advice. Likewise, if you view your client as incompetent and helpless then you are likely to give advice. From the other side of the relationship the client may wish to be in the safe hands of an expert and therefore could ask for advice. Some of the following questions attempt to spring the trap on the pseudo client-centred consultant:

- What would you do in my position?
- You must have experience of such problems; what did you do?
- How do other people solve similar problems?
- I have no experience. I can't possible solve this problem, can I?
- I'm new to this, can you just give me a few ideas?

This 'expert' trap is there whether you are giving advice on a technical task or the way a department is organized and managed. More will be said about these dilemmas in Section II.

The training role can offer opportunities for powerful client-centred work. However, it is possible to train and educate entirely prescriptively. If the consultant diagnoses the difficulty, decides on the solution and trains the client accordingly, this doesn't seem to be very different from advice giving. But in the training and educating role the client-centred consultant helps the client to diagnose the difficulty, may offer theories, models or frameworks to help the client understand the difficulty and what to do about it and may then help the client implement the new methods or ways of working. However, the client always retains the ability to reject the particular theory or model or to adapt it to the particular situation. It follows, therefore, that client-centred consultants have to accept that their pet theories on how things should be done may end up in the bin. Commitment and belief in theories and models is very important – ownership is not!

Client-centred consultants work hard to stay non-directive and to identify and work with a problem-solving approach that gives the client more involvement. This requires the consultant to work hard to stay out of the content of the problem and help the client get some clarity about the problem and the options available. You are there to enable the client to see how many different problems make up the presenting problem, how many strands there are to the same problem and maybe how the presenting problem relates to the real problem. Once that has been done you can help the client to think about alternative courses of action to solve the problem, evaluate these alternatives and the implications and decide which one to choose. The client may need help to decide on a plan of action but the final plan should belong to the client rather than the consultant. It is important to note that this role is not about accepting all that the client says without question. There may be inconsistencies between what the client says and what the client does and this may need confronting. Overall, however, the consultant is there to help the client:

- perceive the situation more clearly;
- devise alternative strategies for solving the problem;
- evaluate the alternatives;
- decide on a course of action (including doing nothing);
- plan the implementation and take action.

Another way in which the client-centred consultant works is to stay entirely within the client's frame of reference to help the client get a clearer understanding of the problem. This includes identifying any feelings which may be forming a block to logical problem solving. The client is therefore ultimately responsible for doing something about the problem of not. The consultant doesn't get involved in the problem, accepts the client as he or she is, works hard to establish a trusting and open relationship but does not give advice. Unless, of course, the client is absolutely floundering, when a prescriptive solution may be all that is left. What the consultant can and must do is to reflect back key words, summarize and paraphrase the client's thoughts and feelings.

While it will be obvious that a consultant can fulfil many roles during any one intervention (and may change from moment to moment) it is important to maintain client-centredness throughout if you wish to enhance your client's problem-solving ability and do not wish to be seen as an expert. In order to stay client-centred you need to address the following types of questions:

- Do I get defensive when challenged or confronted?
- Does my self-esteem depend upon being seen as an expert?
- Do I like giving advice to people to influence their behaviour?

That was just to get you in tune. A more complete checklist for client-centredness is given at the end of this chapter – you might like to try it now.

Who Are the Clients?

At first sight this might seem to be an unimportant question with a simple answer. In reality it is probably the most important question to ask, for when you deal with the wrong client the consequence could be at best unproductive or at worst downright destructive. Training consultants often find this out to their cost when they train people in skills which they will not be allowed or given support to use when they return to work. They are really only dealing with part of the client system by missing out the manager of the department.

The dictionary tells us that a client is 'a dependent, a hanger-on, one who employs a lawyer or professional adviser, a customer.' This seems to suggest that anyone who has a problem or difficulty is a client. When people seek help to deal with their difficulty or to solve a problem by approaching someone they think can help, then they become clients. Hence it is possible to think of clients as people who approach doctors or lawyers for advice, who seek technical assistance from a mechanic, help from a psychotherapist or counsellor or shoppers in a store seeking to satisfy their need for household goods or clothes. Going on from there, it is therefore possible to see all those who help them as 'consultants'.

Clients can be individuals who ask for help with their own particular problems, e.g. how to deal with a difficult manager or subordinate or how to plan the next career move. The danger here for the consultant is to assume that you are dealing with the whole client system. In reality the solutions to most problems affect someone else, colleagues or family members. As most consultants deal with more than one client, we find it more useful to think of a 'client system'. It is also important not to define the 'system' too narrowly. You need to ask yourself which people are likely to be significantly affected by the changes which may take place to solve the problem. The answer may lead you to identify individuals or groups from other sections or departments or even other companies from different geographical locations.

Identifying the client may be complicated for instance, when you are contacted by an individual who complains about a problem, the solution to which, can only be implemented with the co-operation of other people. The client then becomes a group or team of people and you can no longer work with your individual client alone. This becomes even more complicated when the situation concerns a change within one group which will affect the relationships with other groups. Many managers think that they can change the culture or way of working within their own department without it affecting the rest of the organization. Inevitably there will be reactions to such changes ranging from surprise and concern to downright hostility and aggression. Unless the consultant realizes that the issue is really the inter-group relationships the intervention is unlikely to be very helpful.

It is important to recognize that however young an organization is it will have developed a climate and culture based upon traditions, precedents, rituals and practices. These are recognized and acknowledged by everyone but seldom get talked about, at least not openly. However, they serve as boundaries to behaviour and define what is acceptable or expected. Whenever the consultant has to deal with such issues the whole organization is always the client system. No one person or department can change without the agreement of everyone else.

Sometimes the problems are even wider than the organization. They are in the larger social system within which each organization operates. Local government, a university, a health trust with several hospitals or even a very large comprehensive school can be thought of in this way. They operate within a community and have relationships with local businesses, patients' organizations and parents. So it is almost impossible for any such organization to change without considering the implications and impact upon the larger social system within which it finds itself. Likewise they have to be aware of all the changes taking place in the social system which might have an impact upon the way they operate. Once organizations started to develop and publish customers' or patients' charters everyone had to follow suit like it or not.

Blake and Mouton in *Consultation* 1983 make the point that: 'It is important for a consultant to determine "who" the real client is. Trying to focus change on an individual as a *separate* entity is only likely to generate resistance if such personal change would make the client a deviant, rejected by other members of the group who have no understanding and even less sympathy for his or her observable behaviour shift. Under these conditions, the client is the group and its members need to change simultaneously if that behaviour is to be supported. Consultants must focus their efforts on the real client in order to intervene effectively. The *real* client is that individual, group or relationship in which the change is expected to occur'.

Do I Have the Real Client?

Even when you have identified that there is more than one client or that there is a whole client system it is often quite difficult to know that you have reached the point where you are dealing with the real or total client system. Professor Reg Revans of 'action learning' fame (1980) has some very useful things to say about finding the real client. He talks about the artfulness of effective negotiation to find 'Who knows? Who cares? Who can?'. If we apply these three questions to finding out who our real client or client system is, we can ensure that we involve all three if they happen to be different.

Who knows – about the problem or has most of the information that we need to be able to diagnose and help solve it is often the person doing the job. The people working for the manager with the problem will often know most about what is going on. Unless we accept that they are part of the system we shall not get very far.

Who cares – that something is done about it might well be the manager with the problem. It is likely to be the manager who identified the problem or who is bearing the pain due to the ineffectiveness of the department. However, there may be other people who care about the problem who also have to be considered as part of the system.

Who can – do something about the solution? If those with the problem have to ask for authority or approval to implement the solution, if they need more resources in terms of money or time or people and someone else controls those resources, then you had better involve that person as part of the client system at the beginning. Otherwise, just as you are about to talk about implementation, someone may say they have to get board approval and by then it may be too late!

The client system is not complete until it includes everyone who is involved in the answers to the three vital questions: Who knows? Who cares? Who can?

An example we encountered might make the whole thing clearer. An internal training adviser was called in by her personnel and training manager and given an assignment to provide training for a group of employees in another part of the organization. At this stage the work group had no knowledge of these intentions. To complicate matters the original request for training had come from the group's departmental manager who asked the personnel and training manager for help. Furthermore, the budget for such training was also controlled by the departmental manager. In this case, who is the client? Is it the personnel and training manager who made the initial request? Is it the departmental manager who wanted the training and controlled the budget? Or is it the group who were to be trained even if they weren't aware of it? Using Revans's ideas to find the real client or client system, the answers to the questions are as follows:

Who knows? Who knows there is a problem? – the departmental manager and the personnel and training manager.

Who knows the detail about the problem? – the departmental manager.

Who knows about sources of help? – the personnel and training manager.

Who cares? Who cares enough to do anything about the problem? – the departmental manager and perhaps the personnel and training manager.

Who can? Who can do anything about the problem? – the work group. Who has access to the budget to pay for help? – the departmental manager.

We would argue that this sort of situation is common for many internal consultants, in many different organizational settings, and in all kinds of specialist fields throughout industry, commerce, national and local government, education and voluntary groups. Great care is therefore needed to ensure that before you get very far into your intervention you have identified (as far as you can) all the parts of the client system. Also, as far as possible, you will need to work with all these various parts of the system so that you don't get to the end and find that the implementation doesn't go ahead because you didn't identify who had to authorize the necessary finance.

The Internal Consultant

If you are to be a consultant you have to have a client who needs your help with a problem or difficulty. External consultants are usually there by invitation, but this may not be so for the internal consultant. As an internal consultant you may be imposed by the client's boss or by someone who recognizes that there is a problem and has the authority to order a consultation to take place. This is likely to give rise to all manner of difficulties when you are trying to establish a relationship or find out what the client's needs are. The following appear to us to be some of the advantages and disadvantages we experienced when working as internal consultants:

Advantages	*Disadvantages*
• You may be able to take longer gaining entry.	• You are part of the culture you are seeking to change.
• You will probably know the client.	• Your department may have a poor image.
• You may know something about the client's problems.	• You may have a poor image.
• You know the history of the company.	• You may be imposed by the organization.
• You may share the same values.	• You may know things about the client that you can't disclose.
• You may spot non-genuine reasons for calling you in.	• You may have problems over confidentiality.
• You will probably know where to go for more information.	• You may be part of the problem.
• You will be able to find the real client more easily.	• You may have difficulty consulting either above you or below you in grade or status.

- You may already have established a good reputation for helping
- You may be able to ask for help from other internal consultants.
- You may find it easier to get involved in implementation and follow-up.

- You may have to confront people who might take offence.
- You may be discounted as a prophet in your own land.
- You may fear that giving bad news could adversely affect your career prospects.

We have found that many of these disadvantages exist solely in the mind of the internal consultant and are not borne out in practice. However, it is our view that if any of them appear to be potential disadvantages they are best highlighted as early in the consultation as possible.

The Consulting Cycle

Whenever you decide to work with someone to help solve a problem you are beginning a process which is similar to starting a journey together. The journey starts with an initial meeting and hopefully ends with the implementation of a different and more effective way of operating. The phases that make up this consulting cycle are:

1 Starting the consultation – making initial contact and establishing a working relationship (or, as we call it, gaining entry).
2 Contracting – finding out what the client wants and saying what you want.
3 Collecting data – finding out what happens now.
4 Making sense of the data – diagnosing the problem.
5 Generating options, making decisions and planning.
6 Implementing the plans and taking action.
7 Disengaging – arranging any necessary follow-up action.

This presents you with your first dilemma as a consultant. More often than not your client will want to tell you all about the problem and what needs to be done about it at the very first meeting. You, on the other hand, will know the folly of rushing into data collection and problem solving without getting to know your client, letting the client get to know you and reaching clear agreement on what he or she wants you to do, i.e. contracting.

This is likely to be even more difficult for the internal consultant. The temptation to gloss over these early phases is likely to be very strong as you will often be expected to know quite a lot about your potential clients and their problems. Before going any further, perhaps we should give a brief overview of each of the phases in our model of the consulting cycle.

Starting the consultation

This consists of making initial contact with the client and starting to build a relationship – we call it gaining entry. Initial contact in this context means the first meeting with a person you assume to be the client. This may not always be the case but until you gain sufficient entry you will probably not find out one way or the other. To prepare for this meeting you will need to have given some thought to how you feel. Are you ready for the meeting? Are you as well prepared as you might be? What sort of first impression do you want to make? Are you in the right frame of mind to meet your client and deal with any difficulties that might arise?

Gaining entry means you and the client coming together to start to build a relationship of mutual trust and respect. You will want to find out a little about the client and the situation the client is in, as well as getting to know something about the problem you are there to help solve. You will also want the client to find out something about you so that confidence in you can begin to build up.

Contracting

Contracting is about making explicit as many of the client's needs as you can. It is also the opportunity to let the client know, as explicitly as possible, what you are prepared to do and what part you want the client to play in the problem-solving process. It is important for both of you to understand in detail your mutual expectations of the relationship – who will do what and any boundaries that may exist. Contracting is therefore about ownership. One of the main difficulties in contracting is deciding when you have done enough to begin working on the problem. Delay too long and your client is likely to get frustrated with your apparent inactivity. Cut it short and you may find that your mutual expectations have not been specific enough and that too much is left to the imagination. In the context of client-centred consulting, contracting is not an exact science and there are bound to be grey areas. Fortunately, you can usually renegotiate as you progress through the assignment.

Collecting data

This means collecting data about what is happening now. Provided you have completed gaining entry and contracting satisfactorily you should have a clear idea of where the client's difficulty lies. You will then be able to help the client collect data relevant to the problem. There are many sources for this data: factual data from staff or records; feelings and opinions of everyone involved or comments and attitudes of both internal and external customers. Most professions have their own methods of collecting the data they need. So whether

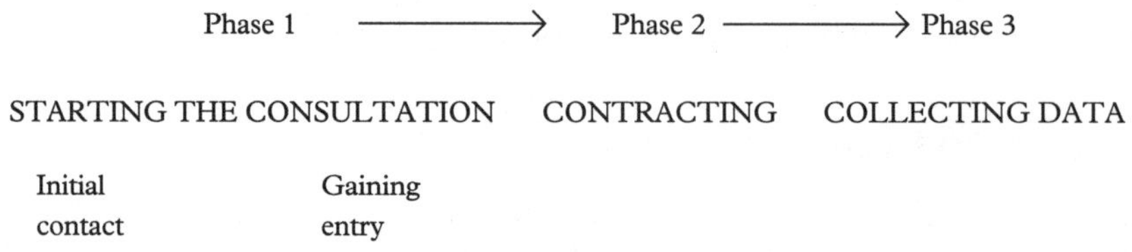

Phase 1 ⟶ Phase 2 ⟶ Phase 3

STARTING THE CONSULTATION — CONTRACTING — COLLECTING DATA

Initial contact — Gaining entry

Figure 1.1 The first three phases of consultation

you are a work study engineer, an operational research scientist, an auditor, a safety adviser or a personnel officer you will know what data you need to help you in your particular specialist field. However, apart from that, you will also be collecting data that gives you an impression of how the problem is managed, what organizational constraints are in place, what policies and procedures help or hinder how the department operates. And even as you collect this sort of organizational data you will have feelings about the staff, the managers and the environment which come to you through your intuition. All this data can be useful and can be fed back to the client.

Up to now the phases in the consulting cycle have been linear, following each other in a sequence as shown in Figure 1.1. While it is often necessary to go back and forth from one to another it is generally possible to complete one before going on to the next. By the time you reach the point where you begin to help the client collect data, the cyclical part of consulting has begun.

Making sense of the data and diagnosing the problem

This phase of the cycle (see Figure 1.2) involves helping the client to spend time reflecting, questioning and discussing the data in order to make sense of it in terms of the difficulty being faced. Where there is insufficient data you may have to return to the previous phase and collect some more, where there is sufficient data or too much data, you may have to help the client determine what is important and relevant. In this case the data may need sorting or presenting in a clearer, more understandable way. It may be possible for you to offer the client data-presentation frameworks such as critical path analysis to help the client decide what extra data is needed. Whatever way you choose to help, the decision about which data or information to collect must come from the client.

This phase presents another significant dilemma for the client-centred consultant. On the one hand, you want to stay with the client's diagnosis so that you don't take ownership of the problem. But on the other hand you will often realize that the client is dealing with symptoms rather than the real problem. Often the client will stay firmly in the content or task aspects of the problem when the real difficulties are embedded in issues about how the problem is managed and how people feel about it. This issue about the real problem may have to be confronted before the client enters the next phase.

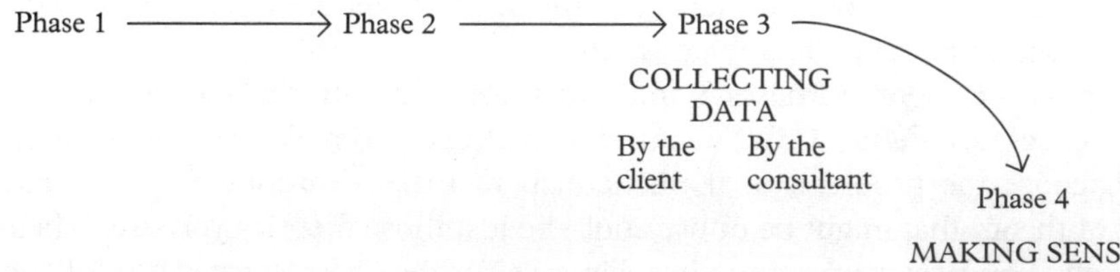

Figure 1.2 The fourth phase added

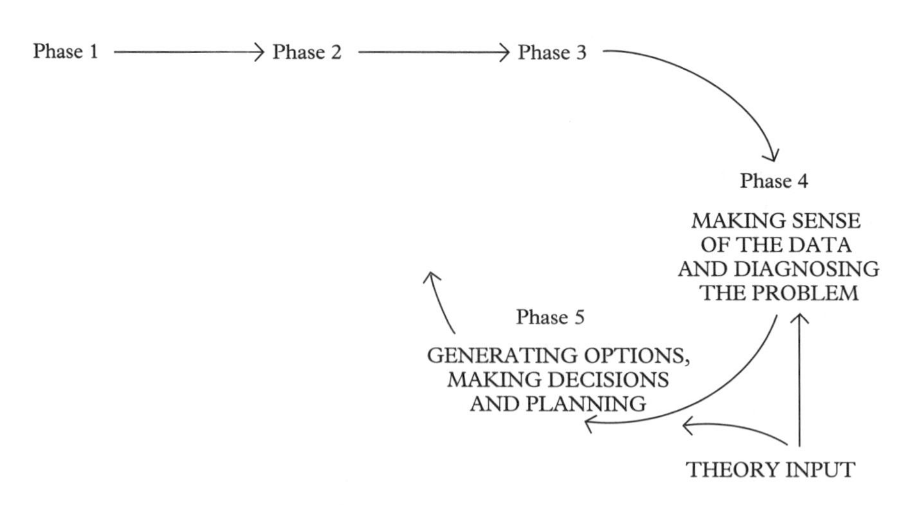

Figure 1.3 The fifth phase added

Generating options, making decisions and planning

Once the problem has been diagnosed you should be in a position to help your client generate the maximum number of options or possible solutions. In client-centred consulting it sometimes happens that you can see more options than the client can. Great care has to be taken about introducing these options, or the client may adopt one without really thinking and then blame you when it doesn't solve the problem. So in many situations it is better to stick with the client's chosen option even though you can think of a 'better' one. Your job is to challenge and confront so that your client doesn't just take the easy option. You may also have to help your client think through the implications of the decisions he or she makes so that there is as little doubt as possible that the right decision has been made.

Having made the decision the next step involves planning. Without a detailed plan of action very little is likely to happen to solve the problem. It is your job to encourage the client to question every aspect of the plan, to try to foresee what might go wrong and to anticipate the resources required (including time and financial costs). You are also there to help the client get commitment from the whole client system before implementation.

Helping the client in Phases 4 and 5 might involve introducing some theory to the client (see Figure 1.3). Such theory might help to make sense of the data, or diagnose the problem, or it might help to make decisions or plans. The kind of theory that might be of use could be just those theories you use to help yourself. This brings in yet another dilemma for the client-centred consultant. Do you merely use the theory to help the client, or do you spend time *teaching* the theory so that the client will be able to use it to solve similar problems in the future without assistance?

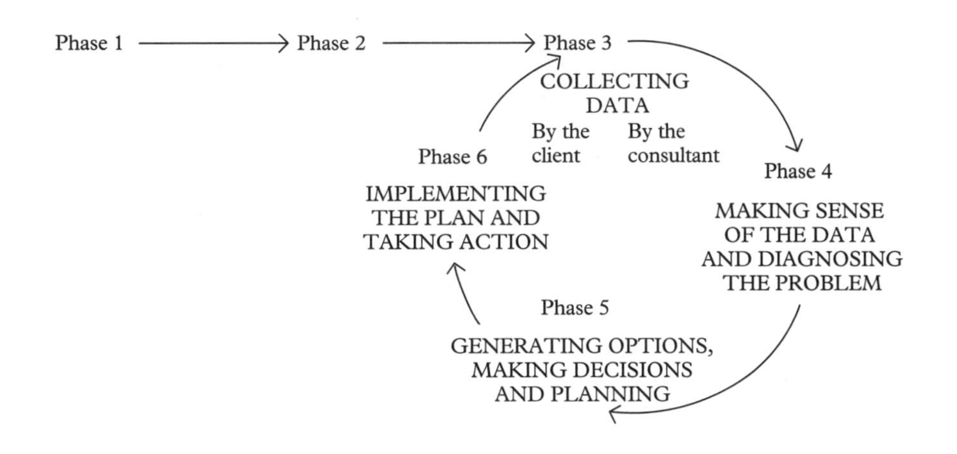

Figure 1.4 The sixth phase added

Implementing the plan and taking action

Many consultants leave before the plans are implemented and action taken. They will often write a report recommending certain action and present it to the client either by post or at a feedback meeting. Sometimes they will then be told 'leave it with us' or 'thank you, that's really helpful – we will let you know what happens'. What you really know is that that is likely to be the last anyone hears about the report or its recommendations. The only way you can be sure that the plan is implemented is to be there while it happens. You may agree to be part of the implementation team but not to be in charge. Your job is to be there monitoring, mentoring, encouraging, supporting, confronting, opening doors or counselling and training, but not to take ownership. It may be very tempting to take a leading role during implementation especially if you think there is a danger of all your hard work being wasted. We always try to remember that the problem belongs to the client and so does the solution. Figure 1.4 shows how Phase 6 completes the cyclical part of consulting.

In our experience most barriers to implementation are about four key issues: capability, organization, ownership and leadership. Briefly, this means that people do not have the skills and knowledge needed, or believe that they don't. They may not be really committed to the plan either because they were not involved or because their attitude to the problem and its solution is one of apathy or mistrust, and therefore there is no ownership. Alternatively, the leadership may be such that people do not believe that the organization or its managers are committed and fear they will not provide the support necessary for the solution to work. Equally, where people involved in the implementation come from different disciplines, how they are organized can become a problem. Unless these issues are addressed during the planning stage, successful implementation is highly problematic.

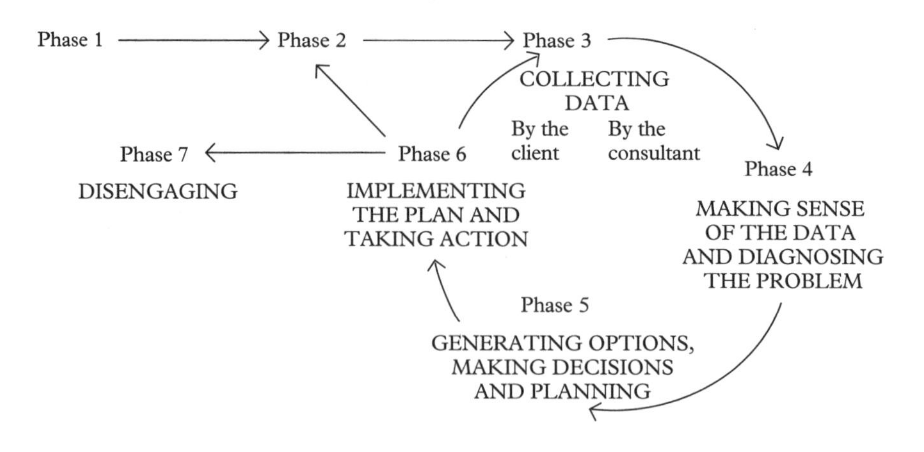

Figure 1.5 The seventh phase added

Disengaging

Once the plans have been implemented and action taken it is necessary to check that the new way of working is what is required and has replaced the old way which was causing the problem. If it has then you can probably disengage with some certainty that the new way of operating will stay in place. If it hasn't then you may have to go around the consulting cycle again until it does. You may have to help the clients examine the options or generate more. You may have to help them make different decisions or amend their plans. You may have to go further back into the process to examine the data, make different inferences from it and amend the diagnosis. You may even have to go back to collect more data or revisit the contract to check whether or not it contributed to inadequate implementation. Figure 1.5 shows the position of disengagement in the consulting process.

However, and whenever, you disengage it is vitally important that you do it well. Your aim should be to bring the consultation to a satisfactory end for both the client and yourself. It is especially important for the internal consultant to leave on good terms with the client, however successful or unsuccessful the outcome of the consultation. Your reputation and that of your colleagues in your department may well depend on how well you disengage. We were reminded of this recently by a colleague who had omitted to disengage from a project because the project leader was someone she saw every day on the same floor of the same building in which they both worked. She was roundly chastized by the project leader on the Monday following the Friday on which the project ended. 'You never came to say goodbye,' he complained. 'It would have been nice to celebrate what we had achieved.' For those of you who find endings of any sort hard, remember that your client may find them equally difficult.

Follow-up

Follow-up may often be needed to help the client maintain the implementation to the required standard. It may be that you have to arrange monitoring and support for the client either in the short term or on a continuous or occasional basis. However, it is very easy to get seduced into being available long after you should have left the client alone. Client dependency is easy to develop but very hard to stop. If your follow-up action happens some time after the implementation you may well find yourself having to start a new consultation from initial contact and gaining entry.

Section III – Managing Relationships with Clients Using the Consulting Cycle, will examine each of these phases in detail in order to equip you to carry out more successful consulting assignments.

Learning Styles and the Consulting Process

Understanding your learning style is likely to help considerably in increasing your learning power and will enable you to get the most from your interventions as a consultant. It will also help you understand the learning strengths of your clients and therefore their abilities in the various stages of the consulting cycle.

We have, for many years, helped our clients to see the relevance of their learning styles and their applicability to their problem-solving and consulting ability. In this respect we have been greatly influenced by Kolb (1981, 1985) and believe it is worthwhile spending some time assimilating his ideas. Basically, Kolb argues that there are four distinct stages in the learning cycle, as shown in Figure 1.6.

- *Learning from feeling*
  - Learning from specific experiences
  - Relating to people
  - Sensitivity to feelings and people
- *Learning by watching*
  - Careful observation before making a judgement
  - Viewing things from different perspectives
  - Looking for the meaning of things
- *Learning by thinking*
  - Logical analysis of ideas
  - Systemic planning
  - Acting on intellectual understanding of a situation
- *Learning by doing*
  - Ability to get things done
  - Risk taking
  - Influencing people and events through action

From these descriptions you will realize that no one style fits you completely. This is because each person's learning style is a combination of some or all of the four basic styles. However, most people have one or more styles they are

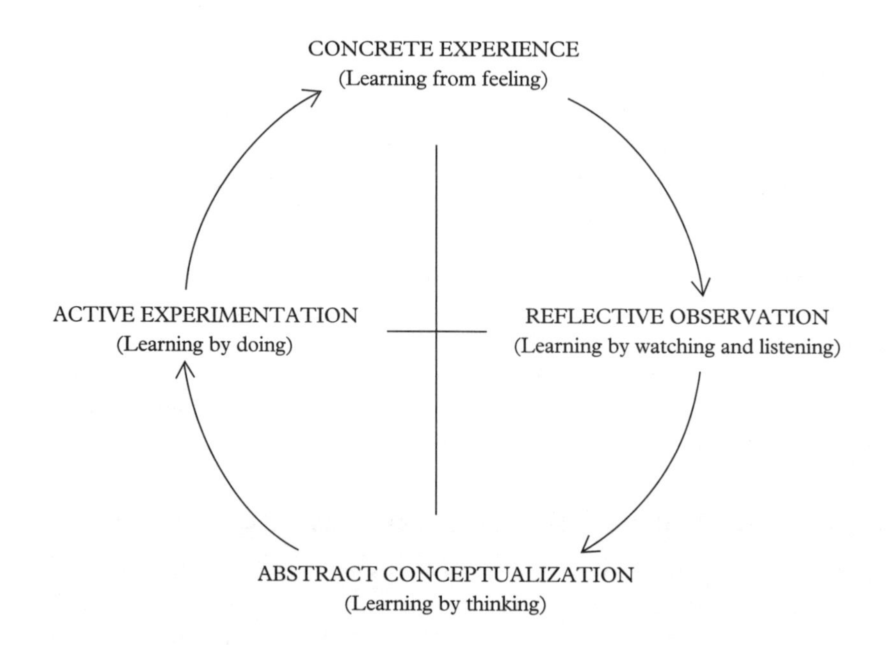

Figure 1.6 Kolb learning styles
Source: David Kolb, **Learning Style Inventory**, McBer & Company (1985). This material may not be reproduced in any way, except with the written permission of McBer & Company, 137 Newbury Street, Boston, MA 02116, USA (617) 437-7080.

comfortable with and this may well distort their ability to learn and also tend to pull them towards particular phases of the consulting cycle. Combinations of the four basic descriptions provide the styles described below.

Combining *concrete experience* with *reflective observation* generates a style called *diverger*:

- Sees concrete situations from many points of view;
- Understands people and is sensitive to feelings;
- Recognizes problems but observes rather than takes action;
- Open-minded, adaptable to change, lots of imagination.

Combining *reflective observation* with *abstract conceptualization* generates a style called *assimilator*:

- Collects and understands a wide range of information;
- Puts information into concise, logical form;
- Focuses on abstract ideas and concepts rather than people;
- Logical soundness more important than practicality;
- Creates models and plans and develops theories.

Combining *abstract conceptualization* with *active experimentation* generates a style called *converger*:

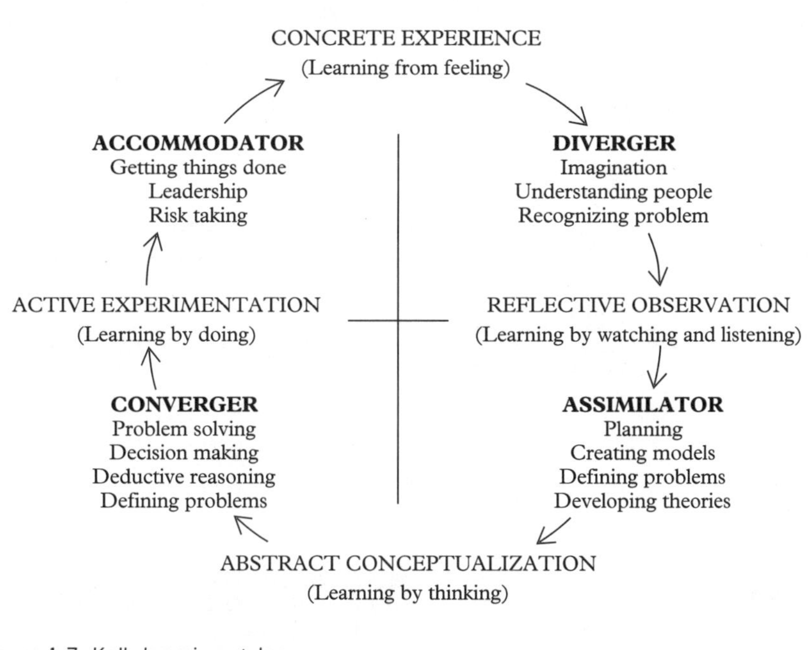

Figure 1.7 Kolb learning styles
Source: Reproduced by permission of McBer & Company

- Finds practical uses for theories and ideas;
- Able to solve problems and make decisions based on finding solutions;
- Better with technical problems than interpersonal issues;
- Deductive reasoning.

Combining *active experimentation* with *concrete experience* generates a style called *accommodator*:

- Implements plans involving new challenges;
- Acts more on intuition than logical analysis;
- Relies on people rather than technical analysis for information;
- Risk taking.

Figure 1.7 illustrates how these styles fit into the basic model.

Those of you who have studied learning styles using the Honey and Mumford typology (1986) will recognize the similarity with those of Kolb.

Kolb	*Honey and Mumford*[1]
diverger	reflector
assimilator	theorist
converger	pragmatist
accommodator	activist

When the learning styles model is integrated with the consulting cycle it can be seen that some learning styles have particular strengths which are useful in particular phases of the consulting cycle (see Figure 1.8).

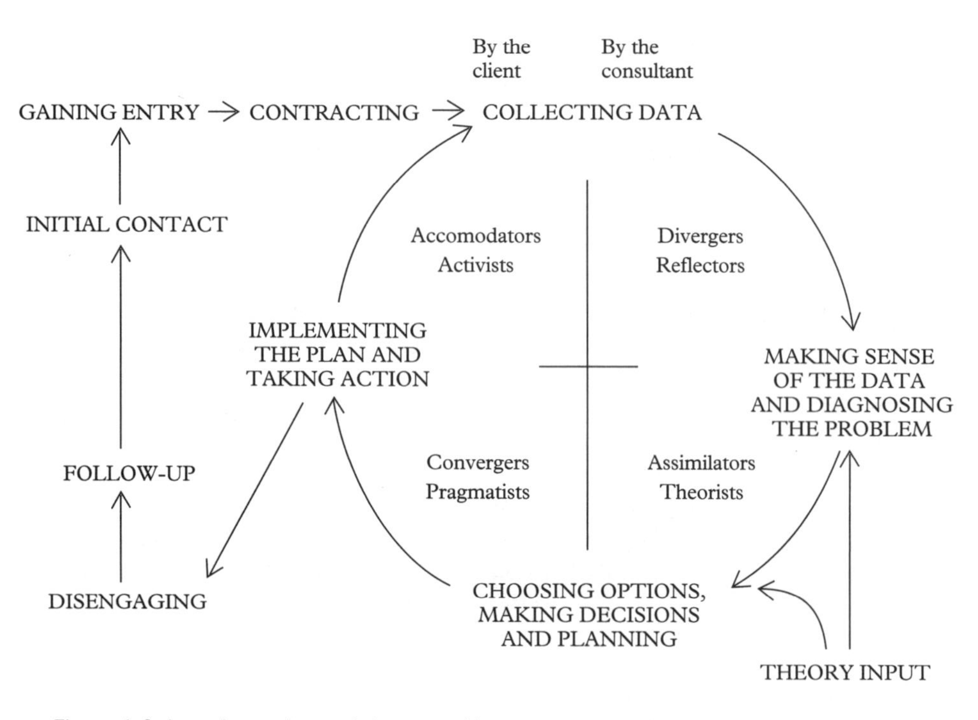

Figure 1.8 Learning styles and the consulting process

When collecting data about what is happening now the *accommodators* and *divergers* will be particularly useful. As you move into making sense of the data and diagnosing the problem you will want to make use of the *divergers* and *assimilators*. As you progress towards exploring options, making decisions and planning, the strengths of the *assimilators* are likely to be supplemented by those of the *convergers*, who are likely to be good at assessing the practicality of the solutions. The *convergers* will need the strengths of the *accommodators* when it comes to implementation. Your own learning style as a consultant is likely to attract you to certain phases of the consulting cycle so it is particularly important that you know what it is and do not hurry through the phases which don't fit with your preferred style. For example, it is likely to be hard for the very pragmatic consultant to keep the client working on making sense of the data and diagnosing the problem if all the time you are keen to get into implementation.

Similarly, if you like generating new ideas and recognizing problems but are not really concerned about putting them to work, you are likely to generate a great deal of frustration in a client who wants action rather than mature reflection.

Intervention Styles

Intervention style is the term used to describe the behaviours that we adopt in our interactions with clients during our journey round the consulting cycle.

Most of us have a particular style we are comfortable with when helping clients. However, if we have only one favourite style to use there are likely to be situations when that style is not effective enough. For instance, consultants in many professions are used to diagnosing clients' problems and prescribing the answers. In many situations where the consultant is the expert and the client is willing and able to take the prescription, the style is appropriate. But there are other equally effective styles available which are essential for the client-centred consultant. There is no part of the consulting process where one or more styles are not appropriate. The main point is that, whatever style you choose, there are consequences and implications. Furthermore, some styles are more important in some situations than others.

It is our experience that consulting styles are rarely even considered, so comfortable are we with our present style. Before looking at the alternative intervention styles available you may like to reflect on your own style preference. Imagine that you have a free choice about the kind of help you give to clients. Rank order the following statements to reflect how you prefer to work. Use 1 for your first choice through to 4 for your least preferred choice.

	Statement	*Ranking*
A	I prefer to work with clients by helping them talk through or sort out how they feel about the problem.	....
B	I prefer to work with clients by helping them gather and sift through information about the problem to help them define the situation more clearly and decide what to do.	....
C	I prefer to work with clients by identifying and highlighting hidden or buried values and attitudes which may be having a disruptive effect on client behaviour or exacerbating the problem.	....
D	I prefer to help clients by carefully examining the situation and then providing answers or solutions that will solve the problem and increase client effectiveness.	....

Following Blake and Mouton's descriptions (1976, 1983) we would distinguish four distinct intervention styles which can be employed in different situations: *acceptant*; *catalytic*; *confrontational*; and *prescriptive*.

Acceptant style

A consultant working in an acceptant style helps clients by empathic listening and by providing emotional support. This style of neutral, non-judgemental support can help clients to relax their defences, confront disabling emotional reactions and find their own way forward. It allows and encourages clients to clear what is blocking their ability to deal logically and rationally with their problem. In many respects it is typical of the early stages of counselling. However, as will be discussed later, it can also be useful in many other situations with individuals and groups.

Catalytic style

A consultant working in a catalytic style helps clients gather more data about the problem, sift through it to decide the relative importance of aspects of the data, or reflect upon it to make a diagnosis of the problem. Not all clients are short of information – some have so much that they can't see the wood for the trees. The intention behind the style is that once the clients have obtained and made sense of the data or information they will be able to choose options and move forward to solving the problem. Although the catalytic style can involve many types of data-gathering methodologies, it is perhaps typified at the interpersonal level by questions which begin with who, what, why, when, where and how. In this sense it is a diagnostic style. However, the important point is that, although catalytic interventions may help clients at the data-gathering stage, the solution is always generated by the clients themselves.

Confrontational style

A consultant working in a confrontational style helps the clients by calling attention to discrepancies between the values and beliefs they hold and how they put these values and beliefs into practice, i.e. their behaviour. Most of us have theories in our head (espoused theories) and yet we behave in ways which are quite contrary (theories in use). The confrontational style points out these differences to clients so that they are able to recognize the discrepancies and have an opportunity to decide if they wish to change.

Prescriptive style

Consultants working in a prescriptive style with clients generally listen to the clients' problem, collect the data they require, make sense of it from their own experience and present the clients with a solution or recommendations. It is probably the most common style used by specialists although it may not be the most effective. Typically, it is the style used by experts or those who think they are experts, e.g. doctors with their patients. The assumption is that the clients do not have the skill, knowledge or objectivity to make an accurate diagnosis or prescription of their own. Unfortunately, this is seldom the case; clients seldom know absolutely nothing about their problem and may have had the particular problem for some time. However, consultants can still use their expertise and experience by becoming a source of data to enable clients to provide their own solution or satisfactory way forward, without removing all freedom of action from the clients. As will be discussed later, there are situations in which the prescriptive style is entirely appropriate.

From our experience we would support Blake and Mouton and suggest that these four styles constitute a practical and comprehensive description of the most legitimate consultant behaviour. However, despite the fact that all the styles can be of value, you will probably feel more comfortable with one or two (as the ranking exercise may have shown). You may also tend to use your preferred style more often than the others. This could be detrimental to the consultant/client relationship as all styles have their uses in different situations and phases of the consulting cycle. The key is being able to recognize when a particular style is needed and then to use it appropriately. To do this effectively you will need to know more about the behaviour associated with each style, the assumptions behind them, their uses, and the associated risks for the client and consultant. These are all covered in Section II on Intervention Styles.

You may like to turn back and have a second look at your ranking now that you have read about each style. Assuming you have a good understanding of how you operate with clients it could provide insight into your favourite styles and highlight areas where you may need to do some additional work to become more client-centred.

Summary

- Consulting is what happens when one person has a problem or difficulty and seeks help from someone with special skills.
- Typically, counselling is a specialized type of consultancy.
- Consulting skills are needed by many specialists, advisers and helpers in organizations. Many managers are also beginning to find they need consulting skills.
- Consultants can be defined as those who find themselves having to influence or advise others without any formal authority or choosing not to use what authority they have.
- Client-centred consultants recognize that being sensitive and responsive to the needs of clients is as important as technical competence.
- The training role, used appropriately, can offer many opportunities for client-centred work.
- Clients can be single individuals, a disparate group or a whole organization. In organizations, it is often more practical to conceive of 'client systems'.
- The real client is defined by:
  - Who knows?
  - Who cares?
  - Who can?
- The consulting cycle follows the path:
  - initial contact and gaining entry;
  - contracting;
  - collecting data;
  - making sense of the data – diagnosing the problem;
  - generating options, making decisions, planning;
  - implementing plans and taking action;
  - disengaging and follow up.
- The phases of consulting, from collecting data to implementation, form a cyclic path and are consistent with current thinking on experiential learning. Indeed, consulting and experiential learning are identical.

- The process of consulting requires a variety of intervention styles. These are:
  - acceptant;
  - catalytic;
  - confrontational;
  - prescriptive.
- Being able to recognize and use all styles is an important element of consultant competence.

Checklist 1.1 Your client-centredness as a consultant

The following checklist is designed for you to assess the degree to which you feel client-centred in your work as a consultant, or how client-centred you think you would be if you are intending to work as a consultant.

Estimate your score before you complete the checklist by placing a cross where you think you will be on the following scale.

I have a high degree of client-centredness			I have a low degree of client-centredness
20	40	60	80

Now complete the checklist as honestly as you can. Try to get in touch with your *feelings* about each statement rather than scoring what you *think*.

Tick whichever column best represents your *feeling*

	I never feel this way	*I seldom feel this way*	*I often feel this way*	*I always feel this way*
1 I should be able to understand my client's problems as well as they do.	....	....	....	....
2 When I am giving advice and suggestions I really feel I am helping my clients.	....	....	....	....
3 I get defensive when challenged or confronted on something I feel strongly about.	....	....	....	....
4 My self-esteem depends upon my being seen and acknowledged as expert in my field.	....	....	....	....
5 I like influencing my clients' behaviour by telling them what to do for the best.	....	....	....	....
6 I believe that my clients are generally not competent and skilful at problem solving.	....	....	....	....

7 I have a lot of experience and therefore I know the answers to most of my clients' problems. ....

8 I feel rejected as a person when people don't like what I do or say. ....

9 I don't like feedback which is negative, unconstructive or against my self-image. ....

10 I enjoy showing how clever I am by being witty and scoring points off people. ....

11 I find it hard to ask for help for myself. ....

12 I believe that most of my clients want me to solve their problems for them. ....

13 It is important for me to get the credit when my clients solve their problems with my help. ....

14 I know better than my clients how to solve their problems. ....

15 The only rationale for my being a consultant is to solve my clients' problems for them. ....

16 I like being in control when helping clients to solve problems. ....

17 I do not believe that most of my clients want to solve their own problems. ....

18 If I have spent years getting my expertise it is a waste not to use it to solve problems for my clients. ....

19 I enjoy having clients who come to me with problems they cannot solve. ....

20 If clients ask me for advice I believe I should give it to them if I can. ....

Score 1 for each answer in the Never column
2 Seldom
3 Often
4 Always

Total your score and transfer it to the client-centredness scale above.

Total [ ]

Rationale The classification of the items in the checklist is not a definitive one and some statements apply to more than one area. Generally, however, we have included statements which seek your feelings about being an expert/advice giver, your attitude to your clients and your self-image and personal power.

Expert/Advice giver:	Items 1, 2, 4, 7, 14, 15, 16, 18, 20.
Attitude to clients:	Items 5, 6, 10, 12, 14, 16, 17, 19.
Self-image and personal power:	Items 1, 2, 3, 4, 5, 8, 9, 10, 11, 13, 18.

If you found yourself ticking most of the *Often* and *Always* boxes and your score is above 50 you may have some difficulty in working in a client-centred way.

If you found yourself ticking most of the *Never* and *Seldom* boxes and your score is below 50 you may find it somewhat easier to work in a client-centred way.

To find out what you need to work on to become more client-centred, circle the items numbers above for all those items where you scored three or four. The pattern which emerges will indicate whether your blockages lie in being an expert/advice giver, your attitude to clients or your self-image. The rationale which follows may give you some indication of the areas to work on.

If your personal power does not depend upon your being seen as an expert;
If you have little desire to be in control;
If you do not automatically operate as a giver of advice;
If you are not concerned to influence other people's behaviour;
If you value yourself and value your clients even though they need your help;
If you have a positive self-image and can handle negative feedback, *then* you are likely to be working in a client-centred way already or you are likely to have little difficulty working in a client-centred way in future.

Note

1 It is important to stress that our comparison of the learning styles used by Kolb and Honey and Mumford is not strictly accurate. Both sets of researchers base their work on the circular pattern of learning and at the general level their descriptions of the styles appear to have much in common. However, Honey and Mumford have built their views of the styles around recognizable statements of managerial behaviour. This has meant that their descriptions of learning styles are, in their view, more detailed than, and differ from, their apparent Kolb equivalents. Suffice to say that we have found that managers readily relate to the Kolb Learning Style Inventory and can use it to find ways of improving the effectiveness of their learning. However, we acknowledge the important contribution which Peter Honey and Alan Mumford have made to the current knowledge about how people learn and how they might become more effective learners, and the influence they have had on our own thinking.

2 Client-centred Leadership

Some years ago we, the authors, started with a mission of 'helping and developing internal consultants – people who facilitate change without formal authority'. We believed that this lack of formal authority was so significant that it required a different set of skills from those of the line manager. In recent years, however, we have had more and more managers and leaders requesting our help. These managers have recognized that the old paradigms of managing people are no longer relevant. Rather than relying on a position of power to get things done they want to manage their staff in a more collaborative, empowering or consultative way. These people also recognize that they are in the forefront of wave after wave of organizational change which has resulted from developments in legislation, the economy, the market place and technology. If, as a manager, you adopt a traditional prescriptive style, you have to keep checking to see if people continue to do what you want. If, however, you want the organizational change to happen without such checking then people have to be committed to it. This can only be achieved by involving people in the decision making process. We have come to accept that the empowering manager needs exactly the same skills and styles as those of the Client-centred Consultant.

The purpose of this chapter is to set the scene for the reader who comes to this book seeking ideas on developing his or her approach to managing and leading people. If that is you, then you are likely to be committed to supporting and developing individuals and teams, as well as facilitating change and doing so without recourse to your formal, hierarchical authority.

Recent Trends in Organizations

The most significant role of today's – and tomorrow's – manager is helping people to initiate change or react to and embrace continually changing circumstances. Many organizations have, or are going through a process of de-layering, that is, stripping away one or more layers of management, leading to a much flatter structure. Inevitably this means increased spans of control for those who are left. Once the change has taken place, it simply is not possible for a manager to supervise perhaps twice the number of direct reports as closely, or even in the same way. Also, for their part, people are expected to take on greater responsibility and become more proactive, empowered and committed. This cannot happen without an equally radical shift in management style. Similarly, introducing the concept of total quality management with ideas like 'right first time', 'continuous improvement', 'customer first', 'customer-supplier chains' – embracing both internal and external customers and suppliers – etc., requires a fundamental shift away from traditional notions of management direction and control. Even changes such as introducing self-managed work teams, or 'value driven' initiatives into an organization cannot be fully realized in an atmosphere of authoritarian control.

However, the big danger with all of these changes is that they may be introduced as purely structural or 'systems, procedures and processes' changes (see Chapter 3 for Organizational Life Model). Such changes are driven simply by designing a different structural configuration to the hierarchy, or introducing a new system/procedure for working. The dilemma in implementing change in either of these ways on their own is that they ignore the human process issues – feelings, attitudes, behaviours – which are an inevitable consequence.

For example, flatter organizations usually mean fewer people doing more, and often more with new technology. Despite the euphemisms of 'down-sizing', for those who are left – both managers and employees alike – it often means:

- increased stress;
- longer hours at work and often taking more work home;
- greater vulnerability;
- discomfort and uncertainty;
- a sense of powerlessness at work;
- lower morale;
- more time spent in displacement activities like swapping the latest rumours and stories of discontent or attempting to second guess what 'they' are likely to do next, gossiping in corners about how badly people are treated etc.;
- higher levels of sickness (particularly through stress related illnesses);
- both absenteeism and presenteeism (where people attend work physically but are mentally switched off).

One of the authors was working with a group of senior managers in a large pharmaceutical company in the throes of a merger and the consequent rationalizations. The Managing Director, without any hint of cynicism told the meeting that 'we must never forget that people are still our most important assets'. 'That may be so' retorted the HR Director, 'but at the moment they feel much more like liabilities than assets'.

In our experience, these types of people issues arise in varying degrees in all of the change initiatives outlined earlier. We believe it is axiomatic that 'where any change ignores the people involved and concentrates solely on implementing a new structure or system, it will, in the long term, backfire, or at best, be seriously impaired'. There may be short-term gains, but in the longer term any gains will be progressively eroded as people become demotivated and lacking in enthusiasm for either the job or the organization. In short, the quick fix rarely lasts.

Clearly change is vital if an organization is to succeed, thrive and grow in an increasingly competitive environment. What is needed though, in tandem with any structural or systems/procedure change, is equal effort in addressing the human process issues. Once again this means a fundamental change in management style.

As a line manager, then, you are responsible for managing in the context of these cultural as well as structural changes. Cultural changes cannot be managed in the same way as changes in structure, procedures and processes. They cannot be controlled in the same way. Indeed it is often said that it is impossible to manage change. What it requires is a willingness to deal with a high level of ambiguity, to acknowledge people's feelings and adopt a range of non-prescriptive styles of working.

Characteristics of High Performing Organizations

Much has been written about leadership and management during the 20th century and no doubt this will continue into the next millennium. There have been innumerable definitions drawn up of the activities of leadership and the styles and skills which leaders need to adopt.

Some people have argued that the leader's role is not really very important as it is only one of many variables that affect the success of an organization. These variables might include:

- the purpose and goals of the enterprise;
- the technology;
- the systems, procedures and business processes;
- the organizational structure;
- the reward systems;
- the environment;
- the market;
- legislation;
- the culture of the organization.

People taking this view often see managers as being so constrained by all these factors that they are unable to make a significant individual impact on their enterprise.

However, we think it is undeniable that as organizations take on the challenges of the 21st century, the role of leaders is becoming even more important. Leaders must become agents of change. They have the potential to transform business, government agencies, government, even countries. One only has to look at entrepreneurs such as Richard Branson and Anita Roddick in the UK to appreciate how an individual's vision, values, energy and determination can influence their organizations. In another area Nelson Mandela's leadership and charisma has been the basis for a remarkable transformation in South Africa. So not only is it possible for leaders to influence their organizations but essential that they do so.

What kind of leaders do we need?

We have already remarked on the ever increasing literature that has been written on the subject, and the many different theories of leadership which have been developed. An important question that must be asked, however, is 'leadership for what?' It is impossible to identify the kind of leadership which is required unless we first of all understand the trends which are taking place amongst high performing organizations.

Over some twenty years we have observed that far too many organizations have repressive and constraining cultures. All too often managers have inadequate interpersonal skills, avoid conflict, behave abrasively and concentrate on controlling people rather than releasing energy. As Thomas Harris believes they tend to work from an 'I'm OK – You're Not OK' frame of reference. Such practices arouse resentment and frustration amongst employees and result in dysfunctional organizations (*I'm OK – You're OK*, Pan Books Ltd (1973)).

On the other hand we think it is possible to identify a number of common characteristics of high performing organizations. They:

- **Recognize the importance of change** and acknowledge that the quality of leadership is crucial to strategic organizational transformation. Most organizations have had to react to challenges from the market place, from the competition, from customers or from pressures to produce more with less resources. They have responded by restructuring, delayering, business-process re-engineering etc. and many organizations are unrecognizable from the way they were ten years ago. Where this has been badly done, employees have been left scared, vulnerable, aimless, angry, unappreciated and demotivated. Where it has been done well, employees feel energized, enthusiastic, committed and have a sense of release from old constraints and bureaucratic shackles.
- **Are customer focused.** They emphasize the importance of the customer/supplier relationship throughout the organization. Traditional cultures in which people work to satisfy the needs and wishes of the boss have been replaced by one where the customer is more important than the boss and delivery and performance are more important than authority.
- **Design organization structures to be as simple as possible** so that communication is simplified and bureaucracy reduced to a minimum. There is a growing drive to enable people to devote more of their energy to doing things that directly affect business success rather than maintaining systems and rules, almost for their own sake. More emphasis is placed on business processes than formal hierarchical structures. This often means that time can be legitimately devoted to managing working relationships, teamworking and developing mutual support rather than feeding the bureaucracy which isolates people from each other.
- **Are horizontal rather than hierarchical in nature.** Organizations are now much flatter than they have been in the past. This reduces the traditional management responsibility for control and replaces it with a need for

everyone in the organization to develop collaborative skills and a sense of responsibility for themselves and their colleagues.

- **Emphasize the importance of self managed teams** of people able to make decisions and implement new ideas. This is the logical outcome of the drive to give responsibility for providing quality products or services, and quality improvement to the work group rather than to inspectors or quality controllers. This of course requires significant investment in training and development, rewards and benefits and effective support systems.
- **Encourage and support innovation.** Such organizations value project teams and support them while they develop new and innovative ways of solving problems, satisfying customers and developing new products. They also recognize that people need practical and emotional support when working on such projects.
- **Develop a learning culture** in which people share best practice, are able to learn from mistakes, and learning opportunities are sought for both individuals and teams. This is a culture in which people feel *genuinely* empowered.

What Do We Mean by Empowerment?

Empowerment is one of those words which has been used and abused in management circles in the past few years. There have been many organizational initiatives aimed at empowering people, many of which died because they failed to clarify what they were really trying to achieve. At its worst, it has led to people feeling abandoned and unsupported, left to deal with problems and make decisions with which they previously would have been helped.

So what do we mean by empowerment? When someone feels empowered they feel excited and enthusiastic about what they do. They have a sense that what they are doing is significant and that they are contributing to something important. They feel valued by others. There would seem to be five elements to empowerment at work:

1 People feel that what they are doing is significant and makes an important contribution to the total enterprise.
2 People feel that they are able to participate in decisions about their own targets and have control over the way they achieve those targets.
3 People feel personally valued by their colleagues.
4 There is a balance between the level of challenge inherent in the work and the person's feelings of competence to meet those challenges. If people are to feel empowered there needs to be significant investment in training, development and coaching.
5 People have a sense of growth and development. This means that each individual needs opportunities to grow within the job and for the job itself to be flexible enough to encompass new opportunities to make different contributions to the enterprise.

Obviously the way you behave as a manager will have a crucial impact on the degree to which people you work with feel empowered. Just like the client-centred consultant, the empowering manager needs a high level of self awareness. There are many psychological needs and barriers that make it more difficult than we think, to work in a way that is truly empowering. In order to work consistently in this way you need to ask yourself the following types of questions:

- Do I need to feel in control of what is going on?
- Do I get defensive when challenged or confronted?
- Does my self-esteem depend on being seen as an expert?
- Do I like giving advice to people to influence their behaviour?

Such questions are just to get you started. There is a more complete checklist on 'Attitudes to Empowerment' at the end of this chapter – you might like to try it now before going on to the next section.

Characteristics of High Performing, Empowering Leaders

The trends which have been briefly outlined in the previous section are having a profound effect on managers and leaders throughout the world. Indeed, we have a chicken and egg situation here. It is undoubtedly true that many of these far-reaching changes have been initiated by visionary leaders who recognize that the old organizations are no longer equal to what is required of them. This came home forcibly to us a few years ago when working with a group of managers in the electricity supply industry in the UK. It was an industry which had undergone massive changes after privatization, and was still experiencing significant restructuring at the time. During the discussion one of the group seemed quite distressed that his job had been changed and he now had seventy people working for him. At first this sounded like promotion and cause for celebration rather than distress, until he explained that every one of these seventy people reported to him personally. He had no idea how he could possibly manage (i.e. control) seventy people. This situation was echoed by other members of the group who felt similar disquiet. They had been introduced to flatter organizational structures and self-managed teams the hard way. We were able to work with them to help them develop quite different ways of working, which required them to develop new skills, redefine their understanding of their roles and even change some of their assumptions, attitudes and values about people at work. We helped them to move away from some very traditional but constraining ideas about managing people and helped them develop a new, more empowering and satisfying style of leadership. In essence we helped them take on board a client-centred approach to team management.

So what are the characteristics of the managers and leaders required by these new high performing organizations? We think we can say that leaders still have a number of different roles. The first role is probably akin to their traditional one which is that of envisioning what needs to be done, and putting in place appropriate structures and systems to ensure that this happens.

The second responsibility is that of ambassador. For the transformational chief executive that might mean working hard to raise their own profile and that of their enterprise. They invest time and energy developing relationships with their customers and representing their organization in the market place and in the community at large. Many of them become PR experts and are almost synonymous with the images of their companies as Richard Branson and Anita Roddick are with Virgin and the Body Shop. For leaders within the organization, this means working with internal customers and suppliers, developing effective working relationships with them, working collaboratively to improve processes and overcome problems. In so doing the leader works to raise the profile of the department within the organization.

The third role, and the one with which this chapter is chiefly concerned, is that of empowering, supporting, coaching and developing both individuals and teams. Successful leaders now:

- Are much more concerned with releasing creative energy at all levels than with controlling people.
- Believe that people are responsible, creative, energetic and able to solve problems and make decisions individually and together, with support rather than interference, from the leader.
- Take a much more facilitative role, helping and assisting a number of self-managed teams to improve their effectiveness.
- Recognize the importance of coaching, mentoring and supporting people.
- Work in a way that is largely non-prescriptive, helping people to solve problems and make decisions for themselves rather than telling them what to do.
- Work hard to ensure that their people are not dependent on them.
- Allow people to make mistakes and help them learn from those mistakes rather than blaming or punishing, knowing that the person who has never made a mistake has never made a decision.
- Offer emotional support to people. They understand that as leaders they are in the business of organizational change. This means being able to acknowledge the feelings and emotions of people when they are involved in such changes.
- Recognize that when people have a sense of control, they feel better about what they do.
- Encourage feedback and open communication. Feedback on performance is seen as essential if people are to perform effectively. Feedback, however, is not a one-way street. The effective leader also needs feedback. Candidness, openness and honesty are welcomed rather than punished, and given without fear, rancour or revenge.
- Are able to develop trusting relationships by continually working to open up channels of communication.
- Engender an atmosphere in which people have fun doing their jobs and are able to celebrate success.

This demands that leaders:

- Have a high level of self awareness. They work hard to understand their own strengths and weakness and appreciate the way they impact on others.

- Have a positive self image and a high level of self-esteem.
- Have a thorough understanding of the ways in which individuals and groups react to change.
- Develop a range of interpersonal skills such as listening, communicating, assertion, managing conflict, influencing, negotiating, supporting, dealing with feelings, feedback, facilitation, problem diagnosis etc.
- Develop a range of non-prescriptive, facilitating and coaching styles. These styles would include acceptant, catalytic and confrontational approaches as well as offering prescriptions when appropriate. (See Section II.)

Ken Blanchard in his *Situational Leadership* training material talks about the 'upside down pyramid'. He argues that in the traditional organization people think that they work for the level above and therefore employees spend a great deal of time and effort trying to figure out what the next level up wants from them. The manager's role in this setting is seen as being responsible, while the employee is expected to be responsive.

Once the pyramid is turned upside down a change in position occurs and the roles of the respective parties are reversed. Now the employee becomes responsible and the manager has to become responsive; that is supporting, facilitating, encouraging and enabling employees to function effectively.

Facilitating Self-directed Work Teams

When working with self-directed work teams the role of coach is to help create a culture within the team in which problems, ideas, difficulties in working together and blockages to effectiveness can be discussed openly in a collaborative, honest and supportive way.

This sounds fairly obvious but such ideas are counter-culture in many traditional organizations. People often see work as a place where they play a role, rather than be genuine; where they hide their true feelings; where they are 'diplomatic' with each other; where conversations take the form of rituals; where there is very little intimacy, or openness. Organizations are often places where it is very difficult to get genuine feedback on how people are seen by others. People are much more likely to talk about a colleague in their absence than give them helpful feedback directly. Some organizations have acknowledged this by initiating systems which help people to get 360° feedback. But even then the feedback is often given anonymously, in written form rather than directly to the individual. This means that the leader will need to spend a significant amount of time building relationships and contracting. Group members will need a lot of help to develop genuinely trusting relationships with each other as well as with the leader.

The group will also need some help to clarify their expectations of each other – the contract. This is likely to include agreement on such issues as who is responsible for what; how they deal with problems, how they work with internal customers and suppliers, and how they work together.

It should be remembered however, that contracting is an opportunity for the group to discuss and make explicit how they intend to manage their relationships with each other and with the manager. They have the opportunity to decide what kind of culture they want to create within the team. They can agree ground rules about how they would like:

- decisions to be made;
- conflicts to be managed;
- new ideas to be dealt with;
- problems to be discussed;
- mistakes to be dealt with;
- relationships to be managed.

An example of such a contract agreed by a self-directing consulting team is as follows:

- The way we work together is the way we want to work with clients – we will give each other feedback about this in addition to other things.
- We will continually work on clarifying where we're going and how we get there. We will aim to keep focused.
- We will share observations of what is happening in the team without judgement or prescription (by 'judging' we mean saying something is right or wrong).
- We will be open about where we are – express difficulties, concerns, feelings.
- We will say what we want and what needs to be said. We can check what is expected of us at any time.
- We have the right to say 'no' and take responsibility for the consequences.
- We will show care and concern for each other. We will be sensitive to each other's feelings and respond to them and help each other work through them.
- We will challenge each other.

The following set of behavioural groundrules were agreed by a management team in the automotive industry, as the basis of how they intended to work together. Agreeing the contract is often the easy part. The leader then needs a high level of facilitating skills to help the group review its effectiveness periodically and check how well people are living up to the contract. Having contracted for a high level of openness, genuine support and 'no blame' it makes it much easier to help the group to get difficult issues out in the open, work on them, decide what to do, and move on.

Behavioural Groundrules

1. Be Supportive:
   - to encourage others constructively;
   - offering help but not necessarily the solution;
   - give recognition.
2. Be Open and Honest:
   - being truthful about ourselves and each other (without personal abuse);

3 Give and Receive Feedback:
   - be prepared to comment and accept feedback.
4 Be Positive:
   - be constructive and accept responsibility.
5 Listening and Hearing:
   - don't interrupt;
   - showing interest;
   - acknowledging the speaker.
6 Be Punctual:
   - time management.
7 Encouraging Participation:
   - giving everyone a share of the air time;
   - ask each other questions;
   - be prepared to comment.
8 Be Open Minded:
   - explore other people's ideas and opinions.
9 Here and Now:
   - keep to the relevant subject matter;
   - focus on this group.
10 Allow people to answer questions.
11 Confront issues including the contract.

When working with self-directed work teams, the leader's role is to help each team be as effective as possible. So what will prevent them being effective? If we examine the Organizational Life Model in Chapter 3 we can see that there are three areas that require attention and energy in any group. Blockages which will prevent effective teamwork will be to do with:

- The task itself – failure to be clear about long-, medium- or short-term objectives – unclear standards, insufficient resources.
- Inappropriate systems, procedures and processes.
- Unresolved human processes – feelings, attitudes, behaviours – issues.

When facilitating self-directed work teams you will need to help the group function effectively at all three levels. As we have seen it is no longer appropriate to work from a purely prescriptive style, especially when you have to support several teams at the same time. You need them to have a facility with all four intervention and facilitating styles outlined in Section III.

Client-centred Consulting and Day-To-Day Management

Day-to-day management is largely a matter of keeping focused on your short-, medium- and long-term objectives, applying your own technical or professional skills to ongoing problems, and finally, managing relationships. We think that most managers would agree that the most difficult of those three is the latter. As organizations become more fluid, more multicultural and multinational, working relationships become more complex. The emphasis on business processes rather than – or as well as – formal hierarchical structures means that your relationships with your internal or external customers and suppliers are at least as important as those with your own team.

In Chapter 3 we refer to John Adair's Three-Circles model for organizational diagnosis. Originally developed three decades ago by Adair, it identifies three elements of leadership:

- concern for the task;
- concern for the group;
- concern for the individual.

The model is as valid today as it was in the 1960s, perhaps more so, as the groups you have to manage become more and more complex and diverse and levels of formal authority decrease. At the individual level the role of management coaching becomes increasingly important. As people's levels of responsibility increase, so does the importance of coaching and developing them. Perhaps it is true to say that as large organizations can no longer offer long-term job security the importance of coaching and developing people is enhanced. After all, if you can't attract and retain people by offering security, the only way of doing so is through high salaries or a guarantee that you will invest in their training and development, thus giving them an increased sense of employability.

Given such a degree of ambiguity in the role of the 21st century manager, it would seem appropriate to draw on consulting and change management models rather than traditional management models which assume high levels of formal authority and power and a degree of stability in the workplace. An amended version of our consulting cycle would then appear to be equally valuable for the line manager both in terms of facilitating groups and when coaching individuals.

Phase 1 – Making Initial Contact and Building Trusting Relationships

W. E. Deming once said 'Trust is mandatory for the optimization of any system. Without trust there can be no co-operation between people, teams, departments and divisions. Without trust, each component will protect its own immediate interests to its long-term detriment and the detriment of the entire system'.

Yet developing trusting relationships is counter-culture in many organizations. Rather than developing straightforward, honest and open relationships at work, we talk about 'work' or 'professional' relationships which are somehow different from those we have in the rest of our lives. 'Working' relationships are often ones in which people hide from the truth, are closed with each other, are unable to ask for help or support, where in short, there is a significant lack of trust. So managers who seek to develop and maintain genuinely trusting relationships with their people face a significant challenge. Yet they are vital if people are to react positively to organizational change. In times of change people are likely to feel all sorts of emotions ranging from anger to fear, they are likely to feel vulnerable and lacking in confidence. If they are to work through these very personal anxieties, they need to be fortunate enough to work with a manager with whom they have developed a high level of *mutual* trust. And we stress here the word mutual. If you are my manager and you expect me to trust you with my ideas, aspirations, hopes, plans, fears and anxieties, all very personal and difficult issues, then it is important that you are prepared to show the same trust in me. It is not enough that you are prepared to listen to my feelings. You need to be prepared to share some of your own. Building mutual trust then, is an ongoing part of any relationship, of which openness is a key element.

Relationships are never static, people change and it requires ongoing effort to maintain, build and strengthen a relationship. Even people who have worked together for many years may be surprised when confronted with information about one another which they had never before even considered, sometimes causing a dramatic re-appraisal of the relationship. Indeed, we have often found that when managers and their team members attend consultancy skills programmes together, they generally start the experience claiming they know one another really well. However, by the end of the experience they usually report that they have learnt so much more about one another and at the same time, begun to realize that there are depths to the relationship which they would never have thought possible in a work setting. Furthermore, they also find that as their working relationship strengthens and becomes more trusting and open, their ability to function effectively together at work increases in similar measure. This is not an easy matter, however, and always takes commitment and ongoing effort.

Phase 2 – Contracting and Clarifying Expectations

As we will see in Chapter 9, contracting is essentially about sharing expectations. Not only expectations which we have of one another, but also expectations of how we are going to work together. This has to be an ideal opportunity for a manager to work openly with employees about their respective roles and responsibilities, expectations of each other, how they want to be managed and what their manager wants from them. Indeed, if organizational change is to be effective then it is vital that changes in roles, responsibilities and expectations, at all levels, are brought into the open and discussed. Furthermore, as in phase 1, this is not a one off affair. Organizations will continue to change, indeed, concepts like 'continuous improvement' are all about continual modification and change. It follows therefore, that to manage ongoing change successfully then contracting and re-contracting has to become both explicit and an accepted way of life. As we identified earlier in this chapter, it will be necessary to create a culture where it is possible to be open with each other and give feedback without rancour or revenge. To do this you are likely to need a clear contract with whom you are coaching whether it be a group or an individual.

Phase 3 – Collecting Data and Giving Feedback

Whether we like it or not, as human beings we are all constantly collecting data. For employees this is often data about topics such as people, situations, problems, difficulties and anxieties, opportunities and missed opportunities. Sadly in the traditional organization such data are rarely taken seriously, fed back or acted upon. The data usually remains with the employees to become fodder for social conversations and idle gossip over lunch and coffee, and in odd moments across the working day. Only rarely is it picked up and utilized as a valuable resource for addressing organizational problems.

However, in organizations which are genuinely attempting to change it is recognized that data held by employees can hold the key to solving all manner of organizational problems. Examples include developing and improving work methods, finding ways to solve recurrent problems, and even evolving new, creative ideas for products and services. In such organizations managers recognize that part of their role is to work with employees to capitalize on any opportunities or ideas which the employees are able to generate. At times this could involve helping them sift through the data they have collected to sort the wood from the trees, and at other times it could mean highlighting where there is an absence or scarcity of data and then helping them think through how any gaps can be filled. In short, the manager will be practising all of the skills required for collecting data and giving feedback.

Phase 4 – Problem Diagnosis – Helping People Make Decisions

In the client-centred consulting model the consultant helps the client diagnose the problem(s) they wish to tackle, make decisions and plan how they wish to proceed. Obviously the consultant will bring expertise to bear if it is likely to prove helpful, but the main onus for diagnosis and decision making rests with the client.

In high performing organizations and organizations that are implementing many types of radical change, this is precisely the role of the manager. All that changes is that the term 'consultant' is replaced by 'manager', and 'client' by 'employee'. Clearly the manager sometimes has access to a different, perhaps wider perspective, or indeed limiting factors of which employees may not be aware, and at times it may be essential to bring this information into the decision making process. But this should not detract from the central idea of facilitating and working with the information generated by the people who are closest to the day-to-day problems, difficulties and hiccups in the system; therein lies the key to motivation and real involvement.

Of course it would be naive to believe that all decisions are made by consensus. Many decisions are rightly and legitimately made by the manager alone. It is important then to have a clear contract about what kinds of decisions will be made by the manager, which will be left to individual members of the team and what kinds of problems will be worked on and decided by the whole team.

When helping the team to work on problems and make decisions, there also needs to be clarity about the role of the manager. Is he or she simply an equal team member or a team member with rather more power and influence than everyone else. Another role the manager may take on is that of facilitator of the group, working acceptantly and catalytically to help the group stay focused on the issue(s), clarify and define the problems and then move on to look at options and make decisions.

Phase 5 – Implementation

In Chapter 12 we will point out that sometimes the consultant may not be involved during the implementation phase. However, this is never the case for the manager; as a full-time member of the department or section, he/she will always be present when change is implemented and indeed, may be an integral part of the change. Nevertheless, if the manager wishes to follow the client-centred consulting model, then their role is no different to that of any other consultant. Principally it involves facilitating, enabling, coaching and supporting their group and individuals as they carry out the implementation process.

Phase 6 – Celebration

Disengagement is the one phase in consulting which is significantly different for the manager. For the consultant, disengagement generally marks the end of an assignment and often the end of the relationship with the client and his/her organization. However, clearly this is not the case for managers. By virtue of the fact that they are employed by the organization on a permanent basis, managers will have an ongoing relationship with their teams. Therefore in some respects it is inaccurate to refer to disengagement in the same way. However projects are completed, customers satisfied, crises overcome and deadlines met. It is important to acknowledge the movement from one phase to another. Perhaps an important and often overlooked principle is that of celebrating success.

When working with a department in the financial sector we found that there was considerable resentment and lack of co-operation between the four separate teams that made up the department. It emerged that two of the teams were responsible for administering the established workload while others worked on developmental and project work. Despite being responsible for most of the profitability of the department, the team doing the established work saw the others as doing the trendy projects and getting most of the attention and kudos. They therefore felt undervalued and unacknowledged. When this was revealed, the whole department contracted to celebrate formally and share all successfully completed projects or targets throughout the department.

Ongoing evaluation of effectiveness is also an important managerial activity. It is important for the team to ask and discuss questions such as :

- What are we doing well?
- Where are our weaknesses?

- What have we learned?
- Are we sticking to the contract?
- How will we work differently next time?

It is easy to do this at the end of a consulting assignment, less easy but no less important, in the day-to-day hurly burly of team management.

Case Study

The company in this case study is a major clothing manufacturer which makes and supplies clothes for one of the most popular high street retailers in the UK. During the last decade they recognized the need to become more customer focused and embarked on a major initiative to introduce Total Quality Management (TQM) and process improvement. At the time we first became involved with them, they had already re-engineered many of their business processes and implemented many important new systems and procedures. For example, they had a clear mission statement which gave sense and purpose to the direction in which the company was heading. All sections of the business had business improvement plans which were congruent with the overall mission statement. Process management had been implemented and a quality council had overall responsibility for driving the change forward and bringing together all manner of quality improvement project teams to tackle particular problems. Yet despite all of these structural and procedural changes, the board decided that something more was required. They recognized a need to tackle the more nebulous area of the organizational culture. Indeed, they realized all of the changes they had implemented would only really bear fruit in a new, more empowering culture. Hence, the intention was to help managers:

- move away from a traditional hire and fire culture;
- manage on a day-to-day basis without relying on the formal authority system;
- empower staff to feel personally responsible for quality;
- empower staff to make significant operational decisions.

The Board also recognized that key players in any attempt to change culture were factory managers, supervisors and HR people. The particular vehicle they chose to help facilitate the culture change was our client-centred consulting model as it seemed to offer the potential to help managers acquire the skills needed to manage staff in a more empowering way.

Several programmes were completed over a period of months, each comprising a diagonal slice across the organization including factory managers, supervisors and HR people. At first we encountered some difficulties as the language and jargon of 'consulting' is very different to that used on the shopfloor in a clothing factory. But as each group began to grasp the ideas we were proposing they embraced them willingly and started to make connections we had never envisaged. Furthermore, many of the links between client-centred consulting and everyday management are as much a consequence of their efforts and insights as they are our own.

So was the initiative effective? Several months after completing our work we were invited back to attend a company wide TQM day during which the quality improvement teams reported on their current projects. The enthusiasm and commitment were clearly evident. There was no question that this was a company that was being driven forward by an increasingly empowered and enthusiastic workforce. What we witnessed was in no way mere window dressing to impress senior management, it was genuine commitment and involvement. Furthermore, considering that the starting point for this organization was as a traditional fear driven, hire and fire company, the culture shift enabled by the day-to-day actions of managers and supervisors was immense.

Since being involved with this project, and several others, we have increasingly realized that what started out for us as a model to help internal consultants, actually has a much wider application. We now have no doubt that client-centred processes are relevant for managers as well as consultants, and can be applied by anyone who seeks to help others in a way which enables and empowers them. However, we would be among the first to acknowledge that for the manager it is not easy. Unlike the consultant, the manager is often directly involved in the change process. Not only is the manager's role to enable and encourage change, he/she is part of such change, and must themselves change.

Summary

- If the change initiatives prevalent in today's organizations are to be successful, then people need to feel involved and committed. This means that managers responsible for implementing change now need skills which are akin to those of the client-centred consultant.
- Successful organizations are those which recognize the importance of change; are customer focused; design simple organizational structures; are horizontal rather than hierarchical; emphasize the importance of self-managed teams; encourage and support innovation and develop a learning culture.
- If people are to feel empowered they need to feel that they:
  - are making a significant contribution;
  - have control over what they do and are able to make decisions;
  - are valued by colleagues;
  - are competent to deal with the challenges inherent in their work;
  - have opportunities to grow and meet different challenges.
- Successful leaders need to combine three roles.
  - Envisioning long-term goals;
  - being an ambassador for the enterprise;
  - empowering, coaching, supporting and developing people.
- Flatter organizational structures mean that managers are often directly responsible for many more people than has traditionally been the case. This has led to the advent of self-directed work teams which require less control and more facilitation.

- When facilitating self-directed work teams the manager will need to work in a similar way to the client-centred consultant using a modified version of the consulting cycle:
  - building and maintaining trusting relationships;
  - contracting and clarifying expectations;
  - collecting data and giving feedback;
  - diagnosing problems and helping people make decisions;
  - implementation;
  - celebration.

Checklist 2.1 Attitudes to Empowerment

The following checklist is designed to help you assess the degree to which you are predisposed to managing in a way which empowers people. It is adapted from the inventory on client-centredness which appears at the end of Chapter 1 (Checklist 1.1).

Please estimate your score before you complete the questionnaire by placing a cross where you think you are on the scale from 20 to 80.

I have a high degree of commitment to empowerment			I have a low degree of commitment to empowerment
20	40	60	80

Now please complete the questionnaire as honestly as you can. Try to get in touch with your *feelings* about each question as well as your *thoughts*.

Checklist on Attitudes to Empowerment

Tick whichever column best represents your feeling.

	I never feel this way	*I seldom feel this way*	*I often feel this way*	*I always feel this way*
1 I should be able to understand my people's problems better than they do.	....	....	....	....
2 When I'm giving advice and suggestions, I really feel I'm helping my people.	....	....	....	....
3 I get defensive when challenged or confronted by my people about something really important to me.	....	....	....	....
4 Being seen and acknowledged as an expert in my field is very important to me.	....	....	....	....

5	I like to help my people by using my experience to tell them what to do for the best.	....	....	....	....
6	I believe that my people are generally less competent and skilful at problem solving than I am.	....	....	....	....
7	I have a lot of experience and therefore know the answers to most of the problems my people have to deal with.	....	....	....	....
8	I feel rejected as a person when people criticize what I do or say.	....	....	....	....
9	I find it difficult to accept feed-back which is against my self-image.	....	....	....	....
10	I enjoy showing how clever I am by being witty and scoring points.	....	....	....	....
11	As a manager I believe I should not ask my people for help.	....	....	....	....
12	I believe that most of my people want me to solve their problems for them.	....	....	....	....
13	I feel devalued when my people get together to solve their own work problems without my involvement.	....	....	....	....
14	I know better than my people, what to do to solve their work problems.	....	....	....	....
15	My primary role as a manager is to know and control what goes on in my department.	....	....	....	....
16	I like being in control when working with my people, to solve work problems.	....	....	....	....
17	I do not believe that most people want to solve their own work problems.	....	....	....	....
18	If I've spent years developing my competence, I must be in a better position than my people to make decisions.	....	....	....	....

19 I enjoy having people come to me with problems which I can solve but which they can't.	....	....	....	....
20 If people ask me for my advice I believe I should give it to them if I can.	....	....	....	....
Total the number of ticks in each column	....	....	....	....

Score 1 for each answer in the Never column
2 Seldom
3 Often
4 Always

Total score [ ]

Transfer your score to the scale on the previous page then check the rationales on the next page to see in which area you might like to work on your development.

Rationales for the Checklist on Attitudes to Empowerment

The classification of the items in the checklist is not a definitive one and some statements apply to more than one area. Generally, however, we have included statements which seek your feelings about being an advice giving expert, your managerial attitude and style and your self-image and personal power.

Advice giving expert:	Items 1, 2, 4, 7, 14, 18, 19, 20.
Managerial attitude and style:	Items 5, 6, 10, 12, 14, 15, 16, 17, 19, 20.
Self-image and personal power:	Items 1, 2, 3, 4, 5, 8, 9, 10, 11, 13, 18, 20.

In our view these indicate the relative importance of the three areas. If managers are to rely less upon their experience and expertise and their positional power and formal authority, then they will need to develop a self-image which relies upon their personal power as people in their own right.

If you found yourself ticking very few of the *often* and *always* boxes and your score is below 40, you will probably find it fairly easy to work at empowering people in your department; you are unlikely to find it difficult to move away from the traditional way of working as a manager and your self-image is unlikely to rest upon your formal authority or status in the company.

However, if you found yourself at the other end of the scale, with a score above 60 you may like to consider some areas for self-development if you are to be happy in the new environment.

To find out what you need to work on circle the item number above for all those where you scored 3 or 4. The pattern which emerges will indicate what you may wish to work on.

The rationale which follows may give you some ideas:

If your power does not depend upon your being seen as an expert,
If you have little desire to be in control of other people,
If you do not automatically operate as an advice giver,
If you are not overly concerned to influence other people to your way of thinking,
If you value yourself and your people even though you need each other's help,
If you can handle negative feedback without being destroyed by it,
If you can take pleasure from your group's success achieved without you . . .

Then you are likely to be well on the road to becoming an empowering manager already.

Facilitating Change in Organizations

3

Organizational Change Agent?

Machiavelli probably hit the nail on the head when he said:

> It must be considered that there is nothing more difficult to carry out, nor more doubtful of success, nor even more dangerous to handle, than to initiate a new order of things.

One major task for all consultants who aspire to be organizational change agents is to help managers design and implement change. Generally speaking, that entails finding out what is going wrong, helping clients make decisions and plan, and then helping them implement the changes so that they stay in place in the long term.

Organizations are complex systems as Waterman, Peters and Phillips demonstrated with the help of Anthony Athos of Harvard University, when they developed their 7s model (*Business Horizons* June 1980) to help us consider the inter-relationships of all the parts and what happens when you intervene to try to change one of them. However, even this model is only a simplified view of an organization. Each of their categories can be subdivided into many sub-systems. Change even one part of a sub-system and it has repercussions elsewhere. Neither do organizations exist in a vacuum. They are part of the global economy and their particular marketplace; they are subject to legal constraints; affected by social and environmental factors and trends as well as ethical considerations.

Understanding Organizations

As organizations are so complex, is it not possible either to govern them or predict how they will behave? From the time when Frederick W. Taylor wrote his *Shop Management* (1911) people have been trying to understand organizations so that they can be analysed, diagnosed and made more effective. Max Weber took us a little further in *The Theory of Social and Economic Organization* and there have been numerous attempts since by students of organizational structure to produce models which will explain what is happening. During the 1930s and 1940s organizational theorists talked about idealized, logically structured models as characterized by Alvin Brown in *Organization of Industry*

(1947). The emphasis was on form and an assumption that people should do what was prescribed for them or what they were contracted to do. Management were assumed to know what was good for workers and the workers were supposed to get on with the job and not put up any form of resistance. Around the 1940s a view started to emerge that maybe it was possible to make organizations more effective by paying attention to the people who worked in them. Early work by Roethlisberger and Dickson in *Management and the Worker* (1939) and Elton Mayo in *The Social Problems of Industrial Civilization* (1945) began to highlight the view of organizations as dynamic systems rather than simple machines. A system in which the effectiveness of the whole depends upon the effectiveness of its individual parts. There can be few students of management who are not familiar with the work of Douglas McGregor who introduced the ideas of Theory X and Theory Y, and was largely responsible for bringing people issues to the forefront of management theory. What all these early writers seemed to forget was that organizations are man-made, subject to and steeped in aims, desires and expectations.

It wasn't until 1965, however, that H. J. Leavitt put forward his moving model of the organization as a system comprising *task – structure – technology – people*, all linked together so that if a change is initiated in one aspect it affects all the other components. This disposed forever of the 'simple machine' concept but you can still meet managers who seem to be unaware of the fact! More often than not 'quick fixes' are an attempt to change one part of the system alone while assuming that the rest of it will be unaffected. Those who operate from this standpoint seem to assume that people will calmly accept changes which are decrees from above, without a murmur.

During the last thirty years or so we have learned a lot about organizations and the often subtle relationships between the various parts. How the structure affects the people and vice versa, how the product can influence the culture, how the technology bears upon the tasks and so on. We have begun to question whether the way the armed services and the church are organized is right for commercial or voluntary organizations. There are still people who emphasize the importance of the structure and others who put an undue emphasis on the people. So how can we pick our way safely through this minefield? How can each of the available models help us in our concern to understand what we are doing when we try to change the organization? Overall, it seems that there is now a greater awareness of the inter-dependence of human and technical factors; that different forms of organization are required in different circumstances and environments. Nobody now expects standard solutions. This makes our job as change agents more difficult in that we shall be expected to take note of all the different circumstances, but easier in that we shall not just be expected to tinker with a simple machine.

A Model of Organizational Life

We have found, over the years, that many models of organizations are unnecessarily complex and therefore quite difficult to understand or explain. This is not

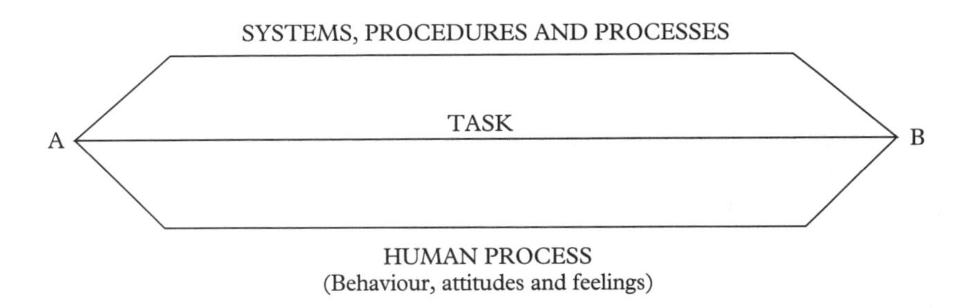

Figure 3.1 Organizational Life Model

to say that organizations are uncomplicated or easy to understand – they are not, but we have found the following model to be one which readily appeals to people who work in organizations of whatever shape and size.

One way to look at it is to focus on the three aspects of organizational life which are involved in getting from Point A to Point B (see Figure 3.1).

These three strands are always present regardless of how many people are involved, the length of time the organization has existed, the complexity of the task or the time available to complete it. The model seems to apply equally well whether examining a group which has come together to achieve a single, simple objective, or an organization of thousands of people which has complex objectives and a long history.

Task

There will always be a task to do: the content of the work or purpose for which the group has come together. It concerns the conversion of information, opinions and ideas of the group members into decisions and recommendations or the conversion of raw materials into finished products. In general, it is about *what* has to be done and why. It is important that all members of a team, department or organization have a clear understanding of what the task actually is.

Often the task is left unstated with everyone assuming that they have the same perception of what is to be achieved. In fact, people could well be working towards slightly different objectives with differing priorities or ones which have changed over time without anyone being aware of them. The result can be organizational chaos. It is important for an organization to have a clear mission statement. People need to know what business they are in, what goals are to be achieved and how success will be measured. When agreeing the task, it is important to ensure that it is realistic and that sufficient resources are available in the form of money, equipment, people, raw materials and time.

The *task* addresses such questions as:

- What is the task?
- Do we all understand it?
- Can we do it?

- Do we have the necessary equipment, space, time, tools, skills etc.?
- When is the finished product required?
- How much product is required and to what quality standards?
- Who needs the finished product – internal or external customer?
- What should we do if something goes wrong?
- Who is responsible for quality control?

The systems, procedures and processes

Even though you are working on a task by yourself you will usually have a plan to work to. Once you have two or more people working on the task there is likely to be an even bigger need for some agreed systems and procedures to regulate how things are done and who is to do them. Some ways of doing things will need to be standardized; some systems need to be followed to ensure that the product is manufactured to the required quality standard and in a safe way; some ways of operating cannot be left to individual discretion. So the Systems, Procedures and Processes strand covers *How* people in an organization need to organize themselves in order to get work done and achieve the Task. In general it covers the mechanics of organizational life such as:

- planning procedures;
- programming and scheduling systems;
- budgetary and financial controls and audit;
- business control systems;
- organization structures and hierarchies;
- job descriptions;
- roles and responsibilities;
- policies and guidelines;
- decision-making processes;
- systems for rewards and benefits;
- personnel systems for recruitment and discipline;
- quality control systems;
- security and safety systems;
- contracting and purchasing procedures;
- legal requirements;
- conflict handling procedures;
- internal and external communication systems.

The *systems, procedures and processes* addresses such questions as:

- How do we acquire additional resources?
- Who does what in this organization?
- Who fills the necessary roles?
- How will we keep to time?
- How will we monitor progress towards our goal?
- How will we review what we have done?
- How do we make changes to the schedule?

The Human Process (Behaviour, Attitudes and Feelings)

When people come together to do a task they need some systems, procedures and processes to regulate how things get done and who does what. However, while the mechanics can be prescribed, they do not take into account human beings with their different personalities, their hopes and fears, their aspirations and above all, their feelings. So this aspect of the model of organizational life takes all these into account. It is about how people work together and the feelings which are engendered by their behaviour and attitudes.

The *human process* issues in organizations therefore cover the *feeling* issues arising from human interactions.

People issues will include:

- Management style and its effect upon the organization.
- Who makes decisions and how they are communicated.
- Communication – one way or two way?
- Perceived powerfulness or powerlessness.
- How people react to new ideas – constructively or not.
- The degree of support, openness and trust.
- Opportunities for development and growth.
- The amount and style of feedback expected and given.
- Is conflict handled constructively or avoided?
- Do people work collaboratively or competitively?
- Are problems over gender, race and disability raised or ignored?
- Are people interested in how other people feel?
- Is there a feeling of commitment and involvement?
- Do people feel involved in decisions about their work?
- Do organizational politics get in the way?
- How much fear is around?
- Is the organizational culture conducive to open relationships or is it one where people keep quiet and don't rock the boat?

What does all this mean?

It will be obvious that a client group which only concentrates on its *systems, procedures and processes* and the *people issues* will have a wonderful time but is unlikely to achieve its *task*. It will not be long before morale will suffer and the group will disintegrate, disband or get taken over. However, concentration solely on the *task* is likely to lead to other more serious problems, at least in the longer term. Arguments may develop about 'who does what', questions will be posed about objectives and bad feelings will probably be the order of the day. Generally people are prepared to concentrate solely on the task when they realize that it is vital for the business. However, they will not expect that to be the order of the day forever and ignoring the process issues for too long is likely to result in the task not getting done at all.

More and more groups are recognizing that choosing to ignore the human process issues in their organization is no longer an option. Dealing with them is not a waste of time, detracting from the time spent on the task. Discussing the people issues openly in a culture which is supportive and allows people to say how they feel, is likely to lead to a more effective organization. It is a sign of group maturity when human process issues are openly expressed and dealt with; when group building is regarded as an integral part of achieving the task.

Although many consultants tend to be called in to help a group be more effective in achieving the task by directly influencing what is done there are many who are also called in to look at the systems, procedures and processes involved. Problems to do with work scheduling, control issues, quality assurance issues or those involving reorganization of some sort. However, whatever the presenting problem, there will inevitably be human process issues which will be much more ambiguous and difficult to handle. Unless you collect data covering these human process issues, present that data to the client and help them deal with it, your impact and your influence will be seriously diminished. If you fail to take account of the human process issues you are unlikely to be able to assess the impact of the problem upon the whole organization.

Of course, persuading your clients to examine and discuss human process issues can be very difficult and time-consuming. They may be reluctant to accept that such issues have a bearing on what is going wrong. You may have to watch out for clients who try to deal with human process issues by instituting more systems, procedures and processes rather than facing them head on.

One final word of caution. When deciding what data to collect it is important to examine your motives for collecting it. The truly client-centred consultant collects data for the benefit of the client *not* to support a pet theory, prove how unpopular or incompetent the manager is, or how clever you are!

We believe that it is important to discuss the boundaries of data collection with the client at the contracting stage. As early as possible it is probably wise to raise the client's awareness of the need to collect all sorts of data including that concerned with human process. Reassure clients about confidentiality but make sure that they are prepared for the possibility that some of the human process issues may make them feel a little uncomfortable. Above all, you have to really believe that these human process issues are important and stick to your guns in the face of the client's reluctance.

Exercise: Try to think of reasons why clients might be reluctant to allow you to collect human process data when you are there, as they see it, to sort out a task or work systems problem? Can you think what reasons might be given for not wanting to face such data when it is collected? Write down as many as you can and them compare them with our list at the end of the chapter (see Exercise 1).

Moving Models of Organizations

An organization is not just what is shown by the organization chart. The cynic would tell us that we should beware of seeing that as anything other than the pecking order. The reality is that the system is more alive, dynamic and irrational than that. In other words, it is a 'moving model'. As stated earlier, the system

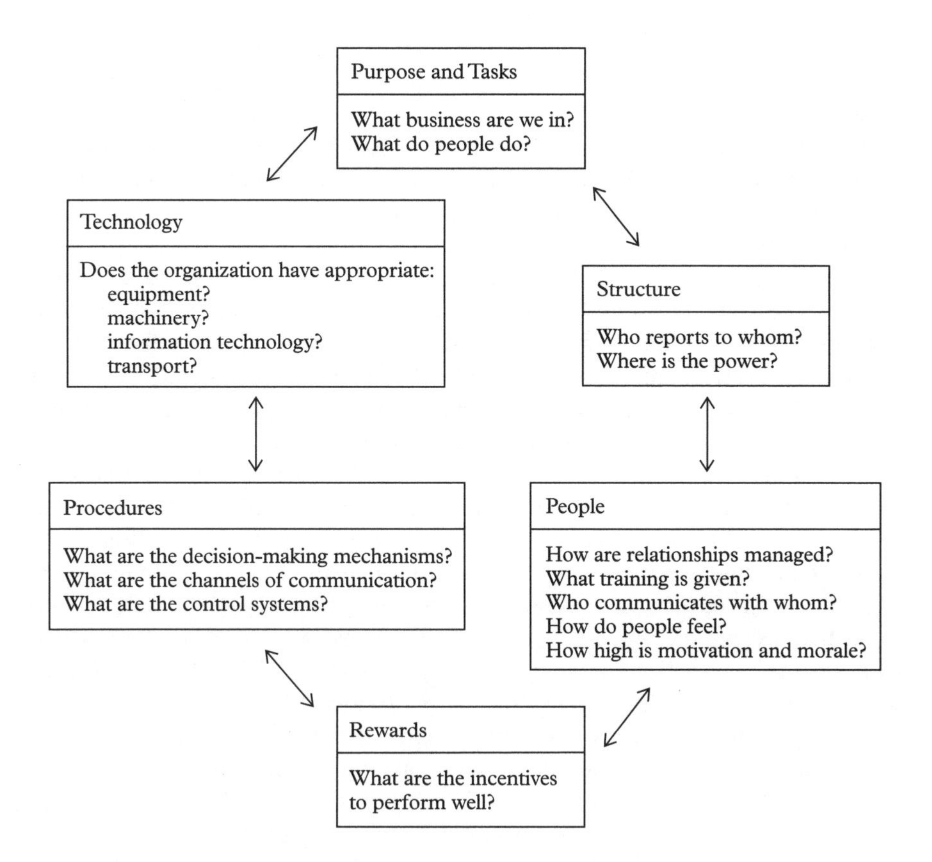

Figure 3.2 Organization diagnostic model

comprises at least four basic components – structure, tools, technology and people. Change one and you affect all the others. The problem for managers and change agents alike is to anticipate the widespread consequences of what could be seen as quite a modest change in one of them.

Thinking about organizations advanced, and Weisbord (1976) suggested that there were six places to look for trouble: *purpose – structure – rewards – helpful mechanisms – relationships – leadership*. By this time we find much less emphasis on structure and a much greater concern with looking at the people side of things, including relationships, leadership and rewards. Much of the analysis has to deal with not only what is but also how people feel about what is.

For a number of years we have used an adaptation of this model as illustrated in Figure 3.2 which uses six aspects of organizational life.

When diagnosing organizational problems you need to be sensitive to all six of these spheres. The symptoms of a problem might emerge in one sphere but some of the causes might lie in others. For example, a construction company identified that it had a problem in the *task* sphere; sales volume was not increasing as it should. The sales force was divided into geographical areas while most of their customers tended to have national operations which meant that orders taken by one sales force might result in work actually being done in a different area. The area sales teams seemed very reluctant to co-operate with each other when dealing with these large national customers. Communication between areas was minimal and no effort was made to keep each other informed or support each other. The problem was diagnosed as a *people* issue and a lot of energy was put into communication and teamworking events. This had some effect but the problems of poor communication and co-operation persisted. What no one had recognized was that at least part of the equation lay in the sphere of *rewards*. The area sales teams were given a group bonus which relied not only on sales volume achieved but also on being more successful than the other teams. The management wanted people to co-operate but they were actually being rewarded to compete with each other. A broader diagnosis would have resulted in an earlier resolution of the problem.

The quest for total quality management (TQM) is also a good illustration of an organizational change strategy which can go badly wrong if attention is not given to all six spheres of activity. The authors became involved with a TQM programme which seemed to be running out of steam. The top team had done a lot of work producing a mission statement (*purpose* and *tasks*). Each department had a clear and agreed departmental purpose analysis (*structure*) which clarified the expectations not only of the manager but of each department's internal suppliers and internal or external customers. A lot of work was done on clarifying quality standards (*procedures*) and systems for ensuring they were met. In addition, quality groups were set up as a way of encouraging employees to develop ideas for solving problems. Finally, it was obvious that the technology was adequate for the needs of the business. So what was going wrong? It became evident that the bits of the jigsaw that were missing were in the spheres of *rewards* and *people*. The company still used a piece-work system so that people were being rewarded for quantity of work not for quality. They were really being rewarded for conforming rather than for taking responsibility for quality or suggesting innovation. This linked of course with the sphere of *people* and how they were managed. The senior team now began to recognize that TQM required the company to work towards having 'TQM people', who feel empowered and valued rather than controlled and mistrusted. The senior team did some work on identifying the kind of people they needed if they were to have a truly TQM business. This led them to think through the implications for management style. They realized that if they wanted employees to work in a TQM way they could no longer use a management style based on coercion, mistrust, closed communication channels, and an emphasis on punishment rather than on rewards – especially psychological rewards. They began to recognize that what they had done so far was important, but to achieve genuine TQM they needed to embark on a very ambitious programme of cultural and personal change if they were to be really successful.

Exercise 2 at the end of this chapter explores the use of the Organizational Diagnostic model in more detail.

In 1980 Peters, Waterman and Phillips, consultants with McKinsey's Organizational Effectiveness practice, produced The 7–S Framework, a model which has proved immensely helpful to managers and change agents ever since. Their 7-Ss are *structure – strategy – systems – style – staff – skills* all linked together by *superordinate goals*. Whether or not these descriptions are still valid is open to debate but what they did was to take us even further away from consideration of mere structural reorganization as the answer to organizational problems. By now all managers and consultants must know that they have to look at everything that goes on in the organization as described above. Yet we still act as if we didn't know it. If we want change we change the structure. We have yet to have a group of consultants and managers together who didn't report that in at least one of their organizations they were being *reorganized*. Maybe we have to accept that the time-lag between the development of new concepts and their acceptance and use is longer than we would like.

What Does This Mean for Change Agents?

First, whenever we get requests from managers to help with any change initiative, our motto must be '*structure is not organization*'. We must ensure that all other aspects of the organization are looked at with the understanding that within a large organization there are going to be multiple tasks, a variety of products, different technologies, differing management styles, different information needs and often very different processes and procedures for getting things done. On top of all this there will be people with different personalities, different skills, different levels of education and ability and different aspirations, attitudes and feelings, especially about change.

Secondly, it seems important to recognize that you can't change everything at once, that during all change processes there is a need for some stability and that unless there is a change in culture every change is a potential 'quick fix'. Organizations are man-made systems and can be changed by man. Change cannot be decreed it can only be achieved by collaboration.

Other Useful Models

With the realization and acceptance that people issues are important in understanding and changing any organization, we should realize the importance of those models which emphasize this.

John Adair's Action-centred Leadership Model

This model, devised and published by John Adair in *Action-centred Leadership* (1979) see Figure 3.3, still holds potential to explain why concentration upon the *task* alone can lead to people feeling ignored and undervalued. Why it is important to listen to people, recognize effort and appraise and train them. Why developing a team to be creative, self-regulating, risk taking and able to manage conflict constructively, has a part to play in getting the task done. This is something most managers know. However, we once worked with an organization which espoused teamworking and were introducing cohesive, self-managed

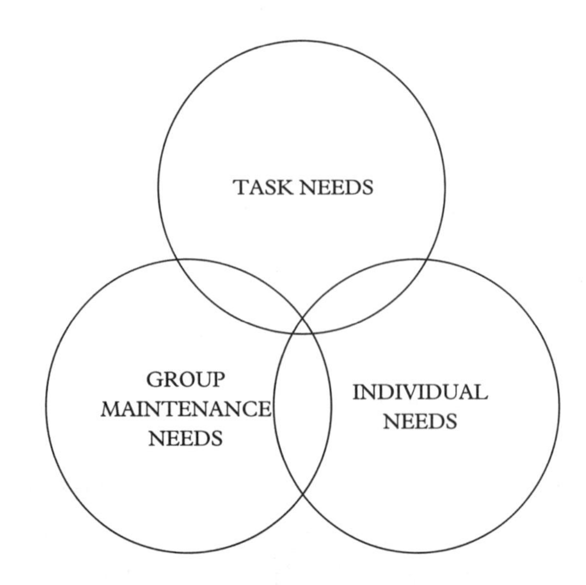

Figure 3.3 Action-centred Leadership Model based upon the work of John Adair

work groups while at the same time putting in a reward system firmly based upon individual performance.

Maslow's Hierarchy of Individual needs

This model, published by A. H. Maslow in *Motivation and Personality* (1954) seems outdated from this distance in time but still has its uses. He described his view of the hierarchy of human needs and suggested that higher order needs could not be met until basic survival needs were met. He described needs as being physiological – safety – social – self-esteem and self-realization/self-actualization. This need/priority model, see Figure 3.4 adapted from the original format, suggests that all human beings have the capacity to climb the hierarchy but that some people never grow beyond certain levels and their lifestyle is geared to satisfaction of lower level, deficit, needs. To Maslow, such cases represent immaturity or stunted growth. Self-realization or actualization on the other hand is a growth need and describes a rarely obtained state of human achievement. What the priority model suggests is that a satisfied need no longer motivates. We all know that people at work are enthusiastically motivated by what they seek more than what they have already. In addition, what people want from their work today may be quite different from what they wanted some time ago or will want tomorrow. Organizations may not provide opportunities for their workers to satisfy all their needs at work, so they may well get what they want from their out of work activities. We have all heard Tom Peters lament the lack of creativity and initiative asked of people at work. He will ask senior managers why their employees run football teams, youth clubs or community associations; serve on local councils or community health boards in their spare

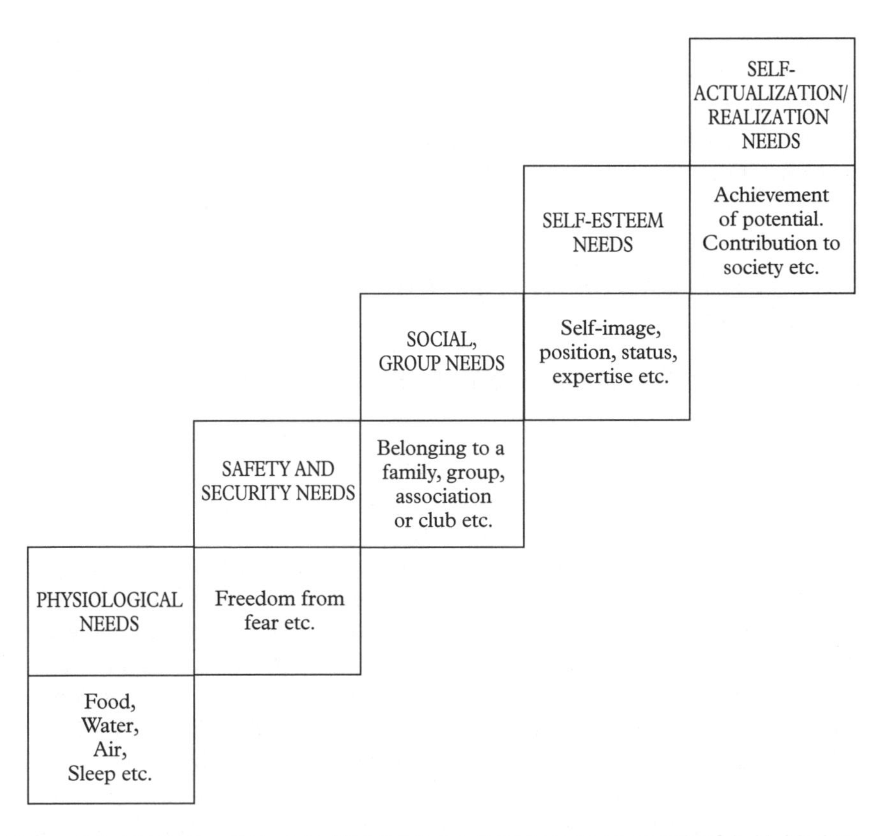

Figure 3.4 Hierarchy of Human Needs Model. Based upon the work of A. H. Maslow

time but are not asked to use the same creativity and energy at work. Yet how many organizations do we know that are still stuck with old fashioned ideas and work hard to satisfy inappropriate levels of need? Maslow's ideas may not be quite so applicable to individuals these days but it may be very helpful to look at what organizations are doing to try to motivate their workforce and find out just how appropriate these measures are.

Our knowledge about organizations and how they behave is still incomplete. We have learned a great deal about how people are affected by the organization and the organization by the people, but there is no checklist available for managers or consultants when trying to change things. All we can do is recognize that when we try to change parts of the organization we are likely to spark off reactions which we never expected and which were probably unpredictable. We should be careful not to overemphasize one aspect over another. We shall meet in our travels, structuralists, technologists, systems and procedures people, strategy consultants and people people. The big issue seems to be how to integrate all these concerns to achieve effective, long-term change. Somehow there has to be a way of agreeing what is right and desirable for both individuals and the organization to achieve their goals at work. It is our long held view that people in general go to work determined to do a good job. More often than not, they know what to do and how to do it. When they don't do it, it is because there are human process issues involving some aspect of their behaviour, attitudes and feelings which are being ignored. Of course, all other aspects of the organization have to be working to the same ends, all contributing to the achievement of the goals. Given that this is the situation, the people themselves make it succeed or fail.

Organizational Change and the Effects of Culture

Why Quick Fixes Don't Work in the Long Term

It is probably fair to say that the evidence that the 'quick fix' fails to achieve lasting change is now overwhelming. Nearly everyone who works in any large organization will be able to provide examples of campaigns variously called 'putting customers first', 'just in time', 'total quality' or 'getting it right first time', which were introduced with trumpets and banners to herald the brave new world. Because they didn't really impact the culture of the organization and dealt only with the presenting problem, they very quickly faded and became known as 'flavour of the month'. Throughout the organization people muttered and moaned and you could regularly hear such comments as 'never mind the customers – what about the staff' or 'whatever happened to "just in time"?' We once worked with a company where the TQM programme had been installed for nearly two years. The shop floor workers told us 'We can't do TQM'. When asked why they replied 'because it gets in the way of the real work'. The TQM programme hadn't changed a thing. Outwardly there had been significant changes. TQM noticeboards were full of reported improvements, the car park was available to the first people to arrive in the morning whether MD or shop-floor worker and there were groups of people labelled quality circles. However, at a deep level, the culture hadn't changed. Managers still managed in the same old controlling style, they made promises they didn't keep and workers' suggestions were largely ignored. No wonder the shop floor said they couldn't do TQM. We had to work quite hard with the management team to help them change not only their behaviour but also their belief system and their attitudes to their workforce, and then help them to convince the rest of their people that they really meant it!

Expert after expert has written about the ineffectiveness of the 'quick fix' yet still they are put in place as a knee jerk reaction to the current issue. In his books, *Beyond the Quick Fix* (1984) and *Managing Beyond the Quick Fix* (1989), Professor Ralph H. Kilmann wrote 'only by treating organizations as living systems rather than simple machines will we ever be able to renew organizations, institutions and nations for the global economy.' The essence of his ideas is that to achieve lasting change it is essential to have a 'completely integrated programme' for improving organizations. This programme must start with culture change and end with continuous improvement, yet we still find people working from back to front. They wonder why their one-day culture change programme on Friday doesn't result in a new culture on Monday, or why beginning work on continuous improvement in a culture where it is not acceptable to say 'I've made a mistake' or 'I need help', doesn't work.

The Humanistic Approach to Organizational Change

So, having decided that it is important for a really effective organization to have a culture in which people are encouraged to 'self actualize', to speak the truth as they see it, respond to each other in a genuinely authentic manner in a climate in which everyone feels safe, we are left with two questions. How can we help to make it happen? and, will this be enough?

There has been a realization that espousing new policies, writing new rules or changing job titles is merely tampering with the systems and procedures to try to achieve real lasting change. Managers still have a choice, to implement the new policies, obey the new rules and do what top management wants, or ignore it all and carry on as they have always done. Espousing an equal opportunities policy will not have any effect upon recruitment behaviour unless people are committed to making it work. Managers with racist tendencies will find devious ways of subverting the policy they don't agree with and only occasionally get caught or taken to a tribunal. However much you try to get managers to change by threatening them with dire consequences, they will only change if they decide to do so. They judge whether or not they will get caught and may decide to accept the risks and consequences of not changing.

The humanistic approach is to veer away from an emphasis on systems and procedures and to concentrate on human process issues in an attempt to get people to behave differently towards each other and to value each other as human beings. The concentration is on such issues as:

- having a positive view of human beings;
- increasing self awareness;
- focusing on the here and now;
- expressing feelings;
- increased openness;
- greater levels of trust;
- increased spontaneity and creativity;
- individual self-fulfilment;
- more genuine communication;
- unconditional positive regard;
- active and attentive listening.

Reactions to Organizational Change

It might be relevant here to consider what happens when we try to change an organization. There is always likely to be one third of the people who are committed and keen to adopt the changes, there will be a third who are doubtful but willing to give it a go and there will be another third who are definitely antagonistic and likely to sabotage the efforts of the other two thirds. So when it comes to implementing the new culture the saboteurs will do all they can to ensure that nothing changes. These saboteurs don't all come from the lower echelons either. Any directors and senior managers who pay lip service to the new ways can just as easily sabotage the change process either deliberately or unconsciously. So, the answer to our second question 'Is it enough?' is a resounding NO. Because if no-one is prepared to take on the saboteurs and confront the discontinuity between what people say they are going to do and what they actually do, whether they be colleagues, senior managers, or chief executive, then they get away with their destructive behaviour. This sends messages which suggest that the new behaviour is not really ok and that keeping your head down, keeping your nose clean and not rocking the boat is what is expected. People will revert to corridor meetings, hiding behind the rules and regulations, withholding information and ridiculing those who are really trying to change. It won't be long before the new culture gives way to the old and we are back where we started. People will find it very difficult to sustain the changes when issues of dependence on authority, personal responsibility for their actions and the fear that is prevalent in many organizations are not dealt with.

So what can be done to make the new culture real and ensure that it replaces the old in the long term? Beverley Stone puts it most eloquently and succinctly in her excellent new book *Confronting Company Politics* (1997) a must for all of us working in the field of organizational development, when she says:

> The humanistic approach creates a climate where individuals are encouraged to satisfy their personal goals of self actualization through the use of their energy and potential in pursuit and achievement of organizational goals. Yet the difficulty in maintaining the climate and the risks and discomfort involved in such a pursuit should never be underestimated. Neither should anyone hold out any hope of avoiding them if they are to succeed in living an authentic and meaningful life. For existentialists each individual has to stand up for their principles every minute of every day, no matter what the cost. Excellent companies have leaders who pursue their vision relentlessly, no matter what the cost to their own popularity. They have zero tolerance of sabotage. Yet, since some leaders are also saboteurs, individuals cannot postpone pursuing their work authentically while waiting for an existential leadership style. Therefore the adoption of an existential approach by each individual who wishes to pursue their values and attitudes which match the desires norms, despite those who don't, is a prerequisite for long-term organizational change.

So, it isn't only about *doing things differently* but about *being different*. How then, can we help the organization to be different in the long term?

In most interventions it will probably be important to deal with some of the issues raised in the section describing the humanistic approach. A safe and supportive climate might well be beneficial to the change process but by itself is probably not enough. The problem facing the 'being different' philosophy – the existential approach – is that it is assumed that most environments are hostile to change. The saboteurs are unlikely to be sacked or changed and so it is left to each individual to behave authentically in the hostile environment. The assumption behind this is that while a supportive climate might well be helpful we are all ultimately alone and must make our own decisions and work through the consequences.

We once worked with a significant number of internal HR consultants with the objective of helping them be more client-centred. The idea was that they should become consultants within departments and work closely with their respective line managers. We worked hard to ensure that the participants and their HR managers knew what we were up to. We understood that as the whole organization was going through a significant culture change the new ways of working would be inline with their new culture. During the programme they all learned how to use the confrontational style and were determined to use it with care when they got back to work. They realized that unless they were prepared to confront managers with the discontinuity between their stated intentions and their actual behaviour they were not likely to be very effective consultants. However, it wasn't very long before people on the programme were talking about the confrontational style as '*the career limiting style*'. So much for the new culture. While everyone accepted the new ideas and ways of working in theory, nobody was prepared to test them out. They all decided that the risk was too great and they were prepared to live with the guilt of not doing what they knew they should rather than suffer the consequences of trying the new behaviour and limiting their career.

We also worked in a hotel where an impressive plaque in the foyer announced 'We are Investors in People' and the car park attendant swore at us and told us the car park was full. When asked for an alternative he said 'That's not my problem – you can't park here!' In another organization we interrupted a briefing at which people were being told how to answer the questions when the IIP assessors came to visit. In both these instances there was apparent change but the culture was still the same.

This means that whoever is facilitating organizational change must be aware of the dangers inherent in just helping to create a supportive climate within which people can be open and honest and so on. It is important to help the organization recognize that being different means taking personal responsibility for the change, confronting the saboteurs, pointing out the differences between what people say they will do and what they actually do. It means helping people to take the risk of looking stupid and being laughed at by those who are hanging on to the old ways. It also means helping people to recognize what they are doing to themselves when they know what they should be doing, but don't do it. They have to choose between the guilt of doing nothing and the risk of doing something which may or may not work.

Beverley Stone again states that 'before anyone embarks on a culture change programme it seems essential that they first understand the assumptions about human nature and learning that underlie the consultant's model and dictate their view of the ideal leadership style and climate. Next, they need to understand their own assumptions, and finally they need to make clear to everyone in the organization that it is these assumptions that they are committing themselves to if they are to join in the creation of the appropriate environment to change behaviour'.

What is Culture and Can it be Changed?

Trying to define culture is extremely difficult. Is it just 'the way things are done around here' or the 'rules that determine our way of life'? Can it be determined by identifying the myths and legends, the symbols, the rituals, beliefs and language? Or is it more about what all these things mean to people, how they are interpreted in everyday life; in other words, what are the 'theories in use'?

This is not meant to be a treatise on culture change but merely a means to point out some of the dilemmas when trying to identify organizational culture. The problem arises when you try to help an organization achieve radical, high order changes such as different attitudes to customers and markets, different attitudes to the tasks in hand, increased creativity etc. What often happens is that what is achieved is only lower order change; outward appearances indicate that things are different but the underlying patterns, beliefs and values stay the same. It seems that, if we are not careful, all we succeed in doing with our change programme is to achieve 'more of the same'. If we conceive of culture as patterns of meaning which provide a world view for the organization's members, it will be obvious that for them to think outside that view will be very difficult. How they think and deal with problems will constrain them in trying to change. This is demonstrated at an individual level by many senior executives who are feeling stressed by overwork and worried about the possibility of premature heart disease. They decide to play squash or tennis, go jogging or exercise in the company gym. They then do this with the same driving attitude which has produced the stress at work in the first place. They try to improve the number of miles they run each day, they time their achievements and exercise however tired they are. Strangely this doesn't relieve the stress but adds to it. Now they begin to feel guilty when they can't exercise and they take more work home to be able to find time during the day to get to the gym. In other words, this is lower order change. Higher order change would have been to make a significant change in their home/work life balance. However, this requires a substantial and fundamental revision of values and attitudes, a rethinking of the importance of family and friends, a new approach to work and its importance in the scheme of things. But such rethinking is constrained by the way the executive works now.

Achieving this higher order change when you, as a consultant, are part of the organization is clearly quite difficult. It requires consultants to be powerful as described in Chapter 16. In other words you need a high degree of self awareness, a high tolerance of ambiguity and the ability and the determination to confront the discrepancies between your clients' stated intentions and their deeds. You have to be prepared to take the risk of taking a lot of flack while you do what you know has to be done. You have to be careful not to be seduced by the existing culture, for unless the organizational change programme achieves higher order change it will probably not last and the investment will not be a good one. This seems to imply that if the existing culture is a barrier to change, unless we can really identify it at a deep level, we are unlikely to achieve higher order change. However, in our experience, most people in an organization find it difficult to identify and describe the culture. They know what it is at an unconscious level. They can tell you what it is 'not ok to do', what you will 'never get away with' or what the unspoken rules are, but describing the culture in more concrete terms is very difficult. So how can we help members of the organization to be more specific and explicit about the culture, and remove or reduce the blockages to change? It seems unlikely that there is ever a need to change everything. Change has to be appropriate and some of the ways we operate now have to be preserved. During any change process there is, paradoxically, a need for some stability.

By means of exercises, simulations, apocryphal stories and jokes, it is possible to get a real feel for, and understanding of, the culture. We have found it useful to have groups make lists of what they like about the organization and what they don't, what things they think the organization is good at or not so good at, what they would like to take with them to a new company, what they would be glad to leave behind and what they would like done differently in the organization. It is possible to get to a deeper level by asking for reasons why and examples which illustrate the points. During this whole process we believe it is important to avoid concepts like 'right and wrong' and 'good and bad' and to suspend judgement as far as possible. We try to get people to talk about things as 'helpful or not helpful' or as 'appropriate or inappropriate'. Blaming others and concentrating on who is responsible is counter-productive. Even when thinking about what should change it is often easy for individuals to avoid personal responsibility and talk about how powerless they are to influence the organization. If it is always somebody else's responsibility to effect changes then you have a very good indication of how the current culture is blocking an approach to a new one.

Summary

Quick fixes as a way of achieving lasting change don't seem to be very effective. Without a change in culture we are not likely to have people saying what they really think and even less how they feel. It is important to have an integrated programme in any attempt at organizational change. The humanistic approach to change is fine as far as it goes. It is probably quite a good idea to have an organization in which everyone is valued and where openness and honesty are the norm. However, this is seldom enough. There will always be people looking to sabotage the achievement of the change. Unless people are prepared to take personal responsibility for confronting the saboteurs and working with the new culture, it will eventually decay and we will all be back where we started. This will give the saboteurs the opportunity to say 'I told you it wouldn't work'. Being prepared to live with the anxiety of trying out new behaviour even though it may not work has to be seen as preferable to living with the guilt of doing nothing.

Attempts to change the culture are likely to be hampered by the existing culture. It is therefore very important for people in the organization to get an understanding of the culture, at as deep a level as possible, before ever you start trying to work towards the new one. Whatever you do to facilitate change you must start with the culture and work towards continuous improvement not the other way around.

Focal Issues in Organizations

Over many years as internal and external consultants we have found that whenever people talk about the problems or issues they need to address they always come up with the same things. It is not helpful to dismiss this with a carefree wave of the hand. In our experience all clients seem to think, and often want to think, that their problems are unique and that no other organization could be having similar difficulties. However, we have found it useful to have a system for putting this wide variety of problems presented by the clients into some semblance of order such that we can understand them and talk to each other about them. Sometimes it is also helpful to explain the system to your clients, but you must be the judge of how appropriate that is. A useful way of categorizing organizational problems was developed by Blake and Mouton (1976, 1983) in their book *Consultation.* They identified four possible 'focal issues' which may be worked on by the consultant and the client. These are:

- power/authority;
- morale/cohesion;
- norms and standards;
- goals/objectives.

Blake and Mouton suggested that all organizational problems have underlying issues that fall into one or more of these four categories. *Power/authority* seems to be the most frequent focal issue, centring around the location and use or misuse of power in an organization or its management style, often resulting in a feeling of powerlessness amongst employees. *Morale/cohesion* problems focus on how people feel in the organization, how motivated they are, whether they feel important and whether they are consulted and involved in decisions which affect their work. Often, in times of change, there are repercussions about morale and cohesion in the organization. Sometimes you may find yourself helping clients to re-examine their *norms and standards* – how things are done around here. This includes what is considered appropriate and inappropriate behaviour; does everyone leave work at the normal finishing time or is it the norm to work late? Often a change in technology can only be successful if there is an accompanying change in working patterns or practices – a change in norms and standards. The fourth issue you may come up against concerns *goals and objectives.* You could be involved with helping a team identify what it is really trying to achieve or helping a whole department come to terms with the fact that their goals and objectives are no longer valid for one reason or another.

Power/Authority Issues

Power/authority is a prevalent source of difficulty in today's organizations. General power/authority problems are two way. People with power/authority exercise it inappropriately and those on whom it is exercised have trouble in accepting the fact however effectively or ineffectively it is exercised. How people react to power/authority can have the effect of decreasing or increasing their effectiveness, creativity and personal satisfaction. When attitudes towards authority in general or a particular person arouse antagonisms or a feeling of being threatened, then people can become less competent in dealing with their situation. Power/authority can evoke strong emotions in people especially when it is exercised ineffectively. Reactions include expressing feelings of self doubt, fear, alienation, hurt or more severe responses that result in destructive behaviour towards the organization or themselves. When power/authority is the focal issue the consultant needs to intervene to bring the issue more into the client's field of awareness. The client should be helped to collect pertinent data which they can then be helped to interpret and act upon.

Misperceptions regarding the use of power/authority are particularly pertinent focal issues in group functioning. The boss views his or her behaviour in one way but each member of the group is likely to have a different perspective, especially when this impinges upon the person's job responsibility or status in the group. Members can be helped to share these perceptions, pool information, clear up misunderstandings and increase the likelihood of problem solving.

Morale/Cohesion Issues

Feelings and emotions at whichever end of the scale from despair to euphoria can lead to irrational behaviour. These behavioural extremes and all points in between are related to problems of morale/cohesion for individuals, groups and whole organizations. Lowered morale can drastically reduce the ability to cope with the stresses and strains of everyday life, resulting in people becoming apathetic, uncertain and disabled by their feelings.

Problems involving individuals can stem from severe discouragement at work, demotion, redundancy or dismissal; from personal feelings of lack of confidence, shyness, loneliness, isolation or despair. People left in the organization after a large-scale reduction of staff have feelings of guilt for being the ones not made redundant which can result in severe morale/cohesion problems. These emotions, if not recognized and dealt with, result in a very quick reduction in effectiveness. Inappropriate exercise of power/authority can often result in problems of morale/cohesion, not only for those subjected to it but also for those exercising it when they find that however they exercise it, nothing happens.

Issues of morale/cohesion can occur between groups. When groups that must interact feel antagonistic towards each other, each group is likely to feel threatened by the other and may withdraw support needed to get the job done. For instance where two groups find it impossible to co-operate when they should they could easily become more isolated and withdraw from each other.

Each group may develop its own resources rather than rely upon the other. We, the authors, came across a group which needed the assistance of specialist staff 'owned' by another group within the same company. The other group refused to help on the pretext of being too busy. Finally the original group attempted to recruit similar specialists from outside even though there was not really enough work for them. Finding this difficult they then raised the stakes and recruited people from the other group! Low morale/cohesion can become an issue for a whole organization either as a result of some traumatic event such as a hostile takeover or as a result of a series of small events or disappointments over a lengthy period. Consequences could include apathy, indifference, or feelings of rejection resulting in withdrawal of commitment.

Acceptant interventions permit long suppressed hostilities and anxieties to be shared and slowly it becomes possible to deal with the human and non-mechanical barriers to organizational effectiveness.

Norms and Standards Issues

Norms and standards are usually reinforced by feelings and emotions and are therefore resistant to change. Consequently it is important, when working with such issues, to identify the real issue that is provoking the emotional reaction. It is probably unproductive to work to change such norms and standards by promulgating new policies or issuing new rules without addressing the feelings which are underpinning the norms and standards. For instance management might issue a policy that in future the best person for a job must be appointed regardless of their gender or race. If the norms and standards of the recruiting managers are such that they do not accept this, the policy will not be put into operation and they will find all sorts of ways to frustrate it. We once worked at an assessment centre for graduates into personnel, where there was an equal number of male and female candidates and the company had a well documented and widely distributed equal opportunities policy. However, during the final selection meeting one representative said, rather apologetically, that his boss had said 'I don't care what anybody says I don't want you to come back with any b . . . . y women'!

Norms and standards can also be organization wide. In many instances organizations can agree cultural changes in which there will be more openness, more honesty, improved upward communication, an open door policy so that anyone can say anything to anyone. However, organizational life isn't usually like that. There is often a lot of fear around and people distrust each other. There are norms and standards about how to behave if you want to be successful such as 'keep your head down', 'don't rock the boat', 'managers don't want to hear bad news', and so on. If change is to occur, consultants have to help the organization let go of some of the old norms and standards and shift the trust levels so that people can react in the new culture not out of fear and defensiveness but out of feelings of self worth and problem solving. People have to believe that when they behave in the new ways they won't be subject to retribution at a later date. We worked with a group who refused to give their manager open, honest feedback even though he really wanted it. They were eventually helped to say 'Because we believe that you have a little black book in which you record all the things we say and you are storing them up to use against us'. Much work had to be done to establish enough trust to begin the feedback process he wanted.

Norms and standards are often involved in resistance to change. Staff may have always worked in certain ways which have become the established norm. Newcomers who try to work against such norms will soon be disciplined by the group and brought into line. This could well result in a morale/cohesion issue for them. When called upon to work on change which involves norms and standards, prescriptive approaches may well serve to block any possibility of change and reinforce the current norms.

Goals/Objectives Issues

When the presenting problem is formulated as a goals/objectives issue the consultant can use the catalytic style of questioning to help a group list and evaluate alternatives and decide on some more acceptable goals. It is often possible to help individuals work on personal goals and objectives in terms of their career or changes of job whether they are new starters, mid-career managers or people about to be 'released' from the organization. Non-existent or unclear goals can often be a factor in less than satisfactory performance by an individual, a group or a whole organization. More and more organizations are beginning to question traditional goals/objectives when faced with economic and market changes or social threats. However, there are situations where goals/objectives are not the presenting problem. Two groups are unlikely to formulate their difficulties as goals/objectives issues. Each will tend to view their own goals/objectives as appropriate and those of the other group as inappropriate or out of line. It may then be necessary for the consultant to help them see the benefit of working with super-ordinate goals rather than sticking rigidly to their own. Goals/objectives issues recognized by the consultant but not identified by the client group may have to be subject to the use of the confrontational style. This may well result in an emotional response from the client which has to be dealt with acceptantly.

We once worked with a personnel department which was quite convinced that their objective, indeed the whole purpose of their existence, was 'To offer a competent, modern personnel service to managers', and that this was entirely appropriate. Their concern for the workshop in which we were involved was to work on the tasks and roles and responsibilities to achieve this. It took nearly a day and a significant use of the confrontational style before they were able to reformulate their objective as: 'To help managers run a more effective business by offering a modern, competent personnel service'. At first, this didn't seem like a very significant re-alignment of objectives but it gave a very different message to the rest of the organization, especially to their client managers and it did much for their image as helpers. Before that they had been known as the department which said 'No'. Finding out how the whole group felt about this new objective also raised their morale.

Goals/objectives issues are often readily recognized by noticing differences between departments or sections which are supposed to be pulling in the same direction. These differences can often stem from non-existent or unclear goals badly communicated from the top. Comments such as 'we don't really know what we're supposed to be doing', 'I think this is what I'm supposed to do' or 'I have no idea how we fit with department "X"' will indicate goals/objectives issues tied in with power/authority issues when people haven't been involved and changes have been sent down from above. In which case working with the felt needs of goals/objectives could obscure the need to work with the power/authority issue first.

How Focal Issues Inter-relate

It is very easy, when working with power/authority issues with one client, say an individual manager who wants to change the way he exercises his authority to a more collaborative style, to forget that he is in a power/authority relationship with his boss. Change one relationship and it has repercussions throughout the department or organization. Similarly, such a change to a more participative, consultative approach, as many managers are now trying, brings into focus how authority has been exercised in the past. So while working on a power/authority issue in one department you could well find yourself challenging norms and standards in the whole organization. When other managers begin to try something of the same style and it doesn't work for any reason, you might find groups beginning to lose direction and teamspirit and you will be confronting a morale/cohesion issue.

Blake and Mouton point out that all focal issues are interdependent. If you are working in one area it is important to look out for the effects in another. If an organization is expanding rapidly, for example, there are likely to be difficulties in each focal issue. As the organization grows managers are likely to become more remote and a management style suitable for a small organization may not be appropriate any more. The objectives of the organization may become blurred as it takes on more products, services or projects. As new people arrive they may challenge existing norms and standards and finally, those who remember the time when the business was small, personal and exciting may feel resentful or diminished as individuals as they see the organization growing around them.

So you need to remember to help your clients look at problems in a positive way while at the same time discouraging them from expecting you to wave a magic wand and deal with all the focal issues at the same time. Real problems rarely lend themselves to perfect solutions. However, it will help if you can try to identify real problems rather than simply working with the apparent or presenting problems.

Focal issues are a useful way of categorizing organizational problems. All organizational problems have underlying issues that fall into one or more categories. The most frequent focal issue is power/authority. Feelings and emotions are the basis of all morale/cohesion issues. Norms and standards are often the most resistant to change. Non-existent or unclear goals and objectives can often be a factor in low performance. All focal issues are inter-dependent. Identifying underlying focal issues will help to ensure you work with the real problem.

Change – Learning to do Things Differently

One thing that is important for consultants to understand and help their clients appreciate is the significance of the change process upon the people and the organization. Human change is not easy. Learning to do things differently is not a simple matter. If concepts and skills are truly integrated they result in personal, affective, conceptual and behavioural change. For individuals this is often a painful process; for an organization it is often equally traumatic and the pain should never be underestimated. Learning is one of the most natural processes in the world. We do not have to motivate people to learn. Our job as consultants, while facilitating learning, is not to get in the way.

When people truly learn they change. We should be able to learn from everything that happens to us, pleasant as well as unpleasant but we have all been part of organizations which even have difficulty learning from what goes wrong. The number of truly 'learning organizations' is quite small. Why is this? It would seem that changing a system of thoughts, feelings and behaviours results in the death of the old system with all the grief and pain that entails. There is a period of hanging on; denial, anger and bargaining finally leading to acceptance. This seems to be true whatever the size of the system – an individual, a group or a whole organization. It is therefore important to recognize what you are asking people to do when facilitating long-term, organizational change.

All human change seems to go through similar phases:

Phase 1 – We find we cannot do what is required of us with our current knowledge and skill. The systems we have in our heads don't match with the new set of circumstances in reality. We find ourselves out of balance and uncomfortable. What often happens in this situation is that we try to work in the way we have always done only harder, more forcefully and with greater tenacity. In other words 'more of the same'.

Phase 2 – We now continue to keep the same thoughts obstinately and persistently. We refuse to accept the need to change our ideas. In spite of data telling us the opposite we persist in our obsession with the old ways. The work necessary to achieve the change often happens at an unconscious level. It is therefore important that consultants ensure that clients allow sufficient time for this process and are not coerced by the organization into trying to get through it in a hurry. We once worked with the board members of a large public utility who steadfastly refused to listen to evidence from line managers that things were not as the board saw them. Group after group produced evidence for their opinions but were told that 'they had got it wrong' and things were not like that.

Phase 3 – It seems that after this stage some new form of understanding takes place, often without us really being aware of it. It is sometimes considered to

have happened as if by magic. It seems that some form of re-integration takes place as the new ideas are combined with the old. They are incorporated into current thinking in readiness for the next step.
Phase 4 – The new ideas have now taken over from the old and the internal systems now match the external reality. We are ready to experiment with the new knowledge and skills, trying them out in practice to see whether they will really work.

When helping organizations to learn to do things differently we must remember that:

- Change is a holistic and transformational process not an incremental one. We do not change one part of a system without affecting all the other parts.
- Learning is often circular. People need to return to what they once 'knew'. We sometimes take two steps forward and one back.
- People learn in relationships. Other individuals, family, friends, colleagues, managers, directors and consultants all impact the learning in one way or another.
- People learn what they want to learn. They only learn when they are open, receptive and ready to learn. When the culture is such that it is ok to admit that you don't know or don't understand and need help.

Learning is easy, it's the unlearning that's difficult.

What are the Consequences for Change Agents?

- People going through unlearning and learning, which is what happens throughout the change process, need support from many sources; other people involved in the change, managers and consultants. If there is little organizational support – beware!
- The learning process needs to be legitimate. People sponsoring the change and consultants facilitating it, need to understand what people are going through and appreciate that it is valuable. Behaviour which, at first sight, seems inexplicable and deliberately unco-operative should be seen as normal in the light of the unlearning process.
- To generate a system of continuous improvement, people undergoing the change need to be capable of self monitoring. The responsibility for continuing the change and embedding it in the organization must somehow be left with the practitioners.
- No amount of threat of punishment, sanctions, imprisonment or even the 'firing' squad can make people change if they don't want to. In a civilized society nobody can be made to change; the client always has a choice.

However, we have come across a very senior manager, responsible for organizational change on a grand scale who believed that change could be 'driven home' – to quote his words – and that the work to deal with all the human process fallout would happen in four or five years' time. Needless to say it was only successful to a limited extent and the resultant staff morale was pitifully low.

We believe there are four essential considerations if change is to be planned and implemented to ensure commitment rather than compliance:

- education beforehand and communication of ideas to reduce resistance – sharing the vision;
- participation and involvement in design and implementation – sharing the decision making;
- facilitation and support in providing training in the new knowledge and skills; listening and providing emotional support by counselling – offering training and development;
- negotiation and agreement about rewards, job satisfaction, prospects and working practices – participative management.

So if, as a consultant, you come across a client organization which:

- is experiencing periods of stress and anxiety that block their learning;
- have feelings of disorientation, inadequacy and low self-esteem which cause them to resist change;
- or feel lonely and isolated and unable to accept the new ways of working;

you will understand that these are normal reactions under the circumstances. You will know that you have much work to do to help them surface and deal with their feelings, before trying to work on new behaviour and skills.

We hope that you won't meet any organizations or groups in this state, but if you do, you will know that the change process leaves a lot to be desired. We suspect that you may also have some work to do with the instigators of the change!

Summary

Change often results in personal, affective and conceptual change. Organizations go through the same painful process as individuals when trying to change. All human change seems to go through the same four phases. Change is holistic and transformational and affects all parts of the system. People and organizations only learn when they are receptive and ready to learn. For change to be effective people need to understand the need for change, be involved in the process, be supported while they try it out and have a participative management. No-one can be forced to change – the client always has a choice.

Exercise 1 Why are clients reluctant to deal with human process issues?

Earlier in this chapter we asked you to list all the reasons you could think of why clients may be reluctant to work on human process problems. Below is our list. It's not intended to be definitive by any means and we are sure you will have thought of a lot of reasons that we didn't.

- Exploring process issues is messy and ambiguous.
- It can feel very personal and uncomfortable, even threatening.
- People often think that if they acknowledge the existence of a process problem, they may be opening a Pandora's box.
- It is difficult to control.
- No one knows where it will lead.
- Once the problem is out in the open it can no longer be ignored.
- Dealing with process issues may be seen as the responsibility of the personnel or training department.
- Dealing with process issues involves acknowledging people's feelings and it usually isn't legitimate to share feelings at work.
- People often believe that they are not competent to deal with other people's feelings.
- There is often a myth that 'stress is good for people'.
- It is seen as prying into personal affairs.
- 'We have quality people – they can cope.'
- Process issues are often embodied in the culture of the organization and include a lot of widely believed myths, e.g. about what can and can't be said.

Exercise 2 Organizational Diagnosis

Introduction

It would seem to be an important prerequisite to organizational change, in whatever size of system you are working, to find out as much as you can about the current situation and what appears to be inhibiting effectiveness. This will probably be told to you as the presenting problem or symptoms which may or may not indicate the existence of a problem. They may be intuitive assessments about problems and causes but such data should not be ignored, they will often give you some ideas or hypotheses about where the problems might lie. Your job is to test these hypotheses to help the client find out what the real problems are and help them to decide what, if anything, to do about them.

How to get started

You might like to try the following diagnostic methodology. In the exercise which follows, we have used the organizational diagnostic model (see Chapter 2) with its six aspects of organization, as an example.

It is important to stress three key ideas about using this structured approach:

1 Not only should you look at each individual aspect in turn but you should also look at the congruence between each aspect and each other aspect. In other words, do they fit together? Is there a balance between any two aspects? Problems are often the result of a poor fit among the various aspects. Problem analysis involves defining the problems and diagnosing causes in the patterns of congruence or fit.

2 Using this model ensures that you look at an organization as a system. However, no organization operates in a vacuum and it is therefore important to look at outside effects upon it, to treat it as an open system. These effects will include the environment in terms of the larger organization, the global marketplace, international agreements and restrictions, government regulations, legal frameworks etc. It is also important to look at the resources which are available in terms of finance, people, time and space. There is no doubt that the culture of the organization will have an impact upon its ability or willingness to change so it will be important to discover what it is in as much detail as possible. Internal consultants sometimes find this quite difficult as they can often be unduly influenced by it.
3 Like any model, this one doesn't represent reality perfectly. Its purpose is not to eliminate all ambiguity but rather to help you structure it. You still need to use your perception, observation, intuition and judgement; subjective and unique as they are. The payoff comes in the form of you and your client having a better understanding of the complexities of the organization and you being better able to help your client make sense of the data and make informed decisions to solve the problem.

The diagnosis needs to be carried out at two distinct levels:

Level 1 – consists of asking questions about each aspect of the organization beginning with *purpose and tasks*, then *structure*, *technology*, *systems*, *procedures and processes*, *people and rewards*, to discover what happens now. For example questions in the technology box might be 'Does the organization have appropriate equipment, machinery, information technology and transport?' – among others as will be appropriate to your diagnosis. See Figure 3.1 – Organizational Life Model.

Level 2 – seeks to discover the congruence or fit of each aspect of the organization to each of the other aspects. In other words, the degree to which the needs, demands, goals and objectives of one aspect are consistent with the needs, demands, goals and objectives of every other aspect. We have already quoted a client system in which people and rewards components were out of balance. The company was establishing self-managed teams while at the same time putting in a reward system based upon individual performance. These two systems were mutually exclusive and provoked concern and confusion. This analysis is a potentially lengthy process which involves taking each aspect in turn and comparing it with every other aspect. So, for example, you might look at the fit between *tasks and people* and ask such questions as 'Do the people have the necessary skills and knowledge demanded by the tasks?' 'Are the tasks such that people are sufficiently motivated to do them?' 'How are changes in the tasks communicated to the people who have to do them?' It is unlikely that your client will be able or need to deal with every instance of discontinuity so that you may like to rate the degree of congruence on a scale of say 1 to 5, to indicate the importance of dealing with the lack of fit, backed up by your comments.

The final stage in the analysis is to establish some ideas of the causes of the lack of fit between the various aspects of the organization, so that you can test them out, assess what other data is required, if any, and also point towards potential solutions. You will also have to help your client assess the costs and benefits of the various solutions and the penalties for doing nothing, following the consulting cycle as much as you can.

Section II
Extending Your Range of Intervention Styles

Introduction to Section II

As we saw in Chapter 1, intervention style is simply the name or label which describes your behaviour during interactions with clients. Unfortunately, most of the time consulting style is not even thought about, it is taken for granted as normal, everyday behaviour. Nevertheless, as consultants, whatever name we give to our normal automatic behaviour, it does have consequences for our clients. Traditionally, many types of specialist consultants and many managers have used a prescriptive style of helping. This involves offering advice and giving solutions. It is a valid style and indeed, in some circumstances, it can be very helpful. But as doctors are becoming increasingly aware, very often patients don't take the prescription nor do people you prescribe to heed the advice. One of the difficulties with prescribing is that it takes any involvement or control away from the clients, effectively leaving them impotent. The only choice they have is either to accept or reject the prescription. Also, style is implicitly a statement about how the consultant perceives helping. Prescribing implies that people cannot solve their own problems and/or that the prescriber is in possession of expert knowledge and knows a solution to their problems. These are quite far reaching implications. Your client may end up feeling dependent and helpless rather than empowered. As a consequence, many consultants and managers are beginning to look at other styles of helping which give clients much more power to make decisions for themselves.

A further reason for extending your repertoire of styles beyond prescription lies in the Model of Organizational Life (Figure 3.1), described in Chapter 3. If you choose to work as a technical expert working solely with systems, procedures and processes, then prescription may be valid. You may have expert knowledge about the best system or most appropriate decision available. How people feel about being told what to do is another matter. However, once you recognize that there is always a human process dimension to all organizational problems and start to intervene at this level, then you can no longer be an expert, and reliance on a prescriptive approach becomes more dangerous. What could be more ludicrous than issuing an edict that 'as of next week everyone will feel more motivated', or 'henceforth all managers will adopt a different leadership style' or 'everyone will support each other'? If motivation, leadership or mutual support are significant issues in your organization then you will need a spectrum of styles to be able to deal with them.

Before looking at the styles available it is worth emphasizing that style affects the entire consulting relationship, from initial contact to disengagement. There is no part of the consulting relationship where you do not employ one or more consulting styles. Furthermore, the main point is whatever style you choose, it has consequences and some of these consequences are more important in certain situations than others.

As outlined in Chapter 1, we believe there are four distinct consulting styles which you can employ when working with clients. These are:

- Acceptant – how to help when feelings are involved.
- Catalytic – how to help your client make decisions.
- Confrontational – how to offer support and challenge.
- Prescriptive – how to give wise, kindly advice.

These categories are similar to those described by Blake and Mouton in their book *Consultation: A Handbook for Individual and Organizational Development* (1976, revised 1983). However, we have added modifications and refinements to their original work. Based on our work with many client systems, we would argue that these four styles constitute a practical description of most legitimate consultant behaviour. However, it is still worth emphasizing again that, despite the fact that all four styles can be of value, you will probably feel more comfortable with one or two – as the ranking exercise in Chapter 1 may have indicated. Unfortunately, you may also tend to employ your preferred style more often than the others. This could be detrimental to the consulting relationship as all styles have their uses in different situations. The key is being able to recognize when a particular style is needed and then using it appropriately. To do this effectively we need to know a great deal more about the behaviour, uses, risks and assumptions embodied in each of the styles. The following chapters in this Section will examine each style in detail.

Throughout this section we will present each of the intervention styles one by one; however, they are rarely used in isolation. To do so would be like driving a car in first gear only, when there are other gears available. In most assignments the styles are used in combination. You will need constantly to adapt your approach to meet the needs of your clients and their particular circumstances. Although there are no hard and fast rules which dictate any order in which the styles can be combined, typically we would expect to use the acceptant and/or catalytic styles fairly extensively throughout most assignments. Confrontation is different and is generally – though not necessarily – used later in an assignment. However, it is nearly always followed by the acceptant style to deal with the feelings which may be aroused. Prescription can be perfectly valid and sometimes very useful but will only be really effective in particular circumstances outlined in Chapter 7. Above all, the main criteria which dictate which style to use are the needs of the clients and their particular situation.

4 The Acceptant Style – How to Help When Feelings are Involved

On the surface an acceptant intervention style appears easy – at first glance it seems to involve simply listening. Yet in practice it is far more complex. An effective acceptant style utilizes a highly sophisticated set of interpersonal skills. In essence it involves setting aside one's own view of a problem or difficulty and instead attempting to understand it from the client's viewpoint. This skill is perhaps best summarized by the expression 'being able to feel how the other person's shoes pinch'. It is about accepting the client, 'warts and all'. The acceptant style is characterized by the skills of empathic listening. In many respects these are similar to the skills used in the early stages of client-centred counselling. They encourage and permit clients to address, disclose and discuss thoughts and feelings which would otherwise remain repressed with other consulting styles.

Virtually every problem, difficulty or change we experience in life is accompanied by some form of emotional response. This is a natural and normal human reaction. Sometimes these emotions are uninvited and unwanted, nevertheless they exist. Where they persist they may disrupt normal objective behaviour making it difficult for us to continue with everyday activities and sometimes denying us the ability to function normally. It is also worth noting that emotions and feelings which disrupt objectivity need not necessarily be negative feelings. For example, euphoria can lead to unbalanced judgements or decisions just as easily as can anger or despair. Imagine some of the problems and difficulties which can result as a consequence of love at first sight.

Individuals or groups that are able to function objectively are not influenced by disabling feelings which warp their perspective on situations. Indeed, the ability to perceive situations or problems objectively is an essential first step in tackling cyclical or habitual behaviour. For example, a member of staff who has been compulsorily transferred to a new department, working for a new manager he dislikes, may be so angry at the change that he may be unable to function in a job which should be well within his normal capacities. Alternatively, the woman who is made redundant may have reached such a low level of self-esteem that she is no longer able to project her abilities in new job applications or at interview. A third common example is the individual who is so overwhelmed with private or domestic problems that he can no longer function at work. The list is endless.

Problems, difficulties and change affect everyone emotionally to some degree, and sometimes this can skew the ability to think and act rationally. This is as true for issues at work as it is elsewhere in life, and occasionally one can have a 'knock-on' effect on the other – problems at work can affect domestic life and vice-versa.

The first stage in helping involves recognizing and acknowledging the feelings which exist. These may be feelings about the situation, feelings about the problem, or feelings about self and others. Only by expressing and working through disruptive feelings can the client begin to make progress. Sometimes these feelings are quite mild but on occasions they may be overwhelming, so that they may take proportionally shorter or longer lengths of time to work through. Similarly, different individuals will take varying lengths of time to come to terms with the same change simply because of individual differences and different personal circumstances. There are no hard and fast rules. However, working through the feeling content of any problem is an essential prerequisite to problem solving.

Sometimes, with a purely acceptant style, helping clients work through the feelings is all the help they need. Having recognized and worked on the feelings, clients find they have sufficient resources of their own to engage in problem solving and find their own way forward. On other occasions some other consulting style may also be needed. But when changing style you must be sure this meets genuine client needs rather than your own style preference.

It is also worth remembering that helping clients might involve helping them to accept some negative event in life. Not all of the difficulties or changes that people experience have nice neat solutions. The most obvious examples of this are with 'life crisis' problems such as bereavement, debilitating illness, or serious sensory or motor impairment. However, situations also arise in the work setting which cannot be resolved, in the sense of everything being put back to normal, for example where skills or roles have become obsolete or have disappeared, or where new automated systems have replaced older manual systems. Staff may long for everything to be put back as it was before the change, but this is no longer an option. The 'solution' lies in their accepting and coming to terms with the change and then learning new skills or finding new roles. There is also little doubt that negotiating these kinds of transitions in life is undertaken more easily with the benefit of skilled help. In this respect, when you are able to use an acceptant consulting style effectively, you become one of the client's most powerful allies.

Underlying Assumptions

The acceptant consulting style is underpinned by a few important assumptions:

1 The first is that the clients *want to talk through a problem or difficulty* they have to deal with. Although their feelings are important, in this case they are not

disabling or getting in the way, they simply want a sounding board to test out their thoughts and ideas. Typically they will not be seeking opinions, alternatives or other ideas, they merely want to verbalize their own thoughts to reassure themselves that they are on the right lines. The principal form of help they need is someone who can assist them in talking through the detail of what they want to do without judging, demeaning or trying to add their own personal experience. An acceptant style is ideal in this kind of situation; in effect it acts as a mirror allowing clients to look at what they are saying and make their own evaluation without inputs from any other source.

2 A second, quite separate assumption is that clients *are impaired or disabled from coming to terms with the problem or cannot find a way forward because of their feelings*. In this case it is assumed that the feelings prevent the clients from carrying out any effective problem solving or decision making to help resolve the issue. The principal form of help which the acceptant style offers is to give clients an opportunity to discuss and either work through or come to terms with how they feel. If carried out effectively, an acceptant style will address the feelings and enable clients to diagnose and resolve their own situation more objectively.

3 A third implicit assumption is that *clients have sufficient resources to find a way forward once they have either verbalized their situation, or acknowledged and resolved their feelings about their situation.* Your role is principally to help and support your clients as they address either of these issues. This is radically different from most interpretations of helping. Conventionally, helping is construed as giving more direct assistance in the form of opinion, advice, suggestions or practical help. These forms of helping are the complete opposite of an acceptant style. Under an acceptant approach clients are helped to find their own way forward without external prompting.

4 A fourth assumption is rooted in the very name of this style. It is that all of us need to be accepted. Acceptance of the client is fundamental to the helping relationship. This is what Carl Rogers called 'unconditional positive regard'. It means that if we are to develop truly helping relationships with our clients, we must value them unconditionally, regardless of their behaviour or their problems. So an acceptant consultant needs to remain non-judgemental throughout.

Obviously, if a purely acceptant style is to be of value, these assumptions must be appropriate. Where they are not, you will generally need to use other styles in combination with an acceptant style. However as will be discussed later, an acceptant style can be of value in all stages of an assignment.

How Can I Use the Acceptant Style?

With the acceptant intervention style your aim is to provide clients with sufficient emotional and personal security that they can work through their difficulties and generate their own set of actions. However, a common misconception is that when you use an acceptant style you act like a 'nodding donkey': that is, you simply listen passively and accept everything that the client says. This is not the case. An effective use of the acceptant style involves a wide range of behaviour, including:

- adopting an open, non-threatening body posture;
- using direct non-oppressive eye contact;
- smiling and nodding acceptance of the client's description of their situation;
- using positive, para-verbal signals such as 'uh-huh' to encourage clients to say more;
- attempting to understand the problem or difficulty from the client's point of view and communicating this understanding by either:
  - restating key words or phrases which the client has used,
  - reflecting back the content of what has been said,
  - sometimes paraphrasing the key messages;
- from time to time summarizing as much as possible of what the clients has thus disclosed, enabling them to acknowledge, review and evaluate what they have said. This is often an overlooked, yet particularly powerful, helping technique;
- encouraging clients to say more by using statements such as 'tell me more . . . ' and then confirming understanding;
- encouraging clients to express both their thoughts and, often more importantly, their feelings about the situation. If necessary using direct questions like:
  - How do you feel about that?
  - How do you feel?
  - How do you feel in that situation?
- picking up 'feeling' words which clients may have used and reflecting them back. In a sense, giving clients permission to explore the feelings more if they wish;
- listening when clients use descriptive phrases that mask how they feel and then giving them the opportunity to explore the feelings further if they wish. For example, clients may use phrases like:
  - 'walking on a knife edge'
  - 'hanging in mid air'
  - 'being used like a doormat'
  - 'walking on eggshells'
  - 'feeling like the filling in a sandwich'

  Statements such as these (and many others) are expressions which could hide a raft of much deeper feelings which could merit further exploration. Therefore, subsequently it may be important to ask:
  - What do you feel like when you find yourself walking on a knife edge?
  - How do you feel when you're left hanging in mid air?
  - How do you actually feel when you are used like a doormat?
  - What do you feel like when you are walking on eggshells?
  - Filling in a sandwich? What does that really feel like?
- Picking up how clients might feel as they describe their situation and tentatively reflecting back how they might feel.

- Using all the data offered by the clients – not only their words but also their body language, their tone of voice, their looks, and their behaviour towards you.
- Using silence to allow time for clients to think.
- Staying outside of any discussion or value judgements concerning the 'content' of the client's problem: neither agreeing nor disagreeing with what clients say and not taking sides.
- Accepting that the client's initial definition of the problem is not necessarily the real problem. Nevertheless, the consultant still needs to work with this initial description up to the point where the client either:
  - feels sufficiently secure to disclose the real problem; or
  - have clarified their thinking and redefined the problem.

  Above all, the acceptant style demands that all diagnoses are made by the client.
- Staying completely in the client's 'frame of reference'. This means that whatever you say will be firmly rooted in what the client has already said either in words or through their body language or tone of voice. This means that you focus on summarizing, reflecting and perhaps identifying themes in what the client has said but that they may be unaware of. Exploring the client's feelings is also acceptant. However, asking questions, even open-ended questions about the content of the problem is likely to move the client in a direction they would not have chosen for themselves. So if you find yourself asking questions, other than about the client's feelings, you are likely to have strayed outside the acceptant style.

The important point to note is that *an acceptant consulting style is much more than mere passive listening or repeating over and over, 'How do you feel?'*. Experienced practitioners attempt to listen at three levels: first, listening to what clients are saying; second, listening to what clients *are not* saying; and third, perhaps the most difficult of all, listening to what clients *cannot bring themselves to say* without our help. There is no question that the level of concentration required is very demanding and requires considerable practice.

What Risks are Involved?

Preliminary exercise Before reading the rest of this section you might first like to generate your own list of possible risks for both consultant and client when using an acceptant style.

Although the acceptant style is a very gentle way of working, there are several risks for both consultant and client. Blake and Mouton (1983) identify two:

- It is possible that clients, having acknowledged and worked through the emotional component of a problem, might choose to accept the circumstances that caused the problem rather than taking any action to initiate change. This could well be the case in instances where the amount of change needed appears overwhelming or too much to take on. As a consequence, clients could choose to remain locked in their existing cycle of behaviour.

- The second risk is perhaps more subtle. The acceptant style eases and gives permission for overt expression of feelings within the consulting relationship. It is possible that some clients may carry this permission into other settings and, in a sense, 'go public' in situations where such emotional outbursts are against the norms. As a consequence, they could meet hostility, resentment and rejection, perhaps making the situation worse.

Beyond these two, we feel it is important to highlight a few other risks we have observed while working with a wide range of different client groups; these include:

- Situations where clients touch very powerful feelings, for example: anger, sadness or despair; feelings so powerful that the consultant becomes very uncomfortable and as a result inhibits any natural expression of the clients' feelings. It is essential to recognize that the acceptant style creates an atmosphere which permits open expression of feelings where they exist, and sometimes very strong feelings. In our experience it is not unusual for clients to experience a whole range of powerful emotions when describing how they feel about their particular situation. A few tears or anger are not unusual in either human life or consultation, but it does not help if consultants use expressions like:
  - There's no need to cry.
  - Getting angry isn't going to help.
  - Pull yourself together.
  - I'm sure it's not that bad.
  - Would you like a few minutes on your own?

  Such expressions seek to meet the needs of the consultant rather than those of the clients. They inhibit and effectively say to clients that 'these feelings are not permitted', and from what we have seen previously, this is the direct opposite of what we are trying to achieve with this style.
- Expression of feelings can also raise issues concerned with confidentiality. Clients who choose to recognize and acknowledge their feelings become more vulnerable as a result. They will become aware that the consultant knows a great deal more about them than does anyone else within the organization. This is particularly important for the internal consultant and can become a major problem if confidentiality is not strictly observed.

When Can I Use the Acceptant Style?

The acceptant intervention style can be used throughout most consulting assignments. Feelings and emotions will always be present to some degree in all phases of your relationship with the client. For example, during initial contact and building a relationship, you can use the acceptant style to:

- acknowledge how the client feels;
- discuss any client resistance;
- discuss any fight/flight reaction on the part of the client.

During contracting you may encounter resistance if the client feels threatened in any way. Equally, during data gathering you could use it to help bring to the surface how a client feels. Decision making and implementation invariably involve some form of change and this could easily generate very strong feelings. Similarly, disengagement necessarily involves separation and loss. It follows, therefore, that the most appropriate style to help at all these points is the acceptant style. We have argued earlier that consultation is principally about change, and all change, whether large or small, technical or human, involves feelings. The issue for consultants is not whether there will be an emotional response, but how will it be manifest? An acceptant approach is the only consulting style that will provide real help when feelings and emotions are a significant component of the problem.

Closely linked to the question, 'When can I use an acceptant style?' is the related question, 'Under what conditions will an acceptant style be effective?' The answer to this flows directly from the assumptions made about the style. Firstly, the clients must be ready and willing to talk about their situation, they may need support and encouragement, but nevertheless they must be willing to talk. Secondly, though not necessarily in every situation, the clients may be currently disabled or blocked from thinking clearly and taking effective action as a result of feelings about themselves, other people or the situation in which they find themselves. We say, 'not necessarily', to acknowledge the fact that an acceptant style can be equally effective in simply helping clients talk through and examine their situation without necessarily being overwhelmed by strong feelings. In a sense they are merely seeking a sounding board to test their thinking. The third condition, which is vital for the style to be effective, is that the clients must have sufficient resources to be able to find their own way forward. An acceptant style offers no direct input or practical help in a traditional sense; instead it offers a mirror to allow clients to reflect on, clarify, evaluate and make decisions about their situation without being judged or censored in any way. This often proves to be an extremely helpful and empowering process, leaving responsibility and all decision making with the client rather than some external expert.

Finally, before leaving this section it may be worth mentioning that the need to use an acceptant approach may not be immediately obvious from how clients sometimes begin to address their situation. A common opening for a client to begin talking may be through a question such as:

- What would you do if . . . ?
- How would you reply if someone asked you to . . . ?
- How would you go about . . . ?

At first sight all these questions seem to request direct advice. However, once the advice has been given, the clients may well carry on by describing how that particular advice wouldn't work in their case. The trap at this point is to try modifying the advice in the hope of adapting it to fit more appropriately with the clients' new description of their situation. Furthermore, the expression they often use to discount the advice starts with the phrase 'Yes . . . but . . . '.

The use of 'yes . . . but' is generally a pretty sound indicator that the type of help you are offering is inappropriate. 'Yes . . . but', usually means 'No'. As a consultant it is vital that you recognize this trap as early as possible and switch to some other style of helping. But what can be done when a client asks for direct advice?

Instead of responding directly it is generally possible to sidestep the request and respond acceptantly by paraphrasing their concern, picking up and reflecting a key issue, or asking them to tell you more about their particular situation. The following extract of dialogue might help illustrate this point a little further:

Client: *What would you do if your boss asked you to do something you felt was unethical?*
Consultant: *I'm not sure, but I think I would have to confront it in some way.*
Client: *Yeah, I know that's what you should do, but it just wouldn't work in my case. He never listens to anything we say.*
Consultant: *I see, it sounds like it's pretty important to you . . . maybe like something that actually happened.*
Client: *You san say that again! Only last week . . .*

The passage opens with a direct request for advice. Caught unaware the consultant in this case responds prescriptively by tentatively suggesting what he would do in that situation. However, this meets with a 'yes . . . but' explanation of why the suggestion won't work. The consultant then switches to an acceptant approach and focuses on the level of concern which the client seems to indicate and links this with the possibility that it may have actually happened to the client. Given this opening, the client launches into the beginning of a much fuller explanation of their particular concern.

However, it is vital to note that the key to enabling the client to speak more openly is the early switch to an acceptant style. For the consultant to continue with more and more suggestions would probably end up going nowhere and with the consultant feeling as if he were banging his head against a brick wall.

Acceptant Style in Practice

Our first illustration relates an experience of one of our colleagues who was involved with helping organizations select, install and come to terms with new computer systems. For us it is an interesting example as it highlights how technological change has important emotional repercussions for the people involved.

The particular client organization had recently installed a new computer system for dealing with customer accounts. The consultant was called in as a result of ongoing staff complaints about perceived difficulties in the system. After making contact and agreeing on an outline contract with the department manager, the consultant realized she would need to talk with the staff who used the system on a daily basis to get to the root of the problem. Initially, her intention was to use a diagnostic, catalytic approach to find out how the staff were using the system. However, it quickly became apparent that the staff were so angry that their responses were skewed by strong feelings of antagonism towards both their management and the new system. In response, the consultant changed her style of approach to acceptant in order to help the group acknowledge and explore their feelings. It eventually emerged that group members were simply unsure how to use the system, but their lack of knowledge was masked by anger and resentment at having the system foisted on them when, in their view, the old system was perfectly sound. For the consultant, further work with the staff group was straightforward, the feelings of resentment and loss had to be worked through. This consisted primarily of helping them really understand why the system was being introduced, then helping them accept the need and adopt the system as their own. However, this was not the end of her work. In order to complete the assignment she needed to provide the management group who were responsible for introducing the new system with feedback on their method of introduction. This required yet another change of consulting style and proved to be the most demanding aspect of the whole project.

In retrospect the consultant recognized that the key to this assignment was her early switch to an acceptant style when working with the staff group. They were angry about the lack of consultation when the system was originally planned and clearly were in no mood to learn how to use the system once it was installed. However, for the consultant, what started as a technical assignment turned out to be one that was more concerned with human relations and management style.

A second illustration comes from our own work with companies which have found it necessary to carry out an outplacement exercise. In such cases the early phases of the consultation, including initial contracting, are usually carried out with the appropriate management group within the client organization. However, the main focus for action is with those whose jobs are to be made redundant. Once the job losses have been announced, usually without warning, we have attempted to make contact with the individuals or groups affected and tactfully offered our services. In virtually every case we have seen, it has been immediately apparent, from body language alone, that the self-esteem of these people has been shattered. The feelings of rejection and loss have often been overwhelming and as a consequence addressing the feelings has taken priority over any other concern.

The consulting style which seems most appropriate in such circumstances is acceptant and we have used this extensively during our early work with affected groups. Only when the feelings of rejection and loss have been acknowledged and addressed have we attempted to move on to more practical steps which could lead the individuals involved to new employment.

In conclusion the acceptant style is useful in:

- helping individuals and groups talk through issues where they simply need a sounding board and do not require advice or input from an external source;
- helping individuals and groups deal with self defeating reactions such as anger, hostility or frustration towards people in authority – managers, supervisors, parents, police inspectors or teachers;

- helping individuals and groups to release themselves from the fear of the unknown consequences if they confront an authoritarian boss, admit a mistake, ask for help, confess to being under stress or lacking in confidence to do the job, in a culture where such things are seen as signs of weakness;
- helping individuals and groups explore, express and heal negative feelings they may have about each other, other groups, the system, equipment which has failed, trade unions, management, suppliers or customers;
- helping individuals and groups come to terms with disabling emotional reactions which may lead to discouragement or demotivation at work; demotion, refused promotion, lack of feedback, poor appraisal, lack of consultation or involvement, rules they see no point in or systems which don't deliver what they are designed to deliver.

Overall, an acceptant intervention style helps people to unload troublesome thoughts, reactions and feelings and allows clients to be more objective about their situation.

Summary

- The acceptant style attempts to convey an understanding of the problem or difficulty from the client's point of view.
- All problems and difficulties in life are accompanied by feelings, and sometimes these feelings distort our ability to make sensible decisions.
- Acceptant helping involves recognizing and acknowledging feelings. It can be used throughout the consulting relationship but may feel uncomfortable for inexperienced consultants.
- Using an acceptant style can sometimes involve helping clients to come to terms with negative life experiences.
- An acceptant style assumes that clients:
  - want to discuss whatever issue concerns them;
  - cannot decide what to do because feelings obstruct or distort their judgement;
  - have sufficient resources to make their own decisions once any feelings have been acknowledged and resolved.
- An acceptant style employs a wide range of behaviour which seeks to:
  - accept and acknowledge the client's perspective;
  - help clients identify and explore their feelings;
  - give clients space to talk without being judged or censured in any way.

5 The Catalytic Style – How to Help Your Client Make Decisions

Many years ago during chemistry lessons at school we were taught that a catalyst speeds up a chemical reaction but is not itself changed as a result of the reaction. By current standards this is probably a naive definition, but in consultation the idea of the catalytic style is to describe a method of interacting with clients which speeds up the rate of change taking place. In situations where this is appropriate clients usually do not have enough relevant data to make a decision about change or have so much data they are overwhelmed and are unable to distinguish the essentials. To move forward they need some form of catalyst to help them either obtain more information, or to sort out the surfeit of information in order to make a decision manageable.

This may sound complicated and highly scientific but it can be a very simple process. For example, one of the authors recalls an instance when his parents could not decide whether to move to a new house. They had discussed the decision for several months, visited the new location, involved other family members seeking their advice, but to everyone's dismay they were unable to make a choice. The decision was finally laid to rest as a result of the author concerned using the catalytic style. In effect he sat down with the couple and helped them to list on a sheet of paper the advantages and disadvantages of moving and, on a second sheet of paper, the advantages and disadvantages of staying where they were. Once the information was rearranged in this form the decision became obvious. His parents chose to remain where they were and the issue never came to the surface again.

This illustration encapsulates one use of the catalytic style, where the consultant used a very simple model for shaping and presenting the clients' data. In this case the author simply helped the clients rearrange the information they had in such a way that it became more meaningful and helpful. It is important to note that he did not add any information himself – by way of suggestions, opinions or advice – he simply helped the couple find a more effective way of looking at the information. Furthermore, as with the acceptant style, the actual decision was made by the clients. The author did not influence them in either direction.

Clearly, in any situation a whole range of data analysis and presentation techniques is available; these could include:

- decision trees;
- force field analysis;
- critical path method;
- cost benefit analysis;
- multi-voting;
- flow charts;
- bar charts, scatter diagrams and histograms;
- ishikawa or fishbone diagrams;
- various control charts.

Some of these techniques are discussed in detail in Chapter 11 and all of them can be used as tools to aid the catalytic style. However, the choice of which is most appropriate will depend on the circumstances surrounding a particular assignment together with the type of data to be presented.

In some cases this process of rearranging and presenting the data will highlight where there are significant gaps in the information available. The client may then need help to gather additional data. This could involve individual or group interviews, questionnaires, direct observation, document analysis, etc. All the data gathering methods discussed in Chapter 10 could be usefully employed. An example of helping the client gather additional data occurred for us with an assignment where we were attempting to help a group develop its teamwork skills. It quickly became apparent that although group members were committed to the task, they were struggling at a feelings level. We were able to help them bring this data to the surface by using a simple review questionnaire which each member completed at the end of the group meetings. The results were tabulated and shared among all group members, and time was set aside at each subsequent meeting for the group to carry out a similar review. This identified areas which the group needed to work on and helped them develop as a team.

Once again, the consultants added nothing other than a review period at the end of each meeting together with a simple technique for bringing previously undisclosed data to the surface. The decisions about which aspects of teamwork the group should tackle were made by the group members following their discussion of the data. However, this example is also important in respect of the type of data collected. In many settings data are regarded as physical – reality, facts and/or numbers. But here the data collected were different – they were information on how the group behaved and how individuals felt. Clearly, this is a much more exotic interpretation of data, but it was vital information which the group needed to address if they were to make progress and develop as a team. In the catalytic approach all kinds of data can be of value, including numerical and factual data, but also feelings, hunches and behavioural data.

It is also important to note that using a catalytic intervention style starts with the client's felt needs. Obviously, as consultants, we hope that by gathering and structuring the information the initial felt needs will be redefined during the consultation to enable the client to address real needs, but this is always a risk. For example, initial felt needs which may prompt a client to request help could include problems such as:

- low productivity;
- poor product or service quality;
- excessive machine down time;
- persistent late delivery;
- high sickness/absence rates;
- rising costs;
- decreasing profits.

However, the real needs underlying these could include:

- inadequate supervisory or management skills;
- poor relationships between departments;
- unmotivated employees;
- poor decision making;
- inadequate information.

Obviously, it is essential that the client's problem, real or felt, eventually be addressed. But within a catalytic approach you must accept the client's definition at the outset – even though you may have a hunch that there is much more to the problem. As you help the client collect and shape the data on the felt problem the deeper issues are highly likely to emerge.

Although it is feasible that the client will not identify the real problem, the main advantage of a catalytic approach is that the client remains in control throughout the interaction. Furthermore, it is the client who identifies the need, and hence the degree of commitment which this engenders is usually very high. Also, as a consequence of the trust that is generally built up during the interaction, you are more likely to get to the real problem.

In summary, although the catalytic style sounds complicated, it is often much simpler than it at first appears. You will see from the subsequent parts of this section that it is also an extremely versatile approach and, like the acceptant style, can be applied in many of the phases of a consulting assignment. Furthermore, once you have mastered how to use a catalytic approach it can become a very comfortable way of working.

Underlying Assumptions

As with the acceptant style, the catalytic style is based on several important assumptions:

1. Perhaps the most obvious, that *the clients want to solve the problem and are capable of exploring various aspects of it (with help if needed).*
2. That *either additional data, or more structured data will have a significant impact on the clients' perception of the situation.* Also, as a consequence of this change in perception, *clients will be able to decide on an appropriate course of action.*
3. That there are *sufficient data within the system for clients to be able to make a decision.* However, it may be difficult to access or interpret the data sensibly at present, or make a decision about change.

4 That *there is likely to be greater commitment to a decision if it is decided by the clients*. Hence, within a catalytic approach it is essential that clients make their own decisions based on the data.

Again, as with the acceptant style, a catalytic approach can only be of value where these assumptions are satisfied. Where they are not you will generally need to use other styles in combination with the catalytic approach.

How Can I Use the Catalytic Style?

The catalytic style seeks to help clients collect or clarify data such that they can make their own decisions about what action to take. Enabling this to happen involves the following types of behaviour:

- Use an open body posture and eye contact similar to that used with the acceptant style.
- Attentive listening and confirming understanding.
- Using open questions to encourage clients to describe their situation – but also accepting the clients' perspective as the legitimate starting point to work on the problem or difficulty.
- Using focused listening and questioning skills to help clients explore their situation and illuminate some aspects of the subject under discussion – in particular using 'who', 'what', 'where', 'when', and 'how' questions. However, you must not lose sight of the purpose of each question, which is to clarify the client's understanding of their problem. If you are simply asking open questions to clarify your own understanding of the issue, you are unlikely to be working catalytically. More likely you are gathering data in order to understand the problem so that you can then, at a later stage, offer a prescription.
- Using 'why' questions very carefully and infrequently in order to avoid creating an interrogatory atmosphere.
- Where required, using data gathering methodologies in order to collect more information about a situation. These could include interview strategies, instruments or scales to measure performance, attitudes, perceptions or beliefs, survey methodology and action research. However, all suggestions must be made very tentatively – specific suggestions are *not* within the remit of a catalytic approach *even about data gathering methods*.
- Giving support and encouragement as clients attempt to define or redefine the problem.
- Encouraging clients to make their own decisions – not allowing yourself to be drawn into making the decisions for them. Equally, not offering your opinion on which decision is best.

Over the years we have noted that many consultants who are new to this way of working sometimes experience real difficulty framing open catalytic questions. Often their attempt at posing a catalytic question emerges more like a veiled prescription (e.g. Have you tried . . . ? You might find it useful to look at . . .). To help overcome this we have listed below a few catalytic openings.

Statements and questions to help identify or explore the problem:
- Tell me about the problem in your own words.
- What do you think caused that?
- Describe the situation now.
- How would you like things to be?
- What difficulties does that cause?
- What have you tried previously?
- What brought it to your attention?
- How do you see the situation developing?
- When did it first come to your notice?
- Who else is involved?
- Where else is it happening?

Questions to help define or redefine the problem:
- Can you restate the problem in a phrase or sentence starting with the words 'how to . . . ?' (This ensures ownership of the problem.)
- How will you know if you have been successful?

Questions to help decision making:
- What are the options?
- What are the advantages and disadvantages of each option?
- What would be the consequences?
- What would be your ideal solution?
- What option will you choose?
- What are the implications in choosing that option?
- How will that option address the problem?

Questions to help implementation:
- How will you implement the decision?
- Who else needs to be involved?
- What steps do you need to take?
- Where will you start?
- When will you do it?
- What resistance might you meet?
- How will you monitor progress?

What Risks are Involved?

Preliminary exercise: Before reading the rest of this section you might like to generate your own list of possible risks for both the consultant and client when using a catalytic style.

When using a catalytic style the risks for the consultant which we would identify are as follows:

- Firstly, as we have already mentioned, perhaps the greatest risk is inadvertently slipping into a style which is more like a veiled prescription. As this is so common we have named these veiled prescriptions 'prescriptive wolves in catalytic clothing'. They include a whole host of questions which at first glance appear to be catalytic, but their real intention is to test out or suggest to the client a particular line of enquiry or way forward. A few examples include:

– Would it be a good idea if . . . ?
– Have you tried . . . ?
– Have you ever thought about trying . . . ?
– Why not try . . . ?
– What about . . . ?
– Why don't you . . . ?
– Do you think you could . . . ?
– How would you feel about trying . . . ?
– Would it be a good idea to try a . . . b . . . or c . . . ?

In all these questions the client is being seduced along a path which the consultant has selected. In some cases it could be an appropriate path, but do not delude yourself into thinking it's catalytic – it isn't!

- A second but small risk for the consultant arises from the nature of the catalytic style. As we have seen, the catalytic approach is restricted to addressing the client's felt needs. It is feasible therefore, that as you see the problem only from the client's point of view you may lose your own perspective on the problem. In a sense the danger is that you can become as muddled and lost in your own thinking as the client. Obviously, if this happens then your value as a consultant is minimal.
- A third risk sometimes arises in situations where you, as the consultant, identify an option or way forward which the client either hasn't spotted or has no knowledge about. This clearly presents you with a dilemma; do you withhold the information and thereby deny the client potentially valuable information, or do you share it? Also, if you share the information, what will the client's reaction be? In our view it would be wrong to withhold information which could be of value; however, as it is information which you have generated you will probably have no option but to offer it either as additional information or as a tentative suggestion for the client to consider. There is nothing wrong with this, but we need to be quite clear that it is not a part of the catalytic style. Furthermore, as the information has come from you, the client may give it undue priority. If subsequently it proves to be of little value, you may be blamed for coming up with useless ideas.
- A fourth risk for the consultant is perhaps a little more subtle. Typically, though not necessarily, it arises in situations where, as the consultant, you genuinely know something about, or have expertise in dealing with the type of problem which the client is describing. For example, you might be an IT or engineering expert and the client is concerned about an IT or engineering problem which you think you have encountered before. While in some instances this can be helpful, in other cases it can get in the way. Your own knowledge of the subject may begin to skew both the type of questions you ask and the way you ask them. Rather than helping the client diagnose their problem, as the expert you diagnose it for them and then, by judicious questioning, lead them towards a solution which fits your diagnosis.

As a general rule remember that if, during the course of a conversation with a client, you find that you think you know what the client *should* do, then beware. Generally it means that you have diagnosed the client's problem and this can affect the outcome. In the catalytic style the main objective is to *help the clients diagnose their own problem*, and in a sense it doesn't matter what you think.

In addition to these risks for the consultant there are a few others for the client; they include:

- If you, as a consultant, lose your perspective, it is quite likely that the client will reject the whole approach. Similarly, it is feasible that clients could reject the idea that restructuring and/or gathering further data will contribute in any way towards resolving their problem.
- As the catalytic approach restricts you to working with the clients' felt needs, it is possible that real needs will not be addressed, in which case you will end up resolving symptoms rather than problems.
- The catalytic style usually leads to some form of decision and action by the client. However, as the responsibility for decision making remains with the client there is no guarantee that change will be in a positive direction. Hence it is important to help the clients think through any consequences of change before they leap into action.
- Finally, if clients regularly call on an external consultant for help it is possible that this will become a standard operating procedure. As a consequence, clients may discount any internal resources within their own organization as a source of help. We are aware of several companies where an internal consulting department is regularly discounted in favour of external help.

Having highlighted the risks, it is important to emphasize that they do need to be kept in perspective. Other than the first, using veiled prescriptions, they are relatively small and in our view outweighed by the benefits of the catalytic style. In most cases clients welcome the approach. It is logical and diagnostic in nature and often matches their expectation of what a consultant should do; perhaps most important of all, the client remains firmly in charge throughout.

When Can I Use the Catalytic Style?

The catalytic style is extremely versatile and, as with the acceptant style may be used at most points during an assignment. For example, during initial contact and building a relationship, the catalytic style can be used to find out more about the clients and their department. In contracting it can be used to explore, clarify and check out contractual details. From the earlier discussion it will be obvious that in data gathering the catalytic style is essential. Indeed, all the data gathering techniques and presentation methods discussed in Chapters 10 and 11 can be used to support a catalytic approach. In decision making the catalytic style can help clients think through the consequences of any decision, and during implementation it can be used to check progress. During disengagement it can be used to explore any possibility for further work.

It is also worth mentioning that where clients are thinking in terms of finding an ideal solution, they may need help to recognize that they may be dealing with a problem rather than a puzzle. Furthermore, they may need help to clarify that a 100% solution might not exist and perhaps the best that can be attained is a 60% solution. In this situation a catalytic approach can be useful in helping the client check out options and outcomes. A simple example is 'how to get the best possible job done within a restricted budget'.

If we now ask the question 'Under what circumstances will the catalytic style be effective?', as in the acceptant style, the answer flows mainly out of the assumptions made about the style. To be effective the clients must genuinely want to work on the problem and be capable of exploring all its different facets. They may need help in this process but both the desire and an adequate level of ability must be in place first. Furthermore, their ability to think must not be clouded by an overwhelming emotional reaction; if there is one, you will have to help them deal with that first. Responding to catalytic questions requires a clear head.

The second set of conditions for ensuring effectiveness concerns the information the client has about the problem. At the outset, the client must either have so much information that he/she is 'unable to see the wood for the trees' or is currently lacking sufficient data to make a decision. However, where there is an absence of data there must be sufficient data somewhere in the system to address the problem, even if at present these are difficult to access. Also, once the data have been sorted and structured they must significantly impact on the client's perception of the problem so that he/she is able to arrive at a decision on what to do next.

The final condition for success concerns client commitment. For a catalytic intervention to be successful the client will need to be prepared to do a significant amount of work, thinking deeply about the problem, looking at it in different ways, redefining the problem and exploring possible options and finally, being prepared to take responsibility for making a decision and being committed to its implementation. If, having worked on the problem, the client is not committed to taking any action, then the problem will persist. As a consultant you can try to guard against this by taking steps along the way to ensure genuine client commitment, for example, by making sure that it is the client who makes all decisions about what should be done. There is no point in you making the decision if the client subsequently ignores it.

In addition, the catalytic style can be of value where clients do not have the confidence to make a decision; for example, where the action is likely to be unpalatable. By using the catalytic approach you can help clients explore the options available in order to build up their confidence in the decision. In this sense the catalytic style can be developmental; it helps clients to make their own decisions in the future.

Catalytic Style in Practice

To conclude this section we include three examples of the catalytic approach in action. The first illustrates how it can help build commitment towards a decision which has already been taken. The organization concerned had already decided at a senior level to introduce a formal procedure for staff development. However, managers at the next level down, who would be responsible for implementing the procedure, were suspicious of the change. Our role involved working with those managers to help them develop skills to carry out staff development. Unfortunately, one particular group spent a great deal of time dwelling on the potential disadvantages of the new system. To overcome this we invited them to discuss and list both the advantages and the disadvantages of staff development. The result was that they began to recognize that the positive aspects to staff development outweighed their reservations. By the end of the exercise they had become much more committed and enthusiastic about implementing the change.

Clearly, choosing to use the catalytic style was risky – the group might have reinforced their negative perceptions about the change. However, we believed that allowing them to arrive at their own conclusion engendered more commitment than if we had tried either 'selling' the new system or telling them that they had no choice about complying. In the event, the risk proved to be worth taking.

The second illustration involved a team development assignment with a group of eight senior managers. Quite early in the work it became apparent that each of them was working to a different agenda. To make progress we invited them to write down individually what they saw as the main purpose for the group's existence. As we expected – but to their surprise – we received eight very different responses and the group had to engage in a considerable amount of further work to agree upon their purpose. Eventually this led to much improved teamwork. Before our action they had assumed they were all working towards a common purpose, and this type of catalytic approach clearly demonstrated that individually they were all going in different directions.

The third illustration involved a newly formed consulting section within a large multinational organization. For some time prior to setting up this section the training department had been receiving an increasing number of requests from line departments for help. Typically this was couched as requests for 'one-off' training programmes across a wide variety of topics. However, as each case was investigated, the trainer concerned usually discovered that what was really needed was someone to work with the department to help them think through their problems more fully before embarking on any training. Furthermore, each success led to an even greater demand for help. Therefore, to meet this demand the senior training management decided to create a separate consulting section specifically to address requests from line departments.

At the outset, the group leader in charge of the project realized that unless the new consulting section had clearly thought through and agreed on a strategy for how they would respond to client requests, they would quickly be overwhelmed by the demand. Hence, one of his early actions following the formation of the group was to work with them as a group to draw out their ideas on an appropriate client response strategy. To make sense of the mass of ideas which emerged from the group, they decided to use the catalytic techniques of brainstorming, multivoting and flow charting to make sense of all the data which were available. What finally emerged after several days of intense discussion was an agreed vision statement and flow chart showing exactly what the group was about and how they would respond to client demand. Furthermore, by adopting this way of working everyone in the group had contributed and felt committed to the collective strategy. Although at the outset the group was under pressure to show quick results, the decision to resist this and spend time working as a group to agree the overall strategy has paid dividends. Every request they now receive can be gauged against the vision and all subsequent actions are clearly understood by everyone concerned.

To conclude, the catalytic style can be useful in:

- Helping managers and their staff explore their expectations of each other so that they have a better idea of their needs, rather than merely relying on job descriptions.
- Conducting a survey to help managers discover which aspects of their management style are considered by their staff to be either helpful or unhelpful.
- Conducting a survey to find out how members of a team view their current performance; helping them generate ideas on how they would like to work and then helping them make decisions about how to achieve what they desire.
- Helping managers and their staff compare and contrast their perceptions and judgements about staff performance, as an alternative to prescriptive appraisal.
- Helping individuals and groups bring to the surface their assumptions and stereotypes about each other when it causes them to adopt a negative and unco-operative approach to one another: Sales v. Marketing, Service v. Sales, Planning v. Operations, Branch Offices v. Head Office, Management v. Trade Unions or Men v. Women.
- Helping groups to improve their creativity by helping them to acquire techniques such as lateral thinking and brainstorming.

Overall, the catalytic style helps clients either make sense of the data they already have, or enables them to assess what extra data they need to make a valid diagnosis of the problem. It also allows clients to increase their knowledge, understanding and awareness of the situation, and develop and distribute information around the system, thereby accelerating the rate of change to a new way of operating.

Summary

- The purpose of the catalytic style is to speed up the decision-making process.
- A catalytic approach helps clients address felt needs by clarifying existing

data and/or gathering additional data. It can utilize a variety of data gathering, analysis and presentation methods.

- Relevant data can include not only objective facts and numbers but also more exotic data such as feelings and behaviour.
- The responsibility for decision making remains with the client.
- The catalytic style assumes that:
  - data absence or overload is causing the difficulty;
  - relevant data exists within the system;
  - clarifying/gathering data will enable the client to progress.
- Using a catalytic style employs behaviour which:
  - accepts and acknowledges the client's felt needs;
  - uses focused open questions and/or data clarification/gathering methodologies;
  - presents the client's data in a meaningful way;
  - gives the client support and encouragement.
- Using the catalytic style involves several risks – but the greatest is that the consultant will slip into using veiled prescriptions.

6 The Confrontational Style – How to Offer Support and Challenge

One common form of confrontation involves situations where the clients are part of the problem and there are discrepancies between what they say they do and what they actually do in practice. Confrontation highlights the mismatch between thoughts, beliefs or values on the one hand and actual behaviour on the other. We are all full of contradictions and mismatches between what we believe and what we do. For example, at a personal level we may believe that 'healthy living' is important for everyone, yet in practice we probably take little, if any, exercise, eat far too much convenience food, and drink more than we should. Or we may say that it is important to value and respect others, yet in practice our listening skills leave much to be desired. We would suggest that for most of us, the authors included, these kinds of discrepancies are commonplace.

The same phenomenon occurs in client systems within organizations. For example, managers may believe that providing customer satisfaction is very important, yet in practice they continually overlook late deliveries, shoddy goods and poor service. Very often, rather than addressing the discrepancy, they make excuses to rationalize the mistakes and then continue in the same self-defeating way. An illustration of this happened recently to one of the authors. He took a punctured tyre to a local garage for repair. The tyre was left late on a Saturday afternoon to be picked up on the following Monday afternoon. As it happened he could not retrieve the tyre on the Monday but called in on Tuesday instead. Despite the fact that the garage advertised 'Customer Satisfaction is our Priority', the tyre was not ready and he was offered the explanation that the garage had too much work on. Rather than confront the discrepancy with the sales assistant, who was probably only a tiny cog in the client system, the author took the tyre elsewhere. This time he chose a garage that did not advertise anything about 'customer satisfaction' but had the job done immediately.

This theme has its parallel with most people in most organizations, although we do not believe that such discrepancies happen deliberately or as a result of malice. It is more that as individuals or organizations we are either not aware of the discrepancies or choose not to acknowledge them. It is only when the discrepancy is pointed out that we might try to change. This 'pointing out' is the substance of confrontation.

One difficulty lies in the confusion between confrontation and conflict. As will be discussed later, there is a danger that confrontation may degenerate into conflict, although, when carried out effectively, confrontation simply highlights discrepancies. It is not about scoring points, punishing people, making value judgements, getting one up on clients, or teaching them a lesson. Confrontation in consulting terms is objective and non-judgemental. Conflict, on the other hand, is often dealt with by trying to win and this can generate antagonism and hostility.

We need to reinforce at this stage, that confrontation is a legitimate strategy for helping people. The purpose of highlighting a discrepancy between what the client says and what they do is to help them acknowledge that their own behaviour is contributing to the problem and also help them deal with the discrepancy. You should always confront for the client's benefit, not to score points, win arguments or to belittle the client. Confronting does not have to be loud and aggressive. On the contrary, it often needs to be very gentle.

However, regardless of how gentle you are when you confront, your client may become upset. Being confronted can be an uncomfortable experience. You might have noticed an emotional reaction within yourself as you read the first paragraph of this section where we mentioned two common discrepancies at a personal level. This gives some indication of the difficulty in using confrontation. Part of the problem is that there is no way of predicting how the client will respond. Even quite gentle confrontation may be perceived as serious criticism and the emotional response can be completely out of proportion to the discrepancy being highlighted. Even positive confrontation can evoke an unexpected emotional response. We can illustrate this with an example drawn from one of our training programmes on consulting skills. During the programme we always attempt to tackle confrontation experientially, often by confronting the group ourselves and encouraging other participants to confront issues which they believe are genuine, significant barriers to the group's learning. The substance of any confrontation is always based on discrepancies as they arise during the programme. This could involve a range of issues such as participation within the group, participants psychologically opting out, talking over the top of one another, or poor listening. During the early stages of one particular programme much of this type of behaviour was evident within the group. However, as time went by the participants started to change, and by the time we reached confrontation their behaviour was consistent with the contract we had agreed on at the start of the programme. They were listening to each other, valuing one another's contributions, participating openly and honestly. We decided therefore, to confront the group by reviewing the initial contract and then describing in concrete terms how they had developed and changed as the programme went along. Our intention was to reinforce the very positive changes that had taken place and encourage them to continue with the behaviour which was now evident. This was eventually the outcome, but the immediate emotional reaction of the group was astonishing. They immediately became very defensive, attempting to deny our observations and generally trying to discount what we were saying. We were surprised because, from our point of view, the confrontation was very positive; needless to say, this was a salutary lesson for us.

This example also illustrates that confronting clients does not involve blame or judgement; it simply acknowledges what was agreed – in this case, the contract – and points out how the clients have subsequently behaved. That is, confrontation highlights what the clients said they would do and what they have actually done. However, the choice of what to do about the discrepancy remains firmly with the clients. Confronting does not involve telling them what you think is best, or what you would do under similar circumstances.

So far we have concentrated on a method of confronting that highlights discrepancies between what clients think and what they do. However, there are three other ways of confronting which are equally useful. The first involves highlighting the implications of continuing with a current pattern of behaviour. For example, you might like to think about your behaviour when you cross a road. If your habit involves looking left, right, then left again, ponder the implications of this if you try to cross a road in France. The second method of confronting clients involves pointing out the impact they are having on you. We recall one particular manager who, when under pressure, unconsciously raised the volume of his voice to a point where he was almost shouting. Our confrontation involved highlighting his behaviour and then describing how we felt on the receiving end of his tirade. From discussion later we discovered that this was the first time he had ever received this kind of feedback, and from then on he consciously attempted to change the habit. The third and final, though somewhat milder, form of confrontation involves calling attention to some particular client behaviour which you find unacceptable, pointing out that you don't understand it and asking for an explanation.

We have already mentioned that confrontation is virtually always accompanied by some form of emotional reaction. Regardless of which method of confronting you choose, clients will *feel* confronted and will probably react in an emotional way. This has important implications for how you act. Firstly, your initial confrontation statement will need to be very clear. If you are confronting about something the client is failing to do, it may well be heard as criticism. Under these conditions it is highly likely that your statement will be misinterpreted. Hence, the clearer your confrontation is at the start, the better. Linked to this, it is essential that your confrontation is based on solid data which you have either observed or experienced. It is foolish to embark on a confrontation which is based on second-hand or controversial data. Likewise, data which are historical are not very useful. Such data are likely to be denied by the client and your attempt at confrontation will fail.

Having confronted the client, you will probably need to switch to an acceptant style to acknowledge and deal with the feelings which have been stirred up. However, this does not mean denying the substance of the confrontation – switching to an acceptant style is simply the most appropriate way of dealing with any feelings.

By now you will probably have realized that confrontation can be a high risk style of consulting. As such it necessitates a solid base of trust between you and the client; in particular the client needs to feel valued and supported. Without this the probability of success will be very low. Also it is worth noting that confronting large client systems, such as groups, can take a very long time to work through. Inevitably, where many individuals are involved, the feelings generated are varied and complex. As a result group confrontation is much more complicated than with the individual client. Indeed, given the level of risk involved, it is always worth assessing your own feelings and motives before starting to confront. Using a confrontational style must genuinely attempt to help the client rather than satisfy any personal need for self-gratification. Also, if you feel particularly uncomfortable using the style, your own feelings can interfere and thus reduce the potential impact of your efforts.

Nevertheless, despite all the difficulties and risks, confrontation is a very important consulting style and at times is essential. It is a very powerful way of working and can prompt clients into action more rapidly than any of the styles previously discussed. As such it should not be overlooked or ignored simply because it is risky. If you don't use the confrontational style when you know you should, you may feel that you have let your client down.

Underlying Assumptions

As with the two styles discussed earlier, confrontation is based on a few important assumptions; these are:

1 *The clients' values, beliefs and/or behaviour are a part of the problem* you are trying to help them resolve.
2 Currently, *the clients either do not have insight into, or choose to ignore*:
   – discrepancies between their espoused values and their actual behaviour – what they say they do and what they actually do – and/or:
   – the impact and implications of their current behaviour.
3 If the discrepancies or implications of behaviour are addressed, the clients *will have sufficient resources of their own to find a solution or satisfactory way forward with the problem.*
4 The *clients have sufficient emotional resilience to undertake an examination of their behaviour and values* and will be able to deal with the feelings likely to be generated as a result.

For a confrontation to be effective all of these assumptions must be satisfied. However, as we have seen, the method is unlikely to be used in isolation. More typically confrontation forms only a small part of your work with clients and is generally used in conjunction with other styles such as acceptant.

How Can I Use the Confrontational Style?

Confronting clients usually involves one or more of three actions; these are:

- pointing out discrepancies between what clients think or say they do and what they actually do;

- pointing out the implications of clients continuing with their current behaviour;
- confronting clients with your own feelings about their behaviour – how they impact on you.

Carrying out these actions requires the following behavioural skills:

- adopting an open body posture, eye contact and attentive listening;
- using direct questions that help clients towards awareness and honesty;
- presenting facts and evidence to support your confrontation;
- confronting clients with discrepancies between their perception and their behaviour and/or between their beliefs or values and their behaviour;
- pointing out to clients the impact of their behaviour on you. This is sometimes known as immediacy or 'you–me';
- helping clients examine any implications which could arise as a consequence of their behaviour;
- being prepared to switch to a different style. You will need to use the acceptant style to deal with feelings as they arise – but, without denying or discounting the substance of the confrontation. You are then likely to switch to the catalytic style to help the client work on ways of moving forward and making decisions;
- presenting alternative frames of reference for clients to consider;
- leaving decision making within the control of the client;
- towards the end of the confrontation, summarizing any decision which has been taken.

What Risks are Involved?

Preliminary exercise Before reading the rest of this section you might like to generate your own list of possible risks for both consultant and client when using a confrontational approach.

We have already acknowledged confrontation as a risky method of working, but to keep this in perspective we need to examine more fully the risks involved. For the consultant the greatest risk is allowing the confrontation to degenerate into argument. Usually this happens if we move away from objective statements about what we have observed or experienced and start making value judgements about what the clients should be doing. In consulting terms this is fatal. Obviously, as human beings we cannot avoid making judgements, but these should not interfere with our behaviour when attempting to confront a client.

Beyond this there are a number of other risks which should be kept in mind:

- There is always a risk that clients will react to confrontation by deciding not to change their behaviour to be consistent with their stated intention. They may decide to change their stated intention so that it is consistent with their behaviour. For example, a manager who considers himself to have a highly participative and consultative style of management may be confronted by evidence to prove that he is autocratic and dictatorial, makes all the decisions

and rarely consults anyone. He now has two options. He may change his behaviour so that he is truly participative and consultative or he may decide to change his stated intention and his view of himself to be consistent with his current way of working. As a consultant you may have a view that a change in behaviour would be beneficial but to give even a hint of this would be somewhat prescriptive. However, you might want to switch to a catalytic style and help him consider the implications of his decision.
- It is also worth remembering that, if you unexpectedly find yourself on the receiving end of such behaviour from your clients, you may have been using a confrontational style even if you hadn't intended to do so.

When confronting groups there are at least two additional risks:

- Confronting a group invariably takes time, and sometimes a long time. As we mentioned earlier, the emotional reactions within a group are varied and unpredictable and take time to work through. It is therefore very risky to start confronting a group if you are faced with severe time restrictions. The results are likely to be incomplete, leading to dissatisfaction all round.
- When groups face confrontation they are highly likely to feel threatened. As a consequence they may 'gang up' on the consultant in an attempt to undermine, deny or ridicule the substance of the confrontation. This may well result in them consolidating their current behaviour.

Needless to say, confronting a group should be undertaken with extreme care. However, for the client there are a few other risks:

- First, the client may feel hurt and perhaps even betrayed. From their perspective you were invited in to help and yet it appears that all you have to offer is personal criticism.
- Linked to personal hurt, there is a danger that the client's self image could be undermined. We all have a picture of ourselves and how we interact with the world. Confrontation could challenge this picture, leaving the client feeling worthless.
- Within confrontation the clients remain responsible for decision making, but there is no guarantee that their decision will improve the situation. It is possible that the problem could become even worse as a result of using the style.
- Finally, poorly judged confrontation could prove too difficult or too much for clients to take in. As a consequence they may simply deny the whole intervention.

Given all these risks associated with confrontation, you may be left feeling that it is not even worth trying – the costs of failure are simply too high. However, despite the risks there are times when confrontation becomes essential. There is no point in continuing with an assignment when it is clear that it will fail; confrontation may be the only option to promote reassessment and change. Furthermore, if it is important to confront the clients and you don't, they are probably entitled to question whether you are as effective as you should be.

When Can I Use the Confrontational Style?

Confrontation is different in both nature and application from the two styles discussed earlier. Unlike the others it is not a style which is likely to be used over a long period of time. Typically the timescale for using the confrontational style is very brief, and in some cases it may consist of only a single sentence. However, the level of feeling generated as a result will more than likely require you to switch to an acceptant style to deal with the feelings which are stirred up. Also, as we have seen, in order for a confrontation to be effective there needs to be a high level of trust between you and your client, and this will take time to build. It follows therefore, that confrontation should rarely be used during the early phases of an assignment (i.e. during initial contact and building a working relationship). Clearly, this cannot be a hard and fast rule and there are exceptions: for example, where part of a client system is being extremely defensive and will not allow you to begin building a relationship with them. The only way forward might be to confront the client group with the implications of their behaviour, despite the fact that this is a very risky strategy. If you haven't spend time building the relationship you have no way of judging whether the level of trust is appropriate, but you might find yourself in a situation where you have no other option. In a sense you are damned if you do and damned if you don't.

More commonly confrontation is needed later in an assignment. During contracting confrontation may be of value as a tool to help clients ensure that all the important items have been covered. Similarly, later on, it could be used to instigate re-examination of the contract where clients are failing to fulfil their side of the agreement. During data gathering the confrontational approach can be used to highlight discrepancies or omissions in the data; in decision making it can help clients face up to uncomfortable decisions or decisions where they need to recognize they themselves are part of the problem. Finally, confrontation can also have a place during disengagement, particularly where clients attempt to procrastinate over the end of an assignment (perhaps as a result of wanting to cling on for additional reassurance).

Once again, we can also ask the subsidiary question. 'Under what conditions will a confrontational style be effective?' Although, as before, the answer is embedded in the assumptions. With confrontation there are a few important prerequisites for it to be effective. Firstly, before starting you must be sure of your own motivation. Confrontation can only be effective when you genuinely want to help the clients move forward and you can see that their current beliefs, values or behaviour are an integral part of the problem, even if for some reason, they are unable to see this for themselves. Secondly, there must be a satisfactory level of trust embedded in the relationship for it to survive the encounter. Thirdly, the information/data you intend to use for the confrontation are accurate and not open to misinterpretation; confrontation on shaky data is doomed to failure regardless of your intent. It is also worth mentioning that if you can present the confrontational information in a concise and concrete form, then all the better. A short, crisp confrontation is always more effective than one which needs a long and tortuous explanation. Next, you need to be sure that the clients will be able to cope with the information presented and find their own solution or way forward. Finally, you will also need to be skilled in using the acceptant style to deal with any feelings that are engendered.

If all this seems like a tall order for anyone to fulfil, perhaps we should end this section by adding that, despite the risks, confrontation is a valuable consulting tool. Exactly how it can be used will become clear from the illustrations which follow.

Confrontational Style in Practice

Our first example of confrontation is interesting in that it illustrates a situation where the problem under discussion was also present in the 'here and now' of the immediate client group. The actual assignment involved helping the client organization to introduce Total Quality Management (TQM). At the time of the confrontation we were working intensively with the senior management team to develop a strategy to introduce the change. The particular issue they were discussing was how to get the staff to participate in the new approach. Our confrontation involved highlighting the fact that the same issue was present within the group which we were helping. They were discussing how to get their staff to participate but had not recognized that several people within their own group had been ignored during the discussion and had stopped participating. Having made the intervention the group immediately reacted defensively, suggesting all the reasons why participation was difficult and claiming that we did not understand their particular situation. In response we switched to an acceptant approach to acknowledge and deal with their feelings, but at the same time held firmly to the content of our confrontation. Eventually, as the feelings began to subside, the group recognized that in order for (TQM) to succeed, fundamental changes had to take place in both staff behaviour and their own management style. One could not happen without the other. Furthermore, it would be highly unlikely that the staff could be encouraged to change unless there was a visible change in the way they were managed.

A second illustration of confrontation involved a colleague of ours who was invited to work with an organization to examine whether managerial behaviour took adequate account of equal opportunity legislation. In retrospect we are convinced that the senior management group believed their organization did not have any problems and that the consultant was engaged merely to 'rubber stamp' what they were convinced was obvious. Unfortunately, however, the more the consultant probed the more she discovered this was not the case. She found that many managers were regularly acting in a discriminatory manner and it was only good fortune which protected them from legal action. Once the data had been collected the consultant confronted the senior group with her evidence. This caused uproar; they attempted to deny the data, discredit the consultant and undermine the data collection method, all in an attempt to maintain the status quo. Fortunately, the consultant was experienced in this kind of work and had anticipated a stormy response. As a result she was able to switch to a more acceptant style to deal with the group's reaction. Eventually the feelings subsided and the group was able to address the information more rationally and plan appropriate changes. In conversation later it was evident that the consultant knew there was no easy option in this assignment. Challenging the senior group's belief about their organization was bound to be a very rough ride, but to have colluded with their view would have been a recipe for professional disaster and would not have brought about any change.

A third, more common illustration of confrontation can be found in many training situations. Most trainers who have used video as a means of giving feedback will have encountered individual or group resistance at some point. It is worth pondering why. There is no doubt that when used sensitively, video can be a very powerful feedback mechanism. However, when individuals are on the receiving end, video confronts them with an action replay of how they behave in any given situation. Even without comments from the trainer this can be highly confrontational. If a consultant's verbal comments can evoke a powerful reaction from clients, it is hardly surprising that the prospect of video on a training course can be equally frightening. Obviously, video has its place in training, but it should be used by trainers who can easily adopt an acceptant style to deal with the feelings it generates.

A final illustration of confrontation occurred with another colleague of ours who was employed as a technical training officer within a large organization. When the problem came to light his department had just completed a long series of courses designed to help the workforce develop their reinstatement skills (i.e., filling in and resurfacing holes which had been dug in public highways to gain access to essential service pipes). The problem started when our colleague was called in by a director to be told that reinstatement was not being carried out properly. Despite the training that had already been carried out, in the director's view, the workforce did not know what they were doing and would require immediate retraining. Our colleague was dumbfounded; he could not believe what he was being told. However, rather than accept the problem at face value he decided to find out more. As a first step he invited into the training centre a sample from the workforce and asked them to carry out a reinstatement exercise. The exercise results demonstrated they knew exactly what to do, and hence the problem was not one of deficiency in skill or knowledge.

Armed with these results he went back to confront the director. Effectively, the confrontation consisted of agreeing with the director that reinstatement was ineffective but also of showing that when tested in the training centre the workforce knew perfectly well what to do. The problem therefore was not one of lack of skills. Eventually the director begrudgingly accepted that the only way to discover the root of the problem was for the training officer to investigate further. The resulting on-the-job interviews and on-site investigation revealed that the problem lay in insufficient availability of tools and equipment, poor scheduling for delivery of reinstatement materials and inadequate supervision. Without the confrontation the organization would have spent a small fortune on unnecessary retraining, the reputation of the training department would have been seriously undermined, and the real causes would not have come to light.

As it turned out, the correct problem was tackled and the reputation of the training department was enhanced.

In conclusion, the confrontational style can be useful in:

- helping a member or members of a group challenge what they see as inappropriate norms of behaviour which the rest of the group accept without question;
- helping an individual or group challenge the difference between what managers say they will do and what they do in practice, so that both parties are able to deal with any potential bad feelings which emerge;
- helping two or more groups to deal with the consequences of a clash between their conflicting norms and standards, which otherwise can often produce rationalization, justification and projection;
- helping two or more groups deal with stereotyping that often leads to discriminatory behaviour, e.g. men and women, blacks and whites, or people with a disability and those without;
- helping a whole organization by challenging assumptions that hinder effectiveness and the process of change that prevent the move towards becoming a quality organization.

Confrontational interventions help people to see the discontinuity between their stated intentions or beliefs and their actual behaviour. They also help clients understand the implications of continuing with their current behaviour patterns.

Summary

- Confrontation should always be used as a way of helping your client. It can often be done very gently and should never be done aggressively.
- Confrontation involves:
  - pointing out discrepancies between espoused beliefs or intentions and action in practice;
  - pointing out the implications of behaviour;
  - pointing out the impact of behaviour.
- Confrontation inevitably invokes feelings which cannot be predicted.
- Confrontation does not involve blame or judgement, neither does it tell clients what to do. As a result all decision making remains the responsibility of the client.
- Effective confrontation requires a firm base of trust with clients.
- Confronting a group is inevitably more complex and takes longer than with individuals.
- Confrontation assumes that:
  - clients are part of the problem;
  - currently the clients do not have insight into the issue to be confronted.
  - once confronted, clients will have sufficient resources to make their own decision.

- Confrontation is a high risk style of consulting, the greatest risk being that it will degenerate into conflict. Confronting a group needs particular care.
- Confrontation is generally used more in the middle and later stages of an assignment, i.e. from contracting onwards.

7 The Prescriptive Style – How to Offer Wise, Kindly Advice

Although prescription is the most commonly used intervention style, it is often used inappropriately. As mentioned earlier, it is the traditional style used in medical consultations between doctor and patient, where the doctor diagnoses the patient's problem and prescribes an appropriate remedy. As a way of helping it is rooted in the concept of the 'expert' – that is, someone who is accredited in, and can call upon, a body of expert knowledge or skill to find solutions to particular client problems. Although traditionally a medical and legal consulting style, over the years it has been adopted by many other specialists, e.g. health and safety, personnel, information technology, financial and training.

When reading the first edition of this book one of our critics argued that we were far too scathing and dismissive in our view of this particular style. Therefore it is important for us to stress at the outset that prescription is a perfectly valid consulting style. When it is appropriate there is no doubt that prescription can be of very real value to the client. It is expedient and usually leads to results more quickly than any other style. Unfortunately, it can be deceptively appealing to clients. Most consultants will report a great deal of client pressure for them to generate solutions to the client's problem. Indeed, why not? If solutions lead to rapid results, then what is the point of wasting time using other styles? In this respect a solution may offer clients a very seductive 'quick fix'. Take, for example, the personal illustration of losing weight. The solution in this case may be for the overweight client to follow a diet. Dieticians, health educators and medical experts can all offer a host of different diets, or the overweight client can buy a book on dieting, and there are hundreds, if not thousands, to choose from. The difficulty is that diets alone rarely work in the long term. The majority of people who diet lose weight initially but within a few months return to their original weight, and probably bemoan their problem and look around for a new diet. The difficulty with weight loss is that it is about changing eating habits (i.e. changing lifestyle) and this is not easy. More effective weight loss programmes tend to be those which support people while they make lifestyle adjustments. But the 'quick fix' diet solution is still very seductive despite the fact that it rarely works. Hence the enormous sales figures for diet books.

In organizations the seductive influence of solution-oriented consulting is the same. Take, for example, early approaches to the management of quality goods and services. The key appeared simply to be the introduction of quality control (QC), but in retrospect we can see that quality control alone took the problem away from both management and staff and placed it squarely with the quality control department. The job of QC was seen as one of overseeing and advising on the quality of the product or service. Unfortunately, 'overseeing and advising' quickly became perceived as more of a policing role. The problem of quality became synonymous with the QC department. By contrast Total Quality Management (TQM) attempts to harness the whole organization in a coordinated effort towards continuous improvement in quality; quality is everybody's responsibility rather than that of a single department. This is a totally different approach to controlling quality and requires a fundamental change in how the organization functions. TQM does not offer a prescriptive 'quick fix', but it does perhaps offer a better route for tackling quality problems on a permanent basis. However, unless TQM is everyone's responsibility it also becomes just another prescription and a further 'quick fix'.

Within the prescriptive style consultants, explicitly or implicitly, perceive themselves as experts in their field, able to diagnose the client's real problem and to advise on an appropriate course of action. The main aim of the advice is to give guidance to the client who otherwise would not know what to do. As we have already stressed, when used appropriately prescription can prove to be a very effective style. However, the prescriptive style does not allow the client any opportunity for development or growth. Admittedly, given an appropriate prescription, the problem will be solved, but the client gains no insight into how the solution was generated. Knowledge of how consultants arrive at a solution is part of their specialist expertise, and is not a subject to be shared outside the profession. As a result, the client will need to call on the consultant again if the problem ever recurs.

Blake and Mouton (1976, 1983) highlight a further difficulty with prescription. When working with client systems that comprise groups or organizations, they argue:

> answers usually are directed to the top of the system so that the system's power/authority-obedience structure can be used to mandate the changes. Under these circumstances, implementation is more likely to occur, but resistance will almost certainly be generated at lower levels. Perceived coercion will eventually cause the prescribed changes to become distorted, watered down or simply ignored.

Finally, it is important to acknowledge the seductive attraction of prescription as an intervention style. Although it can be very powerful, it also offers the consultant a great deal of personal gratification. For many of us there is tremendous self satisfaction in providing an appropriate prescription; we feel as if we have been really helpful. Furthermore, clients may wish to be hidden safely under the wing of an expert who can provide wise and thoughtful answers. Hence, helping clients and at the same time being recognized as the purveyor of help can have immense appeal. The dilemma is how to ensure that our prescriptions are appropriate. Nevertheless, despite all the limitations, there are times when prescription can be the most appropriate consulting style to use. In order to recognize these we will next turn to the assumptions behind the style.

Underlying Assumptions

The assumptions which underlie prescription are a little different from those given for the other styles. First, there is a set of four basic assumptions which lie behind *all* prescriptions. Then, coupled to the basic assumptions, there are three more which relate to particular conditions or circumstances:

Basic assumptions – applicable in all circumstances:

1 The consultant is an expert in the specialism appropriate to the client's problem and is able to give sound, authoritative advice.
2 The consultant has done considerable research and diagnosis before offering the prescription.
3 The consultant is able to provide a satisfactory solution to the client's problem.
4 The client is prepared to carry out the prescription.

Conditional assumptions which depend on particular circumstances concerning either the client and/or their problem:

1 The client is genuinely floundering and does not know what to do, or does not possess the relevant skills to find a satisfactory solution to the problem and/or
2 The situation is critical and requires very rapid action. Under such circumstances it is usually obvious to everyone concerned that unilateral decisions, direction and speed of action are essential for the problem to be resolved. and/or
3 The client simply wants the problem solved and is happy to hand over all control and responsibility to the consultant.

How Can I Use the Prescriptive Style?

The prescriptive style attempts to move the client towards accepting a consultant generated solution. This could involve the following patterns of behaviour:

- Using a strictly professional approach, often paying little regard to social or personal pleasantries.
- Asking probing questions to determine what you need to know about the situation so that *you* can make an appropriate diagnosis.
- Listening to the client – but with a view to diagnosing the problem and offering a solution. In other words, using solution-oriented listening skills.
- Taking control of the discussion by telling clients directly how you perceive the problem or situation.
- Giving expert advice – prescribing the 'best' solution or set of actions for the client to follow.

- Describing your solution with confidence and authority and, if necessary, offering to supervise implementation.
- In instances where clients are unwilling to adopt the solution, threatening to terminate the assignment and if necessary, actually carrying out the threat. However, it is important to leave the door open by suggesting to the client that when they require help they can get in touch.

It is also important to emphasize two further points:

- Few consultants follow prescription in this pure form. More often they offer prescriptions and advice as suggestions or recommendations in the hope that these will be more palatable to the client. Nevertheless, the underlying theme of the approach is the same; all that has changed is the flavour of the medicine.
- A prescriptive approach can describe what to do either as a set of actions to solve a technical problem or as a prescription for behavioural change. Of the two, the technical forms of prescription tend to be much easier for clients to accept and apply.

What Risks are Involved?

Before reading the rest of this section you might like to generate your own list of possible risks for both the consultant and client when using a prescriptive approach.

Some of the risks we would identify for the consultant using a prescriptive style include:

- Rejection of the prescription and/or the consultant. Once a prescription has been given then the client has only two options, either to accept or reject whatever has been prescribed. To use a medical analogy, patients either take the medicine or leave the bottle unopened. They may look at it, smell it, play around with it, ask other people what it's like, but eventually they either take it, take some of it, or reject it completely. In extreme cases they not only don't take the medicine, they also find a different doctor. The same can be true for consultants in organizations, sometimes it is not just the prescription which clients reject, it is the consultant as well.
- Modification/dilution of any recommendations or advice. In large organizations consultants are often brought in to provide advice/recommendations for a senior management group. Unfortunately however, implementation often involves a change of behaviour by employees who carry out the day-to-day work, and between these two groups there are often several layers of managers and supervisors. It follows therefore, that any advice which the senior group decide to implement has to cascade down through several layers to reach the employees where it is translated into action. However, at each stage in the cascade the information content will probably be distorted or modified, and sometimes the cumulative effect means that the result ends up bearing little resemblance to the original prescription.
- In the case of error, being accused of professional incompetence. As

consultants accept total responsibility for diagnosing the problem and generating a solution, their professional competence is under the spotlight. Any mistake or error of judgement could easily lead to accusations of professional incompetence or neglect, in some cases resulting in lengthy and expensive litigation.

- Creating a relationship which fosters dependency. Although an effective prescription could solve the client's problem, the client gains little, if any, insight into how the solution was derived. Hence, if a similar problem arises in future the client must invite the consultant back for further help. You might argue that this is a good way of ensuring further business, but in our experience, when used excessively, this kind of approach does not foster a healthy relationship with the client. Over time, the more that clients become dependent on a consultant, the more likely they are to begin to resent the inequality of the relationship.
- The problem and solution may lie outside the consultant's field of expertise. Many organizational problems are multidisciplinary in nature; that is, the problem can impinge on many different professional disciplines. For example, addressing the problem of 'stress at work' may involve several quite different professional groups – personnel, occupational health, health education, dietetics, counselling, all of which will see the problem from their own particular perspective. Similarly, the problem of 'quality', which we mentioned in the introduction to this section, can impinge on other specialisms, e.g. engineering, personnel, management services, purchasing and supply, operational research, quality control. All of these specialisms may have a valid contribution to solving quality problems, but none will have the complete answer. It follows therefore, that any single specialist solution, despite being well intentioned, may end up addressing symptoms rather than the underlying problem.

In addition to these risks for the consultant there are a few others which affect the client; they include:

- Dependency – We mentioned dependency as a risk for the consultant; however it is also one of the most important risks for the client. All the client receives from prescription is the end result – the final prescription or recommendation. As there is no involvement in the diagnosis or problem solving process, other than supplying the information which the consultant deems to be important, there is no learning, development or growth along the way. Hence, if the problem arises again in the future then the client has no option other than to once again rely on the consultant.
- Despite the fact that the prescription can be exactly what is needed, the client may find that he/she either doesn't have the resources or is not sufficiently competent to implement what is required. As a result the prescription will fail.
- Prescriptions rarely include alternatives – their nature is such that they simply inform clients what to do. It follows therefore, that if, for any reason, clients find the solution unacceptable, then they have no option but to reject the prescription altogether. Furthermore, their situation is not alleviated in any way.

When Can I Use the Prescriptive Style?

More than with any other style, the consultant who uses a prescriptive style is responsible for the complete intervention process: first, he/she chooses what data to gather and focus on and then must make all decisions on behalf of the client. Only the outcome and advice on appropriate action are fed back to the client towards the end of the assignment. Given all of the risks associated with prescription, perhaps more than with any other style, the most important question is, 'Under what conditions can prescription be used effectively?' As usual, the answer must take account of the underlying assumptions. Pre-eminent among these is the consultants' qualification, experience and expertise in a particular field, i.e. the criteria which enable them to call themselves 'experts'.

The established professions have strict entry qualifications for acceptance into the profession; these are usually governed by a professional association. For example, in the UK all medical doctors have to be qualified and registered with the British Medical Association in order to practice, the legal profession is governed by the Law Society, and similarly professional engineering is controlled by one of the recognized professional engineering institutes (civil, mechanical, electrical). These governing bodies try to ensure their members adhere to strict standards of professional conduct. Unfortunately, however, the world is changing very rapidly and new professions and specialisms are constantly emerging. Here the situation is not so tightly controlled and anyone with even a smattering of knowledge can call themselves an expert.

As we have already seen, the situation in organizations is further complicated by the fact that many organizational problems are multidisciplinary in nature. Therefore it follows that in order for prescription to be effective not only must the consultant be a bona fide authority in the appropriate field but also the particular problem must fall within the boundaries of his/her particular profession, e.g. where a medical expert solves genuine medical problems, or a personnel specialist addresses genuine personnel problems.

A second important condition for ensuring effectiveness is that the consultant be able to provide a satisfactory solution to the client's problem. However, becoming an expert in any field usually involves many years of education, training and indoctrination in the history, knowledge and unique traditions of the profession. As a consequence it can be very difficult for a professional to admit that he/she cannot provide an answer; saying 'I don't know' is tantamount to an admission of failure, and no one likes failing – least of all an expert.

A third requirement for effectiveness is that the client is prepared to carry out the prescription. Unfortunately, experience constantly teaches us that this is often not the case. Thousands (perhaps even millions) of pounds are spent every year by organizations retaining or employing consultants to provide reports, recommendations and advice which is either never implemented, or at best, only partially implemented. Even the medical profession has discovered that somewhere between a quarter and a third of all prescriptions for pharmaceutical drugs are either never taken to a chemist or left in a medicine chest unused. The lesson here is profound; no matter what the reason, if the client is not prepared to implement the consultant's advice, then the prescription will be useless.

In addition to these three basic requirements, as we have already mentioned, there are three more which draw attention to particular circumstances where prescription can be used effectively. Perhaps the most obvious of these is where it is essential to act quickly. Obvious examples included crises and emergencies where there is little, if any, time to deliberate or think about alternative strategies in detail; what is needed is an immediate response. Even here the consultant should be careful to make sure that the situation is a genuine crisis rather than one which has been manufactured. Some organizations develop a culture of leaving decisions until the last possible moment so that even routine problems end up as crises. Where this type of crisis management prevails, the unwary consultant may well find he/she is 'sucked into' giving prescriptions which merely address the immediate critical issue rather than tackling the underlying cultural problem.

The second situation where prescription can be used effectively is when the client simply wants a solution and is genuinely not interested in anything else. On the surface this seems to be quite straightforward, however, some clients will say they want a prescription in order to avoid taking responsibility for the problem and/or any solution. Once again, the unwary consultant can be easily trapped into colluding with the request and then be blamed if things go wrong.

Finally, situations can arise in which clients are genuinely floundering and for some reason are unable to help themselves. In these circumstances prescription is then the only option available. As we have seen, all other styles require some input from the client. But when the client is floundering and doesn't have either the knowledge or skills needed, he/she will be unable to comply. Before closing this section it may be worth considering what to do when you find yourself in a situation in which you are required to implement a prescription which has to be adopted by the whole organization. In such situations it is not possible to consult everyone. Both internal and external consultants can find themselves in this situation. Yet all need not be lost, and it might still be possible to carry out the implementation in a client-centred way, using all the other styles.

The adoption of new marketing strategy, a restructuring, a radical change of image, the introduction of new HR, IT, or Quality Systems, may form the basis of an intervention which requires support from consultants. The basic initiative is undoubtedly prescriptive, and legitimately so. However, it is likely to be left to the manager's or consultant's discretion to manage the implementation. They can choose to work prescriptively and simply drive it through. Alternatively they can use a combination of acceptant, catalytic and confrontational styles to help their clients deal with any feelings of resentment and help them to take ownership of the prescribed initiative and be committed to it.

Prescriptive Style in Practice

No doubt you will have gathered by now that although the prescriptive style can be valuable, in our view the situations where it can be used effectively are far less common than with any other style. Furthermore, we suspect that the number of occasions when you will be called upon to deal with critical situations will be very few. Hence the only situations left where prescription is appropriate are those where the client is genuinely floundering or simply wants an immediate solution. As even these situations are very uncommon, our illustrations of prescription in practice are quite limited.

The first example happened to one of the authors when he was working as a personal counsellor within a large industrial organization. At that time many of his clients were individuals who, for one reason or another, were confronted by a number of life/work problems. As a result these people were often suffering from depression and/or anxiety. The emotional problems of one particular client were of an order of magnitude greater than the rest. At the time of the first interview he clearly exhibited extreme anxiety symptoms – obvious trembling, emotionally very upset, unable to concentrate, and at times unable to string a logical sentence together. Although the author was used to helping clients suffering with anxiety, this situation was altogether different. It became evident very quickly that immediate action had to be taken to help control the client's symptoms. The author advised the client to seek immediate medical help from his doctor and offered to make an appointment on the client's behalf. The client gratefully accepted the offer and the doctor made arrangements for an urgent interview. When the client returned a few days later, having received a prescription for medication, he was in a much more stable condition and more traditional counselling could take place. Although the author did not like using a prescriptive style to advise the client, he needed to see a doctor; in retrospect it was probably the most helpful course of action available in those particular circumstances.

A second simple illustration of prescription involved a personnel officer who was approached by a manager for help with a job advertisement. The manager was attempting to fill a job vacancy in his department and had drafted an advertisement for the local press. Unfortunately, the way the advertisement had been written was clearly discriminatory and could have led to problems later. As time was short the personnel officer prescriptively pointed out the discriminatory sections and offered to redraft the advertisement, taking account of current employment legislation. The manager accepted the prescription, recognizing that there were aspects of personnel work which were outside his field of expertise and best left to an expert.

In conclusion, the prescriptive style can be useful in:

- helping clients out of a crisis situation where they might be unable or unwilling to take action, e.g. an emergency such as a fire or the need to abandon ship;
- helping clients out of crisis situations where they are incapable of making their own decisions because they have lost confidence, are immobilized or find themselves unable to cope;
- when you, as the consultant, have the right answer to a problem and withholding the information could lead to the problem not being solved;

- when you have not been able to get clients to generate their own solutions and confronting the issue has not worked;
- preventing clients from taking precipitate action which may prejudice alternative courses of action that could be generated with mature or more objective thought;
- helping poorly functioning clients take decisive steps to get out of a situation which is causing them distress, thereby stopping the restrictive and self-destructive behaviour.

Overall, prescriptive interventions are used to help people who are not in a position to make their own decisions and therefore need someone to diagnose their problems and tell them what to do to solve them. The basic premise is that the consultant is an expert and the client is prepared to accept the answers the consultant provides.

Summary

- Prescription is probably the most commonly used intervention style.
- The prescriptive style is expedient and probably leads to results more quickly than any other consulting style. As a consequence, prescriptive 'quick fix' solutions can be very seductive.
- When using prescription, consultants implicitly perceive themselves as experts able to diagnose the client's real problem and subsequently prescribe an appropriate course of action.
- Using prescription assumes that:
  - the consultant is an expert and can provide expert solutions;
  - the client will accept and implement the solution;
  - the client is genuinely floundering; the situation is critical; or the client simply wants the problem solved without their involvement.
- To use prescription, generally the consultant will:
  - conduct a probing diagnostic interview;
  - give a complete description of the problem to the client;
  - give expert advice on the best solution or next set of actions needed;
  - if necessary, offer to supervise implementation of the prescription.
- Using prescription involves several risks; these include:
  - creating client dependency;
  - client rejection of either the prescription or the consultant;
  - where the prescription is cascaded down, modification, dilution or ignoring the prescription;
  - in the case of error, accusations of professional incompetence;
  - consultants not recognizing when they step outside their field of expertise.
- Prescriptions from 'on high' need not necessarily be implemented in a prescriptive way.

Section III Managing Relationships with Clients Using the Consulting Cycle

Introduction to Section III

The relationship between consultant and client is a complex one. Indeed you rarely work with just one client; you are more likely to be intervening into a large client system which may cross departmental boundaries. This can be equally true for leaders as more and more they become 'process owners' rather than managing a discreet group of people. Having a simple model of the consulting relationship will guide you through the phases of the consulting assignment. In our experience the early phases of the consulting cycle – developing trusting relationships, gaining entry and contracting are crucial. When we look back on our consulting experiences, most of the difficulties we have encountered during assignments can be traced back to one of these early phases; either we hadn't gained entry with the whole client system or the contract hadn't really been clear.

We remember working with two consultants from one of the national public utilities who were doing a series of similar projects with all their regional HQ depots. Each project lasted exactly 22 weeks and involved significant changes in systems, methodology, roles and responsibilities, reporting structure and consequently of management style. We were discussing issues about the entry process when one of these consultants had a flash of insight and said 'Entry? yes that usually takes us about 13 weeks'. His colleague immediately agreed; 13 weeks out of a 22 week project was really about gaining entry. Now that is not to say that they spent all that time drinking coffee and chatting to people. On the contrary a significant amount of work was done during this time. However, what was important, was the acknowledgement of the amount of time it took to build sufficient mutual trust. Moreover if consultants and their clients are to work meaningfully together it is essential that clients take their share of responsibility for the success of the project. We think this story underlines the importance of the entry process and it saddens us to see how often it is ignored in practice.

Again we have separated out each phase of the consulting process and treated each as if it it takes place in isolation from the others, as though there is a clear boundary between one phase and the next. In reality there is likely to be significant overlap between any one phase and the others. As we have seen, gaining entry is not something you can do in isolation; indeed, you will continue the process of building and developing relationships with your clients throughout the assignment. Nor will you necessarily carry out each phase in the same rigid order. You may well start the data collection phase before you even meet the client; you will certainly need to have collected some data in order to agree a contract.

We have deliberately constructed the consulting process in a cyclical rather than a linear form. This is to reinforce the idea that you may need to go back to a previous phase before moving on. Similarly when you move from decision making into implementation, you are likely to need a new contract which clarifies everyone's responsibilities during this phase. You may encounter significant client resistance at any stage in the assignment which should indicate that there are still entry issues that need to be dealt with.

So the consulting cycle is a flexible, not a rigid tool. However, it does help to warn you against some common consulting pitfalls such as:

- ignoring the importance of relationship building;
- responding to the client's initial description of the problem and agreeing to implement the client's proposed strategy without further investigation and diagnosis;
- moving into the assignment without a clear contract;
- moving into decision making without collecting sufficient data or carrying out a thorough diagnosis;
- failing to renegotiate the contract when it becomes apparent that the problem had been wrongly diagnosed at the initial stages or when it is obvious that it is not going to be possible to deliver on time;
- disengaging before the client is able to sustain the system effectively;
- failing to disengage when it would be appropriate to do so.

8 Starting the Intervention – How to Build Productive Relationships

Initial Steps

The question of what to do at the start of an intervention is probably best answered from the client's point of view, i.e. what types of questions will be framed by the client who sits awaiting the arrival of the consultant? However, for the present let us consider the case of the willing participant. It is at this point that people ask if it matters that the person whom you first see is not the real client. Our answer is usually that you have to gain entry before you can find out!

Exercise 1 Try to generate a list of questions which your client may be thinking about prior to your arrival. Here are three to get you started:

- Will I like the consultant?
- Will he/she like me?
- How will he/she treat me?

When you have finished turn to Checklist 8.1 at the end of the chapter and check your list against ours. From the two lists you can probably get a fair view of the client's concerns at the start of a consultation; it follows therefore that you had better start to address some of these before you go any further. When we look back at some of our disasters we can usually point to either an inferior contract or more importantly insufficient time spent at the start on building a relationship. This is what the initial stage is all about.

In Chapter 1 we mentioned that a consultant needs a positive self-image and enough self-confidence, skill and ability to retain it in the face of adversity. It follows that at the start you should spend time on your own self-image. Assuming that the initial contact by telephone or letter was appropriate and has not queered the pitch before you arrive, then it is important to make a good first impression. You will have made sure that you are appropriately dressed, have all your information at your fingertips, have arrived at the right place at the right time and know whom you are to meet. However, all this is rarely enough; you also need to deal with how you feel. Depending upon your particular orientation this part of preparation is usually called grounding or centring. It means getting yourself into a frame of mind to meet your client and deal with any difficulties which may arise while at the same time retaining your self-control.

Meeting your clients for the first time can be a stressful occasion. You are likely to be on unfamiliar territory and this can be just as true if you are an internal consultant visiting a client in the next department or an external consultant making your first visit to a new company.

Preparing to Meet Clients

The initial contact with your client or client group is likely to give rise to all sorts of impressions which may or may not be favourable. So it is important to give some attention to your own needs before you meet. Although you can do little to influence the feelings of your client before you meet (remember the list of questions you compiled in the previous exercise) at least you can assess your own physical and mental condition and get in touch with your feelings. This assessment is concerned with centring or grounding so that nothing knocks you off balance. Tom Crum in his delightful book *The Magic of Conflict* (1989), describes centring as a state 'when the mind, body and spirit become fully integrated in a dynamic balance and connectedness with the world around us. There is a heightened awareness and sensitivity, a feeling that everything is perfect the way it is. The truth of who we are as human beings is revealed.' This might be rather much for mere mortal consultants, but there seems little doubt that to get as near to this as possible would be a good state to achieve before meeting your client.

To do this you can ensure that you arrive for the meeting in plenty of time; you can then spend a few minutes on your own, becoming aware of your heart rate (is it normal or speeded up?), your breathing (is it fast and shallow?), your muscle tension (in your arms, shoulders or where else?), is your mouth dry and do you feel that talking is like spitting feathers? Being aware of these symptoms allows you to do something about them. First you can deal directly with the physical symptoms – take deep breaths, tense and then relax your hands, arms or shoulders to reduce the tension, get a drink of water, and so on. The second action you can take is to ask yourself why these symptoms are present. What wild fantasies are giving rise to these fears and concerns? What unattainable goals have you set yourself? What are your worst fears about the assignment or meeting? By thinking through some of these you will help yourself to make a more realistic assessment of the outcomes of the encounter. Finally, you should be able to meet your client without showing the tensions you may feel inside. You will be grounded and little will be able to knock you off balance. The next step is to think through some of the issues that are around when you meet the client so that the meeting is purposeful and meets the needs of both of you.

A Purposeful Initial Meeting

Let us assume that you have decided that the main purpose when you meet the client is to achieve a meeting of minds and to begin to establish some trust between you. It is likely that this will best be generated by trying to establish a collaborative relationship. First this allows you to be client-centred and share the responsibility for the success of the intervention and secondly you are, whether you like it or not, a role model for your client. If you talk one way and act differently then the client is likely to become confused. Your first impressions of the client are important but they must not be allowed to colour your judgement or your behaviour. It is very easy to dislike clients on sight and then look for evidence to support your theory. Likewise it is possible to view your clients in a favourable light, assuming that their intentions are honourable even when their behaviour leaves something to be desired. As a consequence you start looking for evidence to support that theory instead!

From our experience there are four situations that can be thought through before meeting a potential client. We say 'potential' client because you have to accept that the person you see at the start may not be the real client (or may be only one part of the total client system). However, for the purposes of gaining entry, you must assume that you have at least a potential client. The penalty for assuming that your contact is not part of the system is that you may be inclined to skimp on this phase only to find out later that he or she is indeed the client. The safest course seems to be to assume that your contact is part of the client system and go from there. If you find out later that you have to gain entry with other parts of the client system as well, then what have you lost?

The four situations which may arise are as follows:

A You have been in the department before with that client or with another client.

B This is your first ever visit to the department or with this person.

X You have been invited by the people with the problem.

Y You have been imposed by a person with power and you may or may not be welcome.

Situation A with X. The danger will probably be obvious. If you know the people and have been invited to help you may feel that you do not have to bother gaining entry. However, even if you have worked with a particular client or client system as recently as a week ago it is vital to check out what has happened in the meantime. As an internal consultant you are quite likely to know about significant changes affecting the organization or your client's part of it, but it is still worth checking in case you have been kept in the dark or you know something your client doesn't. If there have been significant changes in the client's private life you may want to check whether or not these are likely to affect his or her behaviour or mental attitude at work. It will be very surprising if they don't. Allowing the client space and time to discuss such issues may well be enough. You might also need to decide whether or not to check with other people who know your client. The culture, norms and standards of the organization will usually tell you how far to go.

Situation B with X. If this is your first visit it is likely that you will have to spend some time building a relationship with the person who is your initial contact. Bearing in mind what we said earlier about making assumptions about real clients, you will need to gain entry to check whether this is the case here. As an internal consultant you may be in a less favourable position than an external consultant; clients often find it easier to admit and share problems with an outsider. For example, company training officers often find it difficult to get participants to share real problems on courses where everyone is from the same department or organization. On public courses where participants are usually the only representative from their organization this is usually much less of a problem. However, as we discussed in Chapter 1, internal consultants usually have many distinct advantages which can work in their favour.

If you have been invited in by the people who have the problem or want something done about it, you are halfway home before you start. You will still have to establish whether or not you can help but the difficulty is more likely to be a different one in our experience. What often happens is that you are not allowed time for gaining entry as the client meets you with 'I'm glad you could come – let me tell you about the problem'. You find yourself rushed headlong into data collection before you even have a contract! So it may well be important to let the client tell you about the problem while you gently probe for information that will help you build a relationship. Questions which somehow take the client back to the beginning may be useful: 'How did the problem come to your notice?', 'Who is involved in the problem?', 'What effect is the problem having on you and the department?' Other questions which focus on how the problem is managed might help: 'How do you feel about the problem?', 'Who else is worried about the problem?', 'What happens when problems come up?', 'Who are the key people involved and how do they feel?', 'How have you managed similar problems in the past?'. Above all, you need to keep your attention on what the client is telling you about the problem while at the same time listening for what the client is not telling you. We will deal with collecting data in Chapter 10 but it is important at this stage to be aware of all the data there is around. Your ears are important in picking up the way the client talks to you and other people as well as what is being said. Your eyes will tell you a lot about the environment, the layout, the furnishing, and the differences attributable to status. You will be able to feel whether the place is a warm or cold place to work in – and this has nothing to do with the central heating or air conditioning! Your intuition should be working overtime during the gaining entry phase. All this is especially important if you are on your first visit.

Situation A or B with Y. If you have been imposed on the client system you will probably have a difficult task just gaining entry. It may make some difference if you have been to the department before, but your main difficulty is likely to be one of non-co-operation and a great reluctance to tell you anything. Before you can start to make any sense of the situation you will probably have to deal with the bad feelings or anger which is around and which may or may not be expressed verbally. It is your job to get these bad feelings into the open so that you can help your client deal with them. If they are not being expressed you may have to indicate how the situation feels to you by saying something like 'I feel very uncomfortable here. There seems to be some unexpressed hostility to me being here. Is that right?' You may well have to listen for some time while the clients play a game of 'ain't it awful', saying what they think and feel and inviting you to collude. Your job is to stay out of the game, stay calm and let the emotion surface. Remember no clients are able to deal logically with a problem while they are emotionally charged. An acceptant style will enable you to remain neutral, be empathic but not take sides, and let the client know that you understand and genuinely want to help.

There is still one more important aspect of gaining entry to keep in mind. While the main objective is for you to gain entry with the client it is also important that the client gains entry with you. Remembering all the questions that may be going through the client's mind before you arrive (as discussed in Exercise 1) can help you steer the gaining entry phase so that you get the client to surface some of the questions, or you may answer them even though they have not been voiced. It is also important that you have given some thought to what you want the client to know about you before you start. It is our experience that clients often see gaining entry as a waste of time given over to social chit-chat. However, without getting into an argument, it is vital to ensure that both you and the client gain enough entry with each other to get a valid contract. You can do this by listening actively and picking up on similar backgrounds, shared values and feelings, similar experiences or interests which will give you the opportunities you need. If the meeting is in the client's office you may gain quite a lot from observing how the office is furnished or arranged, what hangs on the walls, what trophies are displayed and so on. Everything is grist to the mill for the consultant who wishes to gain entry effectively.

Exercise 2 From what you know and what you have read so far, try to make a list of all the reasons why gaining entry is important. Then compare it with Checklist 8.2 at the end of the chapter.

Barriers to Gaining Entry

The barriers to gaining entry are twofold – your needs and the clients' needs. Your needs play a part because it is quite hard to keep coming back to gaining entry issues when the clients are trying desperately to get into data collection and problem solving. It is quite easy to collude with their desire especially if you find gaining entry to be the phase that you like least. In some instances it may be necessary to confront the issue directly and explain to clients that you need to establish a relationship before you can be sure that the rest of the intervention will be successful. Client needs can also be a barrier to gaining entry because, as we have suggested, they see it as time wasting. They may see talking about the way the problem is managed and their feelings about it as idle gossip. Somehow this attitude also needs confronting and clients need to be helped to understand your need to know about the problem and all that surrounds it.

Apart from that there are other obvious barriers and difficulties to gaining entry. Some of these will be to do with the place and the environment; some will be to do with how you both behave to one another, but all the remaining ones are likely to be embedded in feelings: issues of trust, previous relationships, status, cultural norms, confidentiality, etc.

Exercise 3 Try listing as many barriers as you can think of and then compare your list with Checklist 8.3 at the end of the chapter.

What can I do about them?

Generally, you are likely to be into gaining entry before you realize that some of the barriers exist. For example, imagine you are called to a meeting in the client's office and are not given any choice about where you sit. Furthermore you may find that the meeting is attended by more people than you expected, leaving you feeling very uncomfortable. In such situations you may have to grin and bear it or take the first opportunity to express your concern and feelings about the situation. In taking any action you will have to weigh up any risk of not gaining as much entry as might otherwise be possible.

Other barriers can be minimized by preparation before you arrive. For example, you can research the history of your department's relationships with the client's department and so on. This is often a wise precaution if you are going on your first visit, but in our experience it can also lead to preconceptions which may work against you. On balance our recommendation is to go with an open mind, give your potential client unconditional positive regard and be ready to deal with any non-co-operation and defensiveness if it arises. If the barriers are really getting in the way of progress towards a valid contract then you may have to stick at it until such time as you feel sufficient barriers have been removed or reduced. Checklist 8.4 at the end of this chapter gives a list of aspects of your relationship with clients that you can affect directly.

Consequences of not gaining entry

The consequences of not gaining entry are quite severe. For a start you are unlikely to build a relationship based on trust. The consequences may be that you do not get the information you need to help the client solve the problem, or you are given misinformation or even disinformation. A few clients may actually tell you lies just to ensure that you fail. The main difficulty we have experienced is that you are never quite sure that what the client is telling you is the truth. The consequences of that will be obvious. If you are in a situation where you do not trust the client and the client does not trust you, you are likely to be treated with suspicion whatever you do. The client is likely to attribute ulterior motives to you which you have never had and never even considered. Despite this, there are times when you just have to move on, knowing that the gaining entry is incomplete and that you may have to continue gaining entry as the assignment progresses. Indeed, if you are working with a large group you could get to the end of the project and find that there are some people with whom you never gained entry. The crucial decision is – have you gained sufficient entry to ensure you can enter into a meaningful contract?

Is Your Client Ready for Change?

Having decided who the client is, the next important consideration is, are they ready for change? Deciding whether or not the client really needs help, is likely to work with you on the problem in hand and implement what you agree seems, at first sight, to be a contracting issue. However, it is probably better to think about it before that. Often while you are still gaining entry with the client or the department, you begin to get a feel for whether the reasons given for the need to change are genuine or not.

A large variety of problems and difficulties might cause a client to seek help from a consultant, all of which are likely to be presented as genuine needs. It is possible that some problems arise from objectives which are not about improving effectiveness. You may or may not have a choice about whether you work with these stated needs but it is unlikely that you will effect much improvement or problem solving if they are not genuine.

Furthermore, there are many ethical issues for both you and the client if you consent to work with stated needs which you believe are not genuine. If you are to be successful in helping clients to solve their problems it is important that they have genuine reasons for asking for help. They also need to have a genuine readiness for change and a willingness to try more effective ways of operating. Certainly there will be times when you know that you are not really wanted by the client. Their boss may have told them that you are going to be their consultant whether they like it or not. Under these circumstances there may well be genuine needs but you will have to work quite hard before your client accepts them as such. When we talk about less genuine reasons for change we mean reasons which, on the surface, seem genuine but which give you an uneasy feeling that you are not being told the truth. Or you are only being given half truths. The reasons given for wanting help are not what they seem. One thing we know is that people often take on new ideas, identify with the new values and beliefs, even agree to change their behaviour but nothing happens. There has to be a culture in the organization which will allow people to be different. The consequences of change must be such that people will not be fearful and worry about what others will say and do when they try new behaviour. There is a further reference to this in the Section on Culture Change in Chapter 3.

Exercise 4 You may like to list as many genuine and less genuine reasons why clients may seek help with change initiatives. Then compare your list with the Checklist 8.5 at the end of the chapter.

When to Make a Contract

It is possible to work at gaining entry until both you and the client are satisfied that you have built a relationship that is complete. However, this might take a long time and generally you do not have the amount of time available. Furthermore, it might be rather boring if you did. What you need to ask yourself is 'Have I gained enough entry to get a valid workable contract?' If the answer is yes, then carry on to make a contract. If the answer is no, then you will need to spend more time on gaining entry until you can answer yes. There are, however, some indicators to tell you when enough is enough. For example:

- Is there any previous experience with this client or department which you can use as a guide?
- Do you feel able to raise anything you wish to raise with the client?
- Do you have any nagging doubts which you feel unable to surface?
- Are you colluding with the client by not raising issues you feel uncomfortable about?
- Do you think the client is avoiding discussing significant issues?
- Does the conversation feel open and honest?
- What does your intuition tell you about your mutual readiness to make a contract?

Gaining entry and contracting are, without doubt, two of the most ill-used aspects of consulting and, in our experience, whenever we have had failures they can nearly always be put down to missing out on one or the other or both. However, we believe that it is better to err on the side of going into contracting too early than too late. Too early and you can always go back or renegotiate the contract; too late and you risk alienating your client by seeming to procrastinate unduly. After all, you are there to help the client solve the problem not just to build a relationship or make a contract.

Summary

- Gaining entry is the process of building an effective relationship with your clients. Unless you have gained entry and established a relationship of mutual openness, trust and honesty, your clients are unlikely to be sufficiently open about the real problem. The result will be an unsatisfactory contract.
- In the early stages of a consulting assignment clients are likely to be suspicious or resentful of your presence, especially if they feel that you have been imposed on them.
- Meeting clients can be stressful for the consultant as well as the client. It is important to have a positive self-image. You need to spend time 'getting grounded' before meeting your clients.
- To build an effective working relationship with clients you need to be open, share some of your own feelings, and be absolutely genuine. If you are dishonest, exaggerate past successes or try to manipulate your clients, you will only succeed in reinforcing the barriers and increasing mistrust.

Checklist 8.1 Questions Going Through the Client's Mind at the Beginning of the Assignment

- Will I like the consultant?
- Will they be senior or junior to me?
- How will they treat me?
- Will they like me?
- What will happen if I don't like them?
- What will happen if they don't like me?
- Will I have to admit that I have got a problem?
- What shall we talk about when the consultant arrives?
- How much does he or she know about the problem/me/the department/the division?
- Are they here to give me a solution or help me solve the problem?
- How will they operate? Will they know how I feel? Will they care how I feel?
- What will they do with any information I give them?
- How senior are they compared with me – more or less, or the same?
- Can I trust them? Will they trust me?
- I know what I want from them but will they want anything special from me?
- Will they be like the last consultants we had from that team/department/group?
- What will they need in the way of support, resources, space, time, etc.?
- How can I tell them I don't have a problem?
- How can I tell them it's really someone else's problem (boss/subordinate/another department/a colleague)?
- Will I ever be able to get rid of them?
- I wonder what my boss has told them about me?
- Will they want to know what I think of the boss/my colleagues/any other members of staff?
- What will happen if I don't like what they tell me to do?
- Will I be able to cover up what I have been doing for the last month/year?
- Will they help me to get the changes I have wanted for years?
- Who cares about them – they are only consultants!

Checklist 8.2 Reasons Why Gaining Entry Is Important

- Understand something about the client as a person.
- Let the client get to know you.
- Lay the groundwork for trust.
- Achieve a meeting of minds.
- Enable the client to state clearly the need for help.
- Minimize resistance to change.
- Get some idea of the client's readiness for change.
- Find out something of the motive for calling you in.

- Establish rapport.
- Establish your credibility.
- Decide if you can help.
- Decide if you want to help (if you have an option to refuse).
- Start/develop a relationship on which to build.
- Establish common ground.
- Find out how welcome/unwelcome you are.
- Survey the surroundings.
- Get a feel for the place.
- Soak up the atmosphere.
- Help the client let off steam.
- Get some idea of how the problem is being managed.
- Get some idea of the size of the problem.
- Find out how urgent the solution is.

Checklist 8.3 Barriers and Difficulties to Gaining Entry

- Bad first impressions – you of the client, the client of you.
- Your appearance, manner, style may be off-putting or contrary to the client's norms.
- You may not be what the client expected – male/female, black/white, etc.
- You turn up late or the client keeps you waiting.
- The client misses the appointment altogether.
- Previous relationships – personal or departmental – get in the way.
- You are senior to the client or the client is senior to you.
- The setting and surroundings are not conducive to gaining entry – not private, not comfortable, too formal, etc.
- Why you are there – invited or imposed.
- Cultural norms in the department about asking for help are antagonistic to you.
- You are seen as an outsider – and we don't trust strangers.
- You know what the problem is and the client doesn't.
- Confidentiality – can you and the client be trusted to keep it?
- Client may feel out of control, especially of his or her feelings.
- Information can be a source of power – telling you may weaken that power base.
- The client may think the problem can be solved without your help.
- Your intervention may be part of/contribute to the problem.
- Client doesn't actually need any help.
- You are worried that you can't meet the client's expectations.
- You have information about the client that you can't share for political reasons.
- The client has information which can't be shared with you for similar reasons.
- There are no genuine reasons for calling you in.
- The client is not ready to change or even contemplate change.

- One of both of you have hidden agendas.
- Assumptions about what you will do and how you will operate get in the way.
- We don't wash our dirty linen in public.
- You should be talking to someone above me/below me.
- It isn't really this department's problem.
- We are being blamed for someone else's mistakes.
- Every question you ask is met with an evasive answer.

Checklist 8.4 Building a Relationship with your Clients

- Be genuine and honest with your clients.
- Be open about your own feelings.
- Try to be a human being not a role.
- Share something of yourself.
- Share relevant information about previous successes without working too hard to impress.
- Take a genuine interest in your clients.
- Ask questions.
- Clarify and check your understanding of what clients are saying.
- Value your clients.
- Acknowledge the importance of clients' feelings.
- Help your clients to surface and talk about their concerns and reservations about your presence.
- Encourage open discussion about underlying problems affecting your working relationship with clients.
- Ensure that you and your department always present a professional image.

Checklist 8.5 Genuine and Less Genuine Motivations for Change

Compare it with your list and if you come up with any we haven't come across please let us know

Genuine motivations for change

- Real difficulty in getting the job done.
- Feeling that something is wrong but not sure what.
- Find out how well we are doing against the outside world or other departments.
- A need to be more effective or needing new skills: budgeting, managing time, presentations, assertiveness, etc.

Less genuine motivations

- Supporting decisions already taken.
- Doing what management are frightened to do.
- Being an extra 'pair of hands'.
- Surfacing difficulties the manager knows are there but doesn't want to admit to.
- Calling in a consultant is seen as the thing to do.
- To deputize for internal resources which are difficult to get.

Genuine motivations for change – cont.

- Things need to change but don't know how to do it or where to start.
- Productivity is low and needs to improve.
- Low morale indications: absenteeism, sickness, lateness, etc.
- Destructive relationships with other departments.
- Poor internal conflict handling.
- Low trust levels between individuals.
- Poor relationships, sniping, sarcasm, etc.
- Deadlines not being met.
- Overworked and overstressed people.
- Support for personnel decisions: selection, promotion, dismissal, etc.
- A declining marketplace or market share.
- Poor communications across, downwards and upwards.
- Constant 'firefighting', rather than solving the real problems.
- Lack of innovation: technical, product, human resource policies.
- Complacency about what the organization is doing now: 'as is' contentment.
- Strategic ambiguity – nobody really sure where the organization is headed or why.

Less genuine motivations – cont.

- To provide objectivity to an otherwise subjective decision.
- Supporting incompetent managers by covering up their deficiencies.
- Helping to spend money left in the budget at the end of the financial year which will be lost otherwise.
- Covering up serious errors which may be discovered by audit.
- To prove that the problems belong to someone else, or that they are not the manager's fault.
- To lay the blame for the problem on another department.
- We don't really want to change, but we want to look as if we do.

9 Contracting and Clarifying Expectations – How to Agree What You and Your Client Want

What is Contracting?

All relationships between people are based on expectations in one form or another. Sometimes a few of these expectations are explicitly stated and agreed (as in marriage), more often they are assumed and taken for granted. Yet despite the absence of discussion and shared agreement, expectations still exist. If violated they may cause disruption and disagreement and in extreme cases a breakdown of the relationship. For example a friendship may be founded on each person providing support and encouragement for the other. If circumstances arise where one person can no longer provide support, then unless a new basis is found the relationship is highly likely to deteriorate and founder. In consulting, open discussion of expectations is essential as the foundation for good contracting.

In essence, contracting is the stage in the consultation process where, together with the client, you attempt to crystallize and make explicit:

- the issue you are working on together, and how you will measure success;
- your expectations of the relationship;
- who will do what – i.e. commitment to action;
- any boundaries which may exist;
- how you are going to work together.

In this respect, contracting is about ownership. But it is not easy. Given that clients have invited you in to help overcome some difficulty or problem, you could find that they wish to move to problem solving as quickly as possible. Consequently, as with gaining entry, spending time agreeing the details of a contract may be seen as a waste of time. However, we believe it is essential to resist the pressure to move to problem solving even if this causes some anxiety. Unless you are clear where you are going at the outset, you cannot measure how well you are doing or whether you have reached your destination. Similarly with contracting, it is essential that both you and your clients understand where you are going.

It is also important to note that, although contracting has legal overtones, it is not meant to be an instrument for either side to bludgeon the other into compliance. Contracting is simply a process where both parties can clarify what the other wants to achieve.

Who Do I Contract With?

In our view it essential that contracts are agreed with all who are involved in the client system. Bearing in mind that contracting is about ownership and commitment, then unless the whole client system is committed to change, it is likely to fail at some stage. This is commonly seen in training situations. Probably all trainers have had the experience of running a course where participants do not recognize they have a problem and don't know why they are on the course. In most instances where this occurs the agreement about the training will have been confirmed with the participant's manager. Although the manager may recognize the problem he or she will rarely have pointed this out to the staff. Instead, 'training' will have been invited to sort out the problem by designing an appropriate course. Trainers who collude with this approach effectively allow the manager to dump the problem in their lap. Furthermore, regardless of what training methods they choose, if the staff do not accept there is a problem, the effectiveness of the training will be much reduced.

If a more effective outcome is desired, you must ensure that the contract is agreed with all elements of the client system. The scenario described in the previous paragraph is inevitably a recipe for failure. Assignments which involve complex client systems will inevitably lead to contracts with each of the parties involved. It is important, therefore, to ensure that all the contracts complement each other. If at all possible you might try to encourage each of the different parties in the client system to contract with each other.

How to Start Contracting

As we saw from the previous chapter, meaningful contracting can only start once both you and the clients have built up a good working relationship; one where you can talk openly and honestly about concerns, difficulties and problems. The key issue in this is judging when the relationship is established sufficiently to enable this to happen. Unfortunately, as with most other aspects of consulting, there are no hard and fast rules to follow. It is a sign of a mature relationship when you and the client can talk about the relationship itself.

The key question that you need to bear in mind is 'Have I gained sufficient entry to move on?'. As we saw earlier, this is a matter of personal judgement. Having decided to move on, the next question is 'How?'. In many consultations the flow into contracting will occur naturally as clients start to outline what they want. You are then free to respond and bring in other agenda items as appropriate. In other instances you may initiate contracting yourself, in which case it is possible to begin from a number of different starting points. These could include:

1 a direct question about the reason for needing your help;
2 a direct question about why the client chose you from among other consultants who may have been available;
3 initiating a discussion about the expected relationship between you and the client system;
4 initiating a discussion about the relationships within the client system.

Each of these starting points will open discussion in a different area of contracting, and all can be important in different situations. For example, questions about the need for help tackle the substance of the consultation and is probably the most common starting point. Questions concerning 'why choose me?' may be vital in instances where other consultants have failed or been rejected. Questions about relationships tackle the issue of how the client expects to work with you. Whatever your starting point all the issues need to be discussed at some stage.

In a few cases you may find that you are well under way or have completed contracting when you start to encounter the consequences of not having built up a sufficiently solid relationship at the start (as described in Chapter 8). In such circumstances you have little option other than to abandon any progress so far and turn back to working further on establishing a deeper working relationship. This happened to the authors during one particular assignment. At the first meeting with the client an initial contract was apparently agreed. However, a few days later we were called to an unscheduled second meeting. At the meeting a new person was present who was not party to the initial contract agreement. During the meeting he made it obvious that he wanted several new elements added to the contract together with various other amendments. It was clear he was angry at not being involved in the earlier meeting and was deliberately creating difficulties. In response, we abandoned our attempts at contracting and instead tried to gain entry with the new client group. Eventually it emerged that the new member had been deliberately excluded from the first meeting as the others feared he would be 'difficult'. Only when these issues had been worked through were we able to return to contracting, but this time on a more meaningful basis with the whole client system. It is our hunch that had we gone ahead with the assignment on the initial contract (which, in retrospect, was made with only part of the client system) we would have encountered serious problems later – perhaps jeopardizing the whole assignment.

Having examined when and how to start contracting (and what to do if sufficient entry has not been gained), we must consider next what needs to be discussed.

Discussion Points During Contracting

The level of detail that you will need to discuss during contracting will vary from one assignment to the next, depending on the nature of the assignment and the potential difficulties envisaged. Yet it would appear that client and consultant expectations operate on at least two levels. By way of illustration, we recall a conversation with a public relations officer in a large organization during which she commented, 'You can tell who are the outsiders here almost immediately'. In making this observation she was highlighting the difference between the bulk of employees who had started with the company in their youth and worked their way up and a few others who were usually professionally qualified but had joined the organization later in their careers. When asked to explain, she pointed out that the difference lay not so much in *what* outsiders did but *how* they did it – somehow their methods of doing things and ways of working were different. For us, this illustration highlights the two levels that need to be covered in contracting. The first, or formal level, includes the more obvious expectations about *what* will be done. The second, or informal level, concerns mainly expectations and assumptions about *how* you and the client will work together.

The concerns that need to be covered at the formal level are generally more obvious and include:

- What service or activity will you carry out?
- What is the time-scale for the assignment?
- How much will it cost the organization?

As a general rule this level of contracting is easily identified and rarely overlooked. By contrast, informal aspects of contracting are much more subtle and difficult to pin down. Over and above any agreement about the assignment itself, you and your client will have a whole host of other assumptions about the relationship. These could include:

- how you should behave;
- what information you should collect and how you will collect it;
- issues concerning confidentiality;
- level of commitment expected;
- the match between your value system and that of the client;
- what you mean by the words you use;
- how you tackle disagreements and differences of opinion.

It is clear that unless these informal expectations are made explicit and understood at the outset they can obstruct and eventually undermine the whole assignment. Even something as simple as inappropriate dress can put you in a situation where, whatever your expertise, you will be discounted by the client. Similarly, misunderstanding about the words and expressions we use can lead to problems. For example, managers frequently use terms like 'work hard', 'participation', 'confidential', etc., but do they mean the same as our interpretation? The only way we can be sure is to explore with clients what they really mean, in the hope of reaching a mutual understanding of the concepts and constructs we use.

Many of these kinds of issues are taken for granted within organizations and as a result they often do not come to light until they surface as problems during an assignment. It is useful therefore to look at potential difficulties.

Difficulties

There are many assumptions and expectations which could cause difficulty during your assignments. But, before looking at our list, stop for a few moments; use your own experience and thoughts about consulting to generate your list of potential problems.

Our response was as follows:

Previous history
- Is this the first time a consultant has been used?
- What has the client tried before?

Expectations of the consultant
- Why has the client chosen you for this assignment?
- What is your bias?
- Is an outcome expected in terms of results, changes, solutions, recommendations, savings, or a combination of these?

Time/resource allocation
- Is your time fixed or open-ended?
- What time/resources is the client expected to put in?
- How much departmental time will be needed?

Organizational relationships
- Do these enable or constrain?
- Who can you speak/not speak to?
- What can you discuss?
- What topics/information must you avoid?
- Are there any power/authority difficulties?

Methodology
- What methodology are you expected to use for data gathering:
  - action research?
  - questionnaires?
  - interviews?
  - informal discussion?
  - attitude surveys?
- Are any specific data-gathering methods excluded?

Level of commitment/involvement
- Is the client the owner of the problem? What does this mean with respect to commitment and involvement?
- What level or kind of commitment is required from the client?
- Is the client's manager or any other group/department involved?

Confidentiality

- What does confidentiality mean with respect to the problem, the data and any recommendations?
- Can data be collected/reported anonymously?
- Who can share any data collected? The people who supplied it? The client? The client's manager?
- Will any aspect of the assignment be reported on a wider scale or published?

Termination/renegotiation

- Who can initiate renegotiation of the contract if the problem changes or if the problem is found to be outside the original agreement?
- Who can terminate the assignment?

The list is not meant to be exhaustive and inevitably you will run into difficulties which either you never envisaged at the outset or are unique to a particular organization or department. Nevertheless, it should give you a reasonable overview of the kinds of issues you should bear in mind when engaging in contracting discussions. Having looked at the difficulties, it is perhaps sensible to turn next to how you can minimize them.

Minimizing the difficulties

Given that it is highly unlikely you will be able to anticipate all difficulties beforehand, it is important to address what strategies you might employ to ensure that unexpected problems are minimized. A few suggestions include:

- Accept from the outset that the nature of a contract is dynamic and always open to renegotiation from either side. Following from this, it is equally important that clients have a similar understanding. Should difficulties then arise there is permission for either side to request renegotiation.
- Help clients to state what they really *do* want as opposed to what they feel they *ought* to want.
- Be clear about who else will be involved, how they will be kept informed and how their inputs will be managed.
- Remain constantly aware that the problem as defined by the client may not, in the event, turn out to be the real problem. However, 'start where the client is' is usually good advice.

The Optimum Outcome of Contracting

Ideally, the outcome of contracting is some form of agreement on what is to be undertaken, at what expense and under what terms. Although this can be simply a verbal agreement, a written contract can be very helpful in testing mutual understanding (i.e. Is what I think I said the same as what you think I said and is it what we both mean, and vice versa?). Obviously, the detail you include will vary from one assignment to the next depending on the nature of the assignment and the potential difficulties envisaged. However, as a minimum, we believe all contracts should include:

- A statement about the aims and objectives of the assignment. This should be as explicit as possible and include a statement on how you will judge success. This will then permit much easier evaluation of whether the venture has been worth while.
- An outline of the first steps. This should aim to give a clear picture of how both you and the client will proceed.
- Identification of who will be involved in the assignment and the division of responsibilities.
- Any potentially difficult areas if it appears important that these should be included: e.g. methodology, levels of involvement, confidentiality, etc.
- A statement defining the dynamic nature of the contract and giving permission for either party to request renegotiation if this becomes necessary.
- Time-scale of the assignment and the disengagement plan. It may seem somewhat surprising to raise the issue of disengagement before the assignment is really under way, but in our experience the best time to talk about endings is at the beginning. In a strange way it can help to reassure the client that your intentions are honest. The rationale behind this will be discussed more fully in Chapter 13 which deals with disengagement and follow-up.
- Provision of some form of review of the assignment both during the assignment and when it is complete, so that both parties have ongoing and end-point evaluation of the success or otherwise of the consultation.
- An assessment of the cost to the client. In most cases this will include obvious costs such as your time, any additional resources that may be needed and the client's time. Equally, there may be recurrent costs to take into account such as the cost of ongoing back-up or support. Also there could be hidden costs which are very difficult to quantify; e.g. if redundancies are likely as a result of taking on a new system there will be hidden emotional costs not only for those directly involved but also those indirectly involved.

Other contracting issues are summarized in the checklists at the end of this chapter.

An exercise in contracting Think of a relationship with a colleague at work and list on a sheet of paper:

- what you expect of the colleague;
- what you think the colleague expects of you.

When you are responding try to take the following points into consideration:

- why you chose this particular relationship;
- what you gain from the relationship;
- what you would be prepared to do or not do within the relationship;
- what behaviour is acceptable or unacceptable;
- how you expect to manage and resolve differences;

- how much time you expect to give one another;
- boundaries of confidentiality in your conversations.

When you can't think of anything else, review your list and put a tick against all those items which have been explicitly discussed with your colleague. Then consider the implications of what this says about the 'taken for granted' assumptions you have made in this relationship. An even better variation on this exercise is to invite the colleague to do the exercise as well (but obviously from his or her point of view). When you have both finished, compare and discuss your lists. You might even find it helps to develop the relationship between the two of you.

You may like to try the exercise again, this time focusing on a close personal relationship – say, a close friend or your partner or spouse.

Other Outcomes of Contracting

The discussion earlier looked at the optimum outcome from contracting and highlighted the areas of agreement which may be reached. Unfortunately, it is not always the case that the optimum outcome is possible. Indeed, we would suggest that if you are ever in a situation where you feel that you have covered every contractual detail with a client, then beware; in our experience organizational life is rarely so simple. Contracting is often a difficult process and may be spread over a number of meetings. Although the optimum outcome is desirable other legitimate outcomes could include:

- Agreeing the broad basis of a contract covering the main points but (where both parties feel comfortable) leaving the detail until later.
- Situations where you agree to write a tentative draft contract that will provide the basis for further discussion.
- Mutual agreement not to embark on an assignment together with a clear understanding why not.

The important point which arises from this is that you must feel free not to press ahead with any assignment if important contractual details are unresolved. Having said this, we recognize that refusing to accept an assignment could have important implications for the internal consultant.

These include:

- the effect on your career;
- the effect of any bonus or performance-related reward system;
- the effect on your appraisal;
- how will your manager react – will he or she support you?
- the effect on your department;
- will you ever be invited back by that client?
- does the organizational culture support individuals who say no?

Clearly, when deciding whether to refuse an assignment you will need to take these factors into account. We would be the last to condemn anyone who feels obliged to accept a contract which is less than satisfactory. Indeed, in the politics of organizational life there could be perfectly valid reasons for accepting a contract where you are not completely happy. On occasions we have accepted contracts where we were less than one hundred per cent certain in order to gain entry for further work at a later date. However, these were not decisions we took in silence; our reservations were made explicit to the respective client groups. Equally, they were not decisions that were made without assessing the implications. We would argue that our rationale for such decisions is similar to that of the supermarket which offers a 'loss leader'; it may be worth it in the long run.

Consequences of Poor Contracting

At the risk of labouring the point we cannot emphasize too strongly the importance of full and open discussion during the contracting phase. Phillips and Shaw (1989) point out in their book, *A Consultancy Approach for Trainers*, that 'Probably all consultants would agree that problems arising in later stages of an assignment can be traced back to poor initial contracting or failure to renegotiate the contract as circumstances change'.

Even when you recognize all these dangers you could still experience enormous client pressure to move quickly into problem solving once you have agreed the formal aspects of contracting. However, the following illustration gives some indication of the distasteful consequences which could result if you fail to address adequately the informal details of contracting.

The particular assignment consisted of working with a group of highly specialized IT staff. They were all technical experts in their fields but had 'topped out' in terms of their longer-term career prospects. As they all worked in some form of consulting role they were to be offered the opportunity to examine their consulting skills as part of a wider personal development programme. The assignment was offered to the authors only a few weeks before the programme began. By this stage all other details of the programme had been fixed except for a one-day slot which had been left for consulting skills. The contracting meeting was held with the training officer where he insisted it was to be left to our discretion how we wanted to work with the group. After agreeing the formal levels of the contract we attempted to explain our approach. This was to assume a high level of experience in the client group and start where they were. The training officer appeared to accept this and emphasized that he believed that we knew what we were doing and that how we ran the day was our decision. We accepted the work and sent the client a proposal describing how we would structure the day. Although this was accepted, the event proved to be a disaster. Our efforts to work with the group met with refusal and we were clearly informed by the group that the day should have consisted of expert instruction on 'how to consult' together with a few 'war stories'. In effect, our way of working was alien to both the group's expectations and the organizational culture (which revered and rewarded the expert).

In retrospect we should have picked up the cues given out at the contracting meeting and either pushed for more involvement by the client or turned down the assignment. We allowed ourselves to collude with one part of the client system, ignoring the rest. The result was a failed assignment. On a more positive note, we learned a great deal about the importance of the informal level of contracting and resolved to ensure it is never compromised in the future.

Renegotiating the Contract

In the previous example there was no opportunity for us to renegotiate the contract once the assignment had started to go wrong. Thankfully, this is not always the case – with many assignments it is possible to renegotiate as the work progresses. However, you do need to plan for this from the very start.

You can prompt renegotiation as a result of a variety of issues. First, information may come to light during an assignment which changes either the nature or scope of the work. Second, situations do arise where one of the parties fails to deliver their part of the original contract. Both of these situations make renegotiation imperative. However, it is important to recognize that renegotiation is not a sign of weakness or failure on your part. It is simply being open and honest and facing up to the implications of a changing situation rather than carrying on blindly.

Perhaps the best way you can prepare for the possibility of renegotiation is by ensuring that this provision is discussed early in the contracting stage. It is then very easy for either you or your client to initiate renegotiation without loss of face. Of course renegotiation of a contract may be much more complex and may take much longer than one simple discussion. This is the case when you decide to change the whole nature of the way you manage a working relationship.

Some years ago, for example, we worked with the HR department of a multinational organization. The department was undergoing the kind of change that was typical of many HR departments at the time. They were moving away from a highly centralized and specialized structure where HR specialists took responsibility for recruitment, industrial relations, employee services and training. Instead of working in specialized units, a much smaller team of HR professionals became HR consultants offering a generalist service to line managers.

An important part of this initiative was to give back responsibility for HR activities to line managers with HR acting in more of a consulting role. This turned out to be a much more difficult transition than they had anticipated. Line managers resisted taking on what they saw as additional responsibility and they felt quite vulnerable undertaking activities, hitherto within the domain of HR. What was actually happening was quite a long process of renegotiating contracts between HR and line management.

Under the old contract HR maintained a high degree of power, responsibility and control over what they considered to be their domain. Line managers were able to simply pass on people issues to the HR department who would work with them as experts in a very prescriptive way. The new contract meant line managers taking on responsibility for people issues with HR people operating in a support role, offering specialist expertise, but working in a more acceptant and catalytic way, with final decisions remaining with the line manager. Of course the new contract wasn't renegotiated overnight. It took several months of gradually shifting relationships before the new way of working was established.

Similar changes in working relationships happen during shifts towards continuous improvement, self-managed work teams, peer assessment or empowerment of people, where previous ways of working together are changed significantly and previous unwritten contracts need to be renegotiated.

Contracting in Action

Examples of best practice in contracting can be seen in the work done by the Chase Manhattan Bank, Project and Quality Management Team (PQM). They have invested a lot of thought and energy in clarifying the image they wish to project to the rest of the organization, how they want to work with their clients and the kind of working relationships they want with each other. They have done this by developing and publishing three formal documents which tackle a number of contracting issues. These are:

- A set of **PQM Standard Terms and Conditions** which are attached to each contract agreed with every internal customer. These set out the basic principles that underpin PQM's way of working.
- The **Consultancy of Choice** document which has been agreed by PQM consultants as a set of values that underlie the way they all work with their clients, thus facilitating a consistent approach amongst all consultants.

  NB. This is designed to ensure that PQM get chosen as first choice consultants by internal client departments who have freedom to go to outside consultants. This contract is firmly based upon the Consulting Cycle described in Section III of this book.
- The **Group Contract** which establishes a set of behavioural groundrules for working together within the PQM team. The purpose of this is to establish a mature team culture where openness and support are not only encouraged and team members valued by each other but everyone takes personal responsibility for making it happen for real.

These documents are reproduced at the end of this chapter as Checklists 9.6, 9.7 and 9.8.

Summary

- Contracting involves an open sharing of expectations between consultant and client.
- Contracts need to be agreed with everyone involved in the client system.
- Meaningful contracts can only be established when both client and consultant have built up an adequate relationship between themselves.
- Contracts need to embrace expectations at both formal and informal levels.
- Contracting may confront many difficulties.

- There can be several legitimate outcomes ranging from a satisfactory working agreement through to mutual agreement not to embark on the assignment.
- The consequences of poor contracting can lead to severe difficulties later on.
- An option to renegotiate needs to be agreed from the start of any assignment.

Checklist 9.1 The Purpose of the Contract

A good contract:

- helps define the problem further;
- clarifies in both the client's and the consultant's minds the work to be carried out;
- avoids unnecessary work and work on wrong problems;
- provides the consultant with parameters and freedom to act within them;
- gives the client an understanding of how to work with the consultant and what to expect from him or her;
- sets mutual expectations, goals and objectives;
- establishes the ground rules for behaviour between the client and the consultant over such things as anonymity of data, mutual feedback, legitimacy of differences, etc.

Checklist 9.2 Strong and Weak Contracts

A strong contract is central to success. Its characteristics are:

- high commitment by all parties to make the contract;
- clear commitment in terms of time;
- clear statement of objectives;
- mutual trust and respect;
- risks and anxieties in the open.

A weak contract has a different set of characteristics:

- the consultant has uneasy feelings, and is not sure why;
- the client's extent of commitment is unclear;
- the client is under many other stresses, and so the activity has low priority;
- there is inadequate planning time before any event;
- the client abdicates all responsibility to the consultant.

Checklist 9.3 Testing the Contract

It is time to test, and perhaps end, a contract when:

- The client keeps putting things off.
- Agreements are made, and forgotten (by either side).
- The consultant has a higher personal commitment to the outcome than the client.
- The client looks to the consultant to do things he or she should be doing.
- The client is doing well, and does not really need any more help.

Checklist 9.4 Contracting – General Issues

A contract is a way of making expectations explicit, trying to anticipate misunderstandings and setting out each side of the bargain, as it were. A contract need not be in writing but there are certain aspects of your work together which need to be discussed before you start. The following is a list which seems to cover most of the essential aspects. No doubt you can add to it.

- Hierarchical relationships:
  - are we constrained by them?
  - what can I say and to whom?
  - what power/authority problems?
- How much time allocation?:
  - consultant's time/open-ended?
  - client's time?
  - departmental time, etc.?
- How much freedom do we have?:
  - consultant?
  - client?
- What commitment is there?:
  - from my boss?
  - client's boss?
  - owners of the problem?
- What are the expectations?:
  - of consultant?
  - of client?
  - of consultant's boss?
  - in terms of: results;
changes;
solutions;
recommendations;
savings.
- What methods can I use?:
  - data gathering?
  - action research?
  - questionnaires?
  - interviews?
  - attitude surveys?
  - what modes are barred to me?
- Who can share the data?:
  - people who supplied it?
  - client?
  - client's boss?
  - my boss?

- To whom do I report?:
  - who owns the report?
  - client's boss?
  - client?
- Who can end the consultation?:
  - client or client's boss?
  - consultant or consultant's boss?
- The issue of confidentiality:
  - of the problem;
  - of the data;
  - of the recommendations, etc.;
  - can data be anonymous?
- Renegotiation:
  - who can do it?
  - if the problem changes;
  - if the project extends outside the department.
- Starting the consultation:
  - where, when, how?
  - we may not be able to say where we are going but we can say where we start from.
- What has gone before?:
  - is this the first time?
  - what has the client tried already?
- To whom am I responsible?:
  - client?
  - client's boss?
  - my boss?
- Cost:
  - who pays?
  - whose budget?
  - who can authorize more resources in time, money, materials?

Checklist 9.5 An Illustration of a Training Contract

Prior to attending any of our training programmes for consultants we carry out a pre-programme briefing with each participant and his/her immediate manager. The purpose of this briefing is threefold; firstly, to clarify any outstanding questions or confusions; secondly, to give important information about both the content of the programme and how it will be run; thirdly, to initiate a contracting discussion to enable learning from the event to be transferred effectively back to the workplacc. Both manager and participant are encouraged to contribute their ideas to the discussion and a written summary of the conclusions is made. This summary is then subsequently used as the basis for the contracting segment of the actual training event.

Our key contracting questions are:

- What do you want to achieve from this event? (Please be as specific as possible.)
- How will you know when you have achieved your objectives?
- What will you have *to do* to maximize your chances of achieving your objectives?
- What help will you need from others on the programme to achieve your objectives?
- What help can you offer to others to enable them to achieve their objectives?
- How might you sabotage your own learning? (i.e. what are your habitual ways which you use to frustrate your own learning?)

It is also worth adding that once we have completed the contracting section of the training programme we actively encourage everyone attending to use the contracts to steer and guide the event. In other words, the contracts become living documents rather than remaining as idle words which, once written, are immediately forgotten.

Checklist 9.6 Chase Manhattan Bank – PQM Standard Terms and Conditions

Project Management

- Project and Quality Management (PQM) provides client centred consultancy services to its customers within Chase on a project basis to meet defined goals and objectives, within an estimated pre-determined time frame.
- PQM employs applicable Corporate standards supported by its own best practice methodologies in the performance of its work; these include 'the consultancy of choice', 'the project standard' and 'process improvement methodology'.
- PQM will use all reasonable skills and care to deliver the required results, as specified by the goals and objectives in the contract, and to meet or exceed all prescribed quality targets, on time and within budget.

PQM Resources

- PQM will make every effort to ensure that the PQM staff named in the contract are available to support the project during the allotted time frame stated. They will not necessarily be assigned full time to the project.
- PQM will give reasonable notice of any necessary changes in staff assignments and details of replacements.
- PQM may sub-contract performance of any parts of the contract as it deems appropriate.
- PQM will make every effort to ensure staff engaged on the contract are fully competent to perform the work assigned. For the benefit of its customers and staff, PQM invests in the development of its staff and accordingly reserves

the right for them to attend training courses from time to time. PQM will endeavour to minimize any disruption this may cause to the effective execution of the project.
- PQM staff will work under the direction of the project manager and the PQM Relationship Manager, to whom any questions regarding PQM resourcing, timeliness or quality of work should be addressed.

Ownership and Accountability
- The project sponsor maintains ownership for the overall Project and the project manager has responsibility for its success.
- PQM are responsible and accountable to the project sponsor and project manager to deliver the agreed PQM goals and objectives set out in the contract, subject to the provision of the specified support needs on a timely basis and quality standard.
- The PQM relationship manager is responsible for agreeing the terms of the contract with the project sponsor and is the first contact in the case of any issues that may arise in relation to the smooth execution of the contract.
- Any disputes that cannot be resolved between the project sponsor and the PQM relationship manager will be referred to the UK senior country officer, whose decision will be binding on both parties.

Conduct
- All parties to the project will display the Chase Values and follow the Global Bank's Operating Principles, especially an open partnership, constructive collaboration and full commitment to achieve the project's agreed goals and objectives on a timely basis.

Communication and Feedback
- Regular meetings will be held between the project sponsor/project manager and the PQM relationship manager to review progress, team conduct and adherence of all parties to the provisions of the contract.
- Projects, deemed critical, will be monitored, and status reported to senior corporate, GMIO&T and regional management as required.
- PQM expect to give and receive open, honest, constructive and timely communication and feedback in respect of all pertinent matters relating to the execution of the contract and staff performance.
- The project sponsor and/or manager will provide PQM with formal customer feedback at the end of the project, or on a quarterly basis, to help PQM improve its services and act as a performance management and development aid to its staff.

Confidentiality
- All parties will observe the corporate code of conduct in respect of both confidentiality and candour with auditors, regulators etc.
- Unless expressly requested by the customer, PQM will use its professional judgement in respect of sharing information with other members of the project team, PQM and other appropriate Chase management.

Cost Allocations

- PQM allocates its expenses through the monthly cost allocation process to the business and other operating units in the UK on an equitable basis determined from overall estimates of PQM's use of resources covering all its activities.
- Significant out of pocket expenses (e.g. external consultants, overseas travel) for a particular project will be charged separately to the customer. PQM follows corporate policies and guidelines in respect of any travel, entertainment and other expenses.
- Services for units outside the UK will be charged to the customer on the basis of time expended at hourly rates applicable for the respective grades of PQM staff ruling at the time. These rates are calculated on the basis of direct and overhead costs only.

Renegotiation

- Subject to reasonable notice, either party may request changes to the services, goals and objectives included in the contract at any time. Adequate detail of the requested changes must be provided to enable both parties to appraise their impact.
- Until such changes are agreed and the contract amended, both parties will continue to act in accordance with the existing contract.
- All contracts will run for the time specified, but may be subject to renegotiation and extension if both parties agree.

Disengagement

- The contract will apply until the specified PQM goals and objectives have been achieved to the satisfaction of the project sponsor or if earlier, the completion date set out in the contract.
- Both parties have the right to terminate the contract with the consent of the other party.
- Upon completion or termination, the project sponsor and the PQM relationship manager will formally review the execution of the project, record any outstanding issues and identify any lessons learned or potential improvements for future projects.

Checklist 9.7 Chase Manhattan Bank – Consultancy of Choice

Client-centred Consulting

- Remember the customer owns the problem and always has the freedom of choice.
- Use the best intervention style at different times throughout the project (i.e. acceptant, catalytic, confrontational and/or prescriptive styles).
- Employ all relevant PQM competencies, standards and methodologies, seek assistance when required.
- Never usurp the customer's authority, ownership, leadership or management roles.

- Employ the following 6 phase consultancy project template, as appropriate.

Gaining Entry

- Prepare through thorough research, grounding and self-awareness prior to initial meetings.
- Build rapport with the sponsor.
- Identify the whole customer system (who knows, who cares, who can?).
- Recognize and deal with obstacles and barriers (e.g. negative emotions, imposition, lack of time).
- Build relationships of mutual openness, trust and honesty.
- Identify, understand and size the problem from the customers' viewpoint.
- Establish appropriate communication mechanisms, including participants, timing etc.

Contracting

- Agree overall expectations to be derived from PQM's involvement.
- Involve and gain commitment from the whole customer system.
- Define roles and responsibilities for decisions, communication and implementation.
- Recommend open and honest communication and full commitment from all parties.
- Set out formal and informal objectives of PQM's involvement (what, how and when).
- Agree PQM's overall expectations and needs from the whole customer system.
- Establish two-way feedback methodology, including timing, responsibility for follow up etc.
- Clarify general issues such as resources, timing, confidentiality, cost allocations etc.
- Include contract renegotiation and disengagement procedures.
- Establish project evaluation process, including expectations of client feedback on PQM performance.

Data Collection

- Identify most appropriate data collection tools (e.g. brainstorming, 7 quality tools).
- Consider comprehensive quantitative and qualitative data from all areas,
- Observe group behaviour for participation, influence, dealing with sensitivities etc.
- Use correct questioning technique (i.e. open, reflective, clarifying etc.),
- Listen and then confirm understanding of everyone's point of view,
- Classify data using the organizational diagnostic or the organizational life models.
- Provide ongoing, timely and constructive feedback, both positive and negative.
- Involve the whole customer system to ensure appropriate participation and ownership.

Diagnosis, Decision Making

- Identify the most appropriate decision models (e.g. decision trees, force field analysis) and processes.
- Use appropriate consultancy style to help customers reach good decisions.
- Employ the Project Standard and Process Improvement Methodology in planning.
- Transfer skills by using the learning cycle to assist client staff (i.e. experience, reflection, conceptualizing, planning and experimentation).

Implementation

- Ensure the necessary ownership, leadership, capability and organization exist.
- Confirm full customer commitment to focus the group and avoid undue dependency on PQM.
- Identify the most appropriate competencies – knowledge, skills, behaviours and attitude.
- Gain acceptance to change through full communication, participation, trust etc.
- Employ the Project Standard throughout implementation to monitor and report progress.
- Use most appropriate consultancy style, preferably in facilitation and support.
- Provide ongoing, timely and constructive feedback, both positive and negative.
- Measure achievements and accrued benefits and compare against original objectives.

Disengagement

- Agree timing and methodology with whole customer system.
- Use a gradual process with ongoing review, customer support and facilitation.
- Exchange honest and open two-way feedback, both positive and negative.
- Review and share lessons learned for other consultancy assignments with PQM.
- Celebrate success with all customers and their teams.
- Maintain and build positive customer relationships for the future.

Checklist 9.8 Chase Manhattan Bank – PQM Group Contract

Introduction

The group has developed its own group contract for dealing with each other as professionals and for mutual support. Each group member aspires to be a role model in displaying the behaviours outlined by the contract. It was designed through extensive collaboration between all group managers and staff. It encapsulates both the Chase Values and best client-centred consulting methods and practices. It is illustrated in the following table, aligned to the corporate values:

Chase Values	*Group Contract*
Customer Focus	**We will . . .**
• tries all possible ways to solve a customer's problem before referring to others; • helps customers outside of normal working hours; • keeps customers informed of the status of enquiries; • tried to go beyond what a customer asks for; • always seeks ways to improve customer satisfaction.	• act as both client and consultant to each other; • respect and honour each other's confidentiality; • use prescriptive style only where appropriate; • deal with one client or issue at a time; • keep the discussions focused.
Respect for Each Other	**We will . . .**
• listens to constructive criticism non-defensively; • gives feedback in a constructive manner; • shows appreciation of others' efforts; • expresses disagreement tactfully and sensitively; • treats people courteously.	• give and receive open, specific, timely and honest feedback; • ask for feedback and receive it constructively; • actively listen and give each other time; • express feelings and respect others' feelings; • ask people how they feel; • assume good intentions of all team members.
Teamwork	**We will . . .**
• openly share information with others; • asks others how he/she can help them; • willingly puts team goals ahead of personal goals; • compromises with others to get the job done; • works across unit lines to solve problems/create solutions.	• create a non-judgemental atmosphere; • participate fully in all group discussions; • not filter facts; • value and acknowledge the efforts of others.

Chase Values – cont.

Initiative

- challenges the 'way they have always been done';
- generates new ideas and innovative solutions;
- conveys a sense of urgency when appropriate;
- willingly seeks new work challenges beyond own responsibilities;
- takes immediate and independent action when needed.

Professionalism

- asks for feedback from others on how he/she is doing;
- persists in the face of obstacles;
- works constructively under stress and pressure;
- gives candid feedback to his/her superiors;
- holds to the highest standards of performance.

Quality

- produces results that consistently meet or exceed expectations;
- accepts responsibility for successes and failures;
- checks work to ensure accuracy and quality;
- makes decisions based on facts.

Group Contract – cont.

We will . . .

- ask a question if we want an answer;
- deal with all issues as they arise;
- take risks;
- be alert to sabotage and manage conflict:
  - state opinion and listen;
  - discuss and decide;
  - check feelings.

We will . . .

- start on time, assign appropriate time to session and end on time;
- keep our promises;
- respect internal group deadlines;
- recognize barriers and face up to them.

We will . . .

- observe and say what we observe;
- check Group effectiveness;
- ask for what we require;
- say 'I' when we mean 'I'.

10 Collecting Data and Feeding it Back

What is Data?

Once you have a contract the next step is to gather data that will help you and the client clarify the nature of the problem, isolate symptoms, identify causes and lead towards some kind of resolution of the problem. The dilemma, of course, is what kind of data you should collect. What data is likely to be relevant and what irrelevant? To some extent data collection will depend on the technical discipline of the consultant. The accountant will collect financial and control data; the personnel manager is likely to see the client's problem in terms of payment systems, recruitment or industrial relations; the marketing consultant is likely to be interested in the product or service itself and the marketplace in which it is being sold.

We believe, however, that if you remain too firmly rooted in your basic technical discipline then you are likely to disregard important elements of the organizational problem. A good consultant is a bit like a detective in an Agatha Christie novel. The reader is presented with all kinds of evidence, much of which is dismissed as irrelevant. Hercule Poirot or Miss Marple, on the other hand, are able to recognize the significance of seemingly unrelated and irrelevant events, which when put together reveal the identity of the murderer.

The consultant too is often presented with an array of complex information about the client department, the systems, the technology, the structures and the people. Faced with this complexity it is very tempting to focus on that part of the client system that is made easy to understand by one's technical discipline. However, most organizational problems cross functional boundaries. If, for example, a major new system is being introduced there may well be recruitment, training and financial implications. If a new product is being developed there are likely to be technical, financial, systems and human dimensions to the change. Consultants helping with such changes can't afford to remain too firmly rooted in their basic discipline. If you are to be successful as a consultant it is important that you are able to make connections between often disparate pieces of information and put them together so that they make sense and produce the big picture. This way you can help the client to deal with the complete problem instead of tinkering with part of it.

There is one kind of data which is always available but all too often neglected. This is data about the human dimension of the problem. Your *raison d'être* as a consultant is organizational change and such change affects and is affected by people. Many consultants are aware that the managerial style and morale in the client department have a huge impact on the success of the department and on the outcome of the project they are working on. But they feel that they have been asked to explore a 'business problem' and don't want to 'get involved with personalities'. If you do this then you ignore a lot of data which impacts significantly on the business issue. A fall in sales may well have something to do with pricing, quality, advertising or promotional activities. But equally it may be affected by the style of the sales manager; the morale, motivation and commitment of salespeople; political in-fighting between sales managers; an unwillingness to communicate openly with other departments; or a feeling among salespeople of being unsupported. A technical innovation might be less successful if the people involved feel threatened by the change; if they feel that their views haven't been taken into account; that their skills have been devalued or that they themselves are not valued by 'the management'.

This exotic data is very difficult to collect and quantify, and can be ambiguous. However, you ignore it at your peril (Checklist 10.1 at the end of the chapter summarizes questions to help gather this type of data). Ultimately, the success of a consulting project will depend not only on how you handle the purely business problem but also on how comfortable you are dealing with the data you collect about the human beings who will be affected and their relationships with each other. These types of issues are illustrated in the following example.

Some time ago one of the authors was hired to carry out some sales training in the publishing industry. The client company printed newspapers and periodicals. It appeared to be a fairly straightforward assignment. The sales representatives had hitherto been in a distribution role, liaising with wholesalers, retailers and their own head office to ensure that the products passed through the distribution chain efficiently and arrived at the retail outlets on time. Obviously, this is crucially important in an industry where the product has an extremely short shelf life. Henceforth, following a number of structural changes in the company, the role of the representatives was to change and they were being given more responsibility for increasing circulation of the products in their area. This meant they would have to call on retailers to persuade them to give more prominence to the products. To do this they needed training in basic selling skills. When the author arrived to work with the first group, however, there was an atmosphere of anger and resentment. They did not know why they were there, or why they needed these skills. They did not understand the changes that had been made and resented them. Needless to say, they responded very negatively to the training session.

What the author had done, of course, was to ignore some very important data. His first meeting with the national sales manager at head office had been constantly interrupted by telephone calls and people 'putting their heads round the door' seeking urgent information or decisions. The environment seemed to be seething with high activity and urgency, minute-to-minute changes and consequent decisions to be made. It was exciting but it was also frenetic. Subsequent meetings with field sales managers revealed a picture of a group of very able and dynamic people, with lots of energy, but all doing very stressful jobs. What the author did not realize then was that they were spending most of the day at home chained to the telephone in constant contact with various headquarters people. This left them very little time to spend with the representatives. Consequently, the representatives were facing a very uncertain future, they had had very little individual communication about the organizational changes and, inevitably, there were lots of rumours about further changes, cut-backs and redundancies. They had little opportunity to talk through their changing role with their managers and they looked unlikely to get much personal support as they adapted to the new role. Little wonder they reacted as they did. The author eventually decided it was pointless to carry on with the sales training sessions without helping all the clients to examine more fundamental problems of communication, decision making and management style within the department.

Categorizing Data

Having recognized the range and complexity of the data available to consultants no doubt you will need a vehicle to help make sense of it all. This should help you categorize the data so that it becomes manageable and useable. You will then be in a position to feed it back to clients in the form of information that helps them understand the situation more clearly and make informed decisions about the way forward.

In Chapter 3 we introduced some models of organizations which may help you to categorize the data you collect about what is happening. In addition there are also some checklists to get you started.

Data Collection

There is a limited number of ways of collecting data from your client system and they all have potential advantages and disadvantages. The methods are:

- interviews;
- questionnaires;
- direct observation;
- document analysis;
- your own experience and intuition.

Interviews

You can conduct interviews with individuals or with groups. The interview can be open-ended and unstructured or it can be carried out in a more structured way.

Advantages
- The data is very rich. You can pick up a lot of information from the way questions are answered, non-verbal signals, what is not said, etc.
- Sometimes issues emerge during data-collection interviews which could not have been predicted.
- Interviewing people can help you to build relationships, and gain a deeper entry with people in the client system.

Disadvantages
- The cost – interviews can be very expensive and time-consuming.
- Only a restricted number of people can be interviewed.
- It can be difficult to interpret the data.
- Interviewer bias.
- It can be difficult to quantify the data.
- Data can be subjective.
- Data may not be comparable unless interviews are tightly structured.

Questionnaires

A lot of information can be obtained by the use of surveys and questionnaires.

Advantages
- Useful with large numbers of people.
- It is relatively inexpensive.
- People may be more honest if the questionnaire is completed anonymously.
- It can be easier to quantify the data.

Disadvantages
- Predetermined questions can miss important issues.
- People might be suspicious of an impersonal questionnaire. There is no opportunity to give reassurances, to explain the purpose of collecting the data or to point out the potential benefits to the respondent.
- It is possible to over-interpret the results of questionnaires and read too much into them.

Direct observation

If you go out into your client group and watch them at work you can build up a very clear understanding of the way they work now. Sometimes you may be able to observe while they try things differently. This is often the role of the sports coach – acting as informed, critical observer feeding back to the athletes information about their strengths and weaknesses. You may not be an athletics coach but you may well decide to sit in at meetings of your client group, making calls with the salespeople, spend time on the factory floor, look at the technology or experience the working conditions.

Sometimes you will observe and give immediate feedback to the client. At other times you may need to keep a more permanent record of what you have seen in the form of notes. You may also use a camera or a video or tape recorder to gather directly audible or visible data.

Advantages

- You can observe the way people actually behave rather than the way they say they behave.
- You can collect data about what is happening now rather than what has happened in the past.
- Often the outsider can see things that group members are unaware of.
- Issues that could not have been predicted might become obvious during the observation.

Disadvantages

- Direct observation can be time-consuming and expensive.
- The data might be narrow and selective.
- You can only observe what happens while you are present. You might miss significant issues or events.
- Your presence might affect the way people behave.
- Observer bias – if you see someone you like you might assume that what that person does is good.
- Sometimes people's perceptions of events are different from the reality.

Document analysis

A method much used by consultants is to spend time looking at the numbers, the balance sheet, the statistics and written communication. This method can give you a lot of information on things like scrap rates, rejects, absenteeism, lateness, sickness, sales, production, costs, etc.

Advantages

- It doesn't involve the client's time.
- It is inexpensive.
- It can be objective data which has a high degree of credibility with the client.

Disadvantages

- Data gathered by this method is limited to the task, and systems and procedures. It is unlikely to reveal any information on the human process issues which are contributing to the problem.
- This method will tell you *what* is happening but not *why* it is happening.
- You can be tempted to hide behind the documents. This can create the illusion of being busy while avoiding the much more difficult activities of actually meeting people and asking questions.

Experience and intuition

You can collect a lot of useful data about what it is like to work in the department simply by tuning in to your own feelings. The way people manage their relationships with you might be indicative of the way they manage their relationships with each other. Particularly important is your relationship with the manager. The way you are 'managed' can reveal a lot about the manager's management style. Does the manager appear open? How much freedom are you given to talk to people? How often are you expected to check back? Do you feel listened to? All this can be important data about how that manager operates. Similarly, when you are working in the department, how comfortable do you feel? Your own tensions and discomforts might be telling you something about how your clients are feeling. An illustration of this is given in the following example.

We were once asked to do some training on customer relations with a public bus company in a large provincial city. The client was astounded when we suggested that it might be a good idea for us to travel on some of the company's buses to feel what it was like to be a passenger. On entering the first bus we were greeted with an array of commands in the form of a number of notices.

- Don't talk to the driver.
- Don't stand forward of this point.
- Lower your head when leaving your seat.
- Your ticket must be retained for inspection.
- People travelling without a ticket are liable to prosecution (which someone had changed to 'persecution').
- No smoking.
- No standing on the upper deck.
- Enter only by the front door.
- Exit only by the rear door.
- Luggage must not be left in the gangway.

Of course, a good case can be made for the necessity of all these requirements. But what overall message is given to the passenger? We certainly began to feel patronized, distrusted and controlled; the general impression given was that the company would run much more smoothly if it weren't for the passengers, who made life difficult. Using this data gathered from our own experience we were able to help the client redefine the problem which he had previously seen in narrow terms as 'How to train the bus crews in customer contact skills'. Together we redefined the problem as 'How to present a more friendly, comfortable and welcoming image to our passengers'. This changed the whole nature of the subsequent project in which customer contact training, although significant, became one part of a larger problem.

However, perhaps we should return to the advantages and disadvantages of experience and intuition.

Advantages

- The data is very solid. You know what your feelings are and no one can argue with them.
- It helps you identify sensitive issues which are difficult to observe and which people are reluctant to talk about.

- The data is immediate and about the here and now.
- You don't need permission to collect it.
- It may help you to question and challenge other data which contradicts your own experience.
- You can start collecting this kind of data as soon as you make contact with the client.

Disadvantages
- It is very subjective.
- It is open to consultant bias.
- It can be difficult to feed this data back to clients in a way that doesn't make them feel defensive.
- It can be difficult to justify.
- Some people are not very intuitive themselves and are likely to discount this kind of data.
- It can be difficult to trust your own intuition.
- It can contradict other concrete data.

Exercise Try making a list of the kinds of questions you might ask yourself to draw on intuitive data. When you have finished, compare it with our list at the end of the chapter.

Questioning Techniques

Whatever data-collection method or methods you choose you are inevitably going to need to ask questions. You may write these down in the form of surveys or questionnaires, ask them formally as part of a structured interview or very informally as you work with your clients. Asking questions is the single most important tool in the consultant's kitbag. Asking the right questions may appear very easy and yet in practice is often very difficult.

So, what are the right questions? The only answer is – it depends on your objective. However, there is one very important thing we can say about asking questions right from the start. Client-centred consultants try very hard to ask client-centred questions. What is a client-centred question, and how does it differ from those traditionally asked by consultants?

Consultants traditionally ask questions which help them understand the problem so that they can take the problem away from their clients and prescribe a solution with minimum involvement of the clients. If you are simply asking questions about information the clients already know you are probably working in a consultant-centred way.

If you are working in a client-centred way you start with the assumption that you are there to help your clients work on the problem and identify an appropriate course of action. This means asking questions which illuminate the problem for the clients, not just for the consultant. They should be questions that challenge your clients and help them think about the problem differently. Your questions should empower the clients, not diminish them. Questions also relate directly to intervention style, so you will find that many of the questions in this section have been mentioned in Section II in the context of the different intervention styles. It is important to look at the types of questions that can be asked, what results they are likely to produce and when they are helpful or unhelpful.

Open-ended questions

Open-ended questions can be used to elicit general information. They will help you gather facts or explore your clients' feelings, opinions and attitudes. They give clients the opportunity to reply as fully as they wish, using their own words to express their thoughts and feelings. Open-ended questions invariably begin with the words 'how', 'what', 'why', 'when', 'where', or 'who' – although 'Tell me about . . . ' can also produce the same effect.

- 'What do you think has contributed to this situation?'
- 'How did you set about dealing with Mrs Smith's complaint yesterday?'
- 'Why do you do it that way?'
- 'Which part of your job do you enjoy most?'
- 'How does it feel to work around here?'
- 'What options do you have?'

These types of questions infer a non-judgemental, unbiased approach – an attitude of 'wanting to know' rather than 'telling'. Good open questions help clients to explore the situation, think the problem through in new ways and work out ways of moving forward.

Supplementary questions

Supplementary questions can be used to pursue in greater detail some information given in response to an open-ended question. This gives the client an opportunity for deeper explanation and helps to sharpen the focus without losing the natural flow. Such questions usually work best if they are not too obviously probing. Too many at one time can make clients feel pressurized or as if they are being interrogated, but they are essential for getting from the general to the real heart of the matter.

Supplementary questions are often of the 'how', 'what', 'why' type but usually linked back to what the client has just said. You might explore more deeply by asking:

- 'So when you say you were stimulated by that task, what was it that stimulated you?'
- 'So what did you feel like at that point?'
- 'That sounds interesting – could you tell me some more about that part of the job?'
- 'So what exactly did the customer say when you suggested that policy?'

Clarifying questions

Often you need to check your interpretation of the information you are being given. By doing this you can ensure that you have listened and understood what has been said. You might clarify by asking questions like these:

- 'So am I right in thinking that you feel okay with the new system but feel anxious about how it will be received by the staff?'
- 'Are you saying then that it is not the extra work that you're complaining about but the fact that you feel unappreciated?'

Asking for clarification and checking your understanding of what clients have said not only builds up a clearer picture in your mind but can also help clients to crystallize what they actually feel. In the example given above the client may never have mentioned feeling unappreciated, and may not have even been conscious of it until the consultant started using checking and clarifying questions. But be wary of putting words in the client's mouth.

Reflecting

Reflecting is not strictly speaking a form of questioning but it can be a very powerful way of clarifying the importance of the words a client uses. If you listen very actively to what the client is saying he or she may use words that are more significant than they at first appear. This is particularly true when 'feeling' words are used. It is often enough simply to pick up the word or phrase and reflect it back to the client. For example, the client might say, 'I really feel like the meat in the sandwich'. On hearing this the consultant might simply reflect, 'Meat in the sandwich'. Or the client might say, 'I really feel guilty' and the consultant might reflect: 'Guilty'.

This gives the client an opportunity to explore the significance of the word or phrase, to explore more deeply, perhaps, the stresses of feeling pressure from two directions and the causes of it. On the other hand, the client might recognize that the word or phrase doesn't really describe the situation and can now try to describe it differently. Both reactions are helpful and legitimate.

Whereas questions are always framed and therefore controlled by the consultant, by using reflecting techniques and using only the client's own words you can keep the control firmly in the hands of the client, who alone decides on the significance of the words you reflect back.

Asking About Feelings

If our model of organizational life holds true for you it follows that, as a change agent, you will be trying to elicit feelings which will enable you to work on human process issues. This means that you need to have a clear understanding of the differences between thoughts and feelings so that you can be clear about what you are expressing and can help your clients do the same. Thinking and feeling are the two major ways by which we interact with our environment. Both are essential to constructive communication. Generally, thinking (head talk) leads to an *explanation* of the situation while feeling (gut talk) leads to an *understanding* of it.

'Think' statements attempt to define, assert, provide an opinion, rationalize or make causal connections between events. Think statements are bound by the rules of logic; they may be true or untrue. Often a think statement can be proven or disproven. Think statements require words to be communicated. Most of us have been trained to emit think statements exclusively. We are constantly engaged in working with our brains, i.e. cognitive work: observing, inferring, categorizing, generalizing and summarizing. Frequently we are asked for *facts* – 'Where did you put the newspaper?', *opinions* – 'Which tastes better Australian or South African wine?', *speculation* – 'What happens when we achieve our goal?', or sometimes just 'What are you thinking about now?'. Human beings like to think and the ability to do so is what distinguishes us from other animals. Indeed thinking is so highly valued that learned societies are formed to honour those who do it well. When working with human process issues we often want to know how people feel. However, because people are not used to being asked how they feel they will often replace 'think' with 'feel'. This bogus use of 'I feel' often muddles communication. 'I *feel* like leaving the room' is no expression of feelings but a shorthand way of saying 'I'm *thinking* of leaving the room but I haven't yet decided'. Here the word feel is used to express an indefinite thought. 'I *feel* that you are asking us to do something very difficult', is not an expression of feeling but an expression of an opinion. What the person really meant was 'You are asking us to do something that, *in my opinion*, is very difficult'.

An abstract principle cannot really be felt. So, 'I *feel* that everyone is entitled to be treated with respect and dignity', is a statement of a belief or faith in something. It is more accurate to say 'I *believe* that everyone is entitled to be treated with respect and dignity'. It is important to listen to yourself and your clients when you hear 'I *feel that* it is . . . '. It is certainly going to be a think statement, not a feeling one.

Feeling statements try to report our internal, affective, immediate, emotional, gut responses to events. Usually feel statements refer to what is happening inside us. They can't be true or false, good or bad, right or wrong but only honestly or dishonestly communicated. Neither can they be denied. If that's the way you feel, that's the way you feel.

Many of us have been educated and socialized to screen out feelings and so find it difficult to get in touch with what is going on inside. So you may often get mild expressions like interested, alright, OK, confused, which are really thinking states masquerading as feelings. By helping people get in touch with their inner feelings you will enrich their experiences and enable them to deal more easily with human processes/people issues which often block effectiveness for individuals, groups and whole organizations.

An enormous block to the expression of feelings, apart from long experience of not doing it, is fear. Fear of looking stupid, and being laughed at. Fear of going against norms and standards which decree that feelings are not spoken about. Fear of saying the wrong thing at the wrong time and upsetting someone. It is useful to help people realize that they are not responsible for other people's feelings. They are responsible for their own behaviour and the effect it has but not someone's feelings. The popular song may say 'You made me love you' but it just can't be done.

So it is important to establish a climate of trust and openness before people will try expressions of feelings in a group. And from what we have said already, they will only do it as long as they believe that they will not be subjected to ridicule or punishment if they do. One way you can encourage this is to be aware of your own feelings and express them. Effective communication takes place when we take responsibility for our own thoughts, feelings and behaviour; when we own what we do. When we own our own thoughts and feelings the other person knows where we are and can respond more authentically.

Authentic communication consists of both thoughts and feelings. Consider the situation where you are part of a group which agreed to stop at 7.30 and they are still going at a quarter to ten. If a member says 'We agreed to stop over 2 hours ago and I'm very angry that we are still going', you know how they feel and the reasons why. If they had merely expressed their anger you would have no idea of the reason for the anger (though you might guess) and if they had merely said we agreed to stop at 7.30 and here we are still going at 9.45, you wouldn't really know how they were feeling. Both bits of the statement are important for it to be really authentic. As a consultant, you can help by acknowledging the feeling statements and asking for the think statement behind it or acknowledging the thought and asking for the accompanying feeling.

Forecasting or 'fantasy' questions

Sometimes, when working on a change programme, you may need to help clients plan for change. This can involve getting them to imagine how the change will affect them, what they will need to do differently, how they will react to the change and how they will feel about it. The purpose of forecasting or fantasy questions is to help clients explore what 'might be' or a variety of possibilities. For example:

- 'What would have to happen to show you that the organization really valued you?'
- 'Describe the perfect senior management team.'

These questions are only useful if realistic and answerable. They must be used in context, so that clients understand why such questions are being asked. However, be aware of the difficulty of interpreting the response and remember that the more 'fantastic' the question, the more difficult it is to get anything meaningful from the answer.

Less helpful questions

There are also some types of questions asked of clients which are seldom really profitable and can cause confusion or frustration. They include the five types discussed below.

Leading questions In these, the answers are implicit in the question, in other words you almost tell the interviewees what you want their answer to be. For example: 'You find stock-taking difficult, don't you?' or 'Don't you agree that you all need more training?'.

Multiple choice questions There is another form of leading question, but in this case the client is presented with two or more answers and asked to choose between them; e.g. 'Do you think we should send John on a course, give him an attachment or give him a book to read?'. The client may have ideas on another alternative but asking this type of question will limit the choice to the ideas presented. Equally, it restricts the answer to *one* of the alternatives whereas the client might wish to use something from all three.

Embroidered questions This is a common questioning fault, often brought about by nervousness. In this instance the consultant asks a string of questions instead of one, either by constantly amending the phrasing or adding to the question. For example: 'What do you think about him? . . . Do you think he can do it? . . . I mean, is he all right?' This confuses clients, as they no longer know which question to answer.

Unanswerable questions These are usually questions where clients are asked to comment on things beyond their knowledge or experience or which ask for interpretations. For example: 'What do you think made Jane do that?' In this case, Jane is the person to ask.

Statements posing as questions These do not actually need a response and may make clients feel uncomfortable, because they are uncertain whether you wish them to comment or not. Examples are: 'Don't you think that it would be a good idea to . . . ?'; 'Don't you believe that it is best to . . . ?'

Feedback to the Client

Having collected your data from the client system you now need to feed it back to your clients. Providing feedback is a crucial phase in the consulting process. Too often it is at the feedback phase that consulting assignments grind to a halt. The consultant does the research, writes a report and it gets ignored. No action is taken. If, on the other hand, you handle the feedback meeting well, your clients should have an enhanced picture of the problem but they should also have started to explore possible courses of action and be well placed to start making decisions.

Before we explore the issues involved in giving feedback, we would like to clarify what we mean by feedback. Essentially, feedback is a mechanism to enable human beings to develop, improve and change. We all need information about how we are performing whatever activity we are carrying out. We need to know how successful or effective we have been. Sometimes it is easy to get that information for ourselves. Someone learning to use a rifle will shoot at a target and get immediate feedback from the locations of the holes made in the target. That information can then be used as a basis to change and improve. Without that feedback it would be impossible to learn. Sometimes it is not possible to get this information directly; we need another person to give us feedback. This is the function of the sports coach, or the film director; their job is to feed back to the sports people or actors information about their performance that they can't acquire for themselves so that they can use the information as a basis for making improvements.

This is also your role as a consultant: to observe the client group from the outside, examine the way it operates, identify where it is effective and ineffective and feed the information back to the clients in a way that helps them understand what they are doing and make decisions about appropriate change.

One myth we often encounter is that feedback is always negative, that it is always a description of a client's inadequacies and failures. We believe that in client-centred consulting it is as important to feed back successes as it is failures. Positive feedback is as important as negative.

What is important is that feedback should always be constructive rather than destructive. Constructive feedback, positive or negative, is designed to help the client learn, while destructive feedback simply undermines and devalues the client.

These two dimensions (positive and negative; constructive and destructive) can be illustrated diagrammatically, as shown in Figure 10.1.

Positive
(what the client does well)

Destructive (undermines the client)	Constructive (helps the client)
• saying what the client wants to hear • giving unwarranted praise • flattery	information about: • what the client does well • what is appreciated by others • successes • behaviour that is helpful to others
• put downs • insults • non-specific criticism • hurtful comments	information about: • what the client does badly • failures • behaviour that hinders others • behaviour that is uncomfortable for others • specific criticism

Negative
(what the client does badly)

Figure 10.1 Giving feedback

Contracting and feedback

Feedback is usually about making sense of the data and links back to Chapter 9 on contracting. We believe it is important to raise the issue of feedback as early as possible. Both you and your client need to be clear at the contracting phase how feedback will be handled. You need to agree who will be given the feedback report: will circulation be restricted or will everyone who participated in interviews have access to the data that came out of the interviews? You will need to clarify what information will be confidential and what will be in the report. This is also the time when you should discuss with the client the degree to which you will feed back human process as well as systems and procedures information. Don't forget that personal feedback, particularly if it is negative, can be uncomfortable for the recipient. If you feel there is a possibility that the feedback data may be confrontational then it is only fair to prepare your client at the outset. Point out this possibility when you contract so that it doesn't come as a complete surprise when you move into the feedback phase.

Timing

The best time to receive feedback, for both individuals and groups, is as close as possible to the event. It is usually a mistake to keep the data you collect to yourself until you make your final presentation. Remember your role is to facilitate change, not to produce reports. Try to feed back the data as it is collected. This will give your clients an opportunity to think about it, discuss it and make changes. Circulate an early draft of your report to everyone concerned. This gives them an opportunity to make comments and have an input into the final version and so build their own degree of commitment. By feeding information back into the client group throughout the data gathering you also facilitate a more gradual change. This can be much more comfortable for clients than asking them to implement the results of a large report which they feel has been sprung on them.

The report

What should be included in the report? Invariably, a lot more data will be collected than could ever be used and it is tempting to flood the clients with far more than they could handle. You may need to focus on three or four high-priority issues that come out of your research rather than include absolutely everything. Don't be afraid to use your intuition when deciding what to include and what to exclude. Use only enough material to give a clear picture of the situation.

It is important to keep your report as simple as possible; avoid using complicated models. Use your client's words whenever possible to cover the main points rather than technical or professional jargon. Finally, you will increase the acceptability of your ideas if you include positive data which acknowledges the successes and strengths of your clients while at the same time not shrinking from the inclusion of data which may be uncomfortable for them to face.

The feedback meeting

No doubt we have all fallen into the trap of researching a project, writing up our findings, making our recommendations and proudly handing the completed report to a senior manager who we assume will implement our recommendations. This is based on the myth that the more senior a person is in the organization, the greater his or her power to make things happen. This myth goes on to assert that mere internal consultants are powerless by comparison. However, organizational problems (especially ones which have a lot of human process implications) are rarely amenable to an edict from on high. If they are to be solved they need to be discussed by everyone involved in and affected by the problem. If change is to be sustained, at some point a meeting must be called so that everyone concerned can discuss the findings of the report.

The best person to arrange the meeting is usually the person who carried out the project. If you have done the research and written the report you will be intimately involved with the problem. You know where the blockages are, and who needs to talk to whom. To be successful you may need to invite people from different departments or functions, across geographical boundaries and from a variety of tiers in the organizational hierarchy. You need to remember the definition of a client system introduced in Chapter 1 – 'Who knows, Who cares, Who can'. Make sure you have all three at the feedback meeting.

Your role at the feedback meeting is to help your clients clarify their understanding of the nature of the problem, help them understand each other's point of view, and encourage them to make collective decisions to which they are all committed. The meeting should not be a highly polished presentation of your findings and recommendations. Such presentations serve merely to take ownership away from your clients, inhibit discussion and put them in the role of audience rather than decision-making group. Remember that if your clients are to own the data and recommendations they need to feel that they have an opportunity to change them. So it is far better to send everyone a copy of the report in advance so they can read it and at the meeting limit yourself to a simple summary of the main findings of the report. Your role then is to facilitate the ensuing discussion.

There is likely to be some tension and resistance at the feedback meeting. A certain amount of tension is very positive – it means that people are concerned about the problem. However, be cautious if your clients simply glance casually at the data and ask 'Okay, what do we do next?' Such indifference may suggest a lack of commitment or it may indicate a reluctance to discuss the data. Apparent indifference is often a signal of resistance. On the other hand, the clients may appear very hostile, behaving aggressively towards you and your report. Whatever form resistance takes, it needs to be explored. There are often emotional reasons for resistance: people feel threatened, or exposed. They may feel they are being blamed for the problem. They may be fearful of the change that will ensue from the project. Resistance is also likely to increase the further you move away from the technical aspects of the problem and into the human dimension. The group is likely to be comfortable discussing the systems, procedures and technicalities but very uncomfortable talking about how they manage their own relationships with each other and how this impacts on the problem.

During the meeting it is important to help the group discuss any issues contained in your findings. Ask them whether the data makes sense, how the problem looks from their various perspectives, what attempts have already been made to overcome the problem. Don't try to defend the data; if people want to reject it, ask them to supply alternative data from their own experience. It is important to help the clients explore the human process issues in a very supportive way. Make sure that you don't try to allocate blame or take sides. Encourage them to explore their perception of the problem in a collaborative way without trying to blame each other. Your role is to help increase mutual understanding and help them build more open relationships. You will need to use a style of working which supports and does not judge them in any way. However, this doesn't mean you should collude with the group if they attempt to deny their human process and relationship problems. It is important to confront them, remembering that confrontation and support are not mutually exclusive. There may well be 'here and now' data that you can pick up at the meeting which will support your confrontation. For example, if part of the problem is an autocratic leadership style, you might point out that most of the air-time at the meeting is being taken up by the boss; or that no one seems willing to disagree with the boss; or that two people, central to the problem, don't seem to be listening to each other. Highlighting this type of immediate, 'here and now' data to supplement or enrich your confrontation can be very powerful.

As we have said before, the purpose of the feedback meeting is to help your clients to make decisions to which they are all committed. (A summary to help manage feedback meetings is given in Checklist 10.2 at the end of the chapter.) The next two chapters are devoted entirely to these important activities. In them we will describe a number of decision-making models which can be helpful and also a number of tools, ideas and pitfalls associated with building commitment.

Handling Personal Feedback

For many years now, whenever we have run people skills programmes (for a wide range of people including managers, internal consultants, salespeople, technicians and clerical staff, in many organizations), we have always tried to build in a session during which everyone is given an opportunity to receive feedback on how their colleagues on the programme perceive them. They hear what others see as their strengths as well as their weaknesses. They find out how people they have worked with actually feel about them and their behaviour. Almost without exception, participants find this a profound and rewarding experience. They are invariably surprised by the amount of constructive feedback they receive. They say that this feedback, positive and negative, is invaluable in helping them work on strategies for changing their behaviour back at work. What we find sad is that they also say that this is the first time anyone has given them this kind of feedback. Based on this we conclude that people in organizations very rarely share personal information with each other.

A lot of people in organizations are much less effective than they might be simply because some aspect of their behaviour is inappropriate. They may talk too much, constantly put themselves down, trivialize what they are doing with inappropriate humour, or behave in a way which others find threatening and label aggressive. The manager who is perceived as being aggressive, all things being equal, is likely to be less effective than someone who is seen to be assertive. Yet people are often unaware of the way their behaviour impacts on others. This is because, generally, people are inhibited about giving each other feedback on their behaviour and the impact it has on others. The more senior the manager the more difficult it is to get feedback. This is not only true of negative feedback, it is just as true of positive feedback. Just as we are inhibited about telling people what we dislike about their behaviour, we seem equally reluctant to tell them what we appreciate about them.

When you are working with a client group you are likely to pick up a lot of data about how people perceive each other. In the security of an interview, with guarantees of confidentiality, they are likely to share their perceptions and feelings about colleagues, other departments, their boss, senior managers, etc. – sometimes positive, sometimes negative. It would be helpful if there was some kind of mechanism for sharing this data with each other and the others being discussed. Of course, it is inevitable that you, too, will have perceptions and feelings about the way your clients behave towards you.

It follows, therefore, that another dilemma facing you as an internal consultant is how to help members of your client system give each other, and you, constructive feedback on their perceptions of each other, and how to share your own perceptions of individual clients. This is obviously a delicate issue and handled badly it could do more harm than good. There are several important points to remember when giving feedback to others or facilitating the process during which people give each other feedback.

First of all it is absolutely essential that people give each other feedback in an environment where they feel valued. If all I receive is information about what I do badly then my confidence is likely to be undermined and I am less likely to act on the information. If on the other hand I know that you like me and value me, and I know what you appreciate about me, I tend to be much more receptive when you give me negative feedback. So always start by talking about, or getting others to talk about, all the things they value about the recipient of the feedback. This helps recipients to put any negative feedback in context while not discounting what is said about them.

If feedback is to be helpful it should always be given with care. This means that it is given out of a genuine desire to help the recipient. Helpful feedback is not given to avenge some real or imagined slight or to get even but to offer some valuable information which may help others reflect on their behaviour and think of ways they might prefer to behave. One feedback exercise we use is called 'Our Gift to You' (see Chapter 15, Exercise 2, page 243), simply because feedback, when given with care and generosity, is just that, a valuable gift.

Personal feedback is of no value if it is not honest. This is not to say it has to be brutally honest'. You should never be brutal. But if you are withholding information from clients you may be doing them a disservice. Feedback should also be immediate; telling me how you feel about something I have just done is more helpful than telling me how you felt about something I did yesterday, last week or last year!

Feedback needs to be clear. We often hear people who resist giving feedback say that they get it and give it 'all the time' through tone of voice and gestures. But non-verbal feedback needs to be interpreted and there's no guarantee that the message we receive is the one being given. Even verbally it is often difficult to find exactly the words we are looking for, and even then the words may have different meanings to the recipient from the ones that were intended. Words need to be chosen carefully: describe the behaviour and the feelings you have, and then check to find out what the recipient has actually heard.

Finally, remember that when you give someone personal feedback it is never 'the truth'. It is simply your perception, and your perception may or may not be shared by others. For example, a sense of humour which you find attractive may be irritating to others. Do encourage the recipient to check out any feedback he or she receives with other people to get a clearer, and perhaps more balanced, picture.

Giving personal feedback and encouraging others to give it can be very difficult. It involves a high degree of commitment, emotional involvement and risk. It is often counter to the culture and mythology of the organization. Very often people need to overcome tremendous inhibitions in order to start giving feedback at all. But in the end if we can help people to see themselves as others do we have done them a great personal service. (For a summary of the essential points about giving personal feedback see Checklist 10.3 at the end of the chapter.)

Summary

- Gathering data which relates solely to your technical discipline is likely to ignore important elements of organizational problems.
- Exotic data such as feelings and intuition is often ignored, but is always present in any assignment.
- Making sense of complex data often requires organizational models, such as the organization diagnostic model and the model of organizational life.
- The organization diagnostic model divides activities into six interdependent areas:
  - purpose and tasks;
  - structure;
  - people;
  - rewards;

  - procedures;
  - technology.
- The model of organizational life uses three categories:
  - task;
  - systems, procedures and processes;
  - human process.
- Data can be gathered through:
  - interviews;
  - questionnaires;
  - direct observation;
  - document analysis;
  - your own experience and intuition.
- Helpful questioning could include:
  - open-ended questions;
  - supplementary questions;
  - clarifying questions;
  - reflecting;
  - asking about feelings;
  - forecasting or 'fantasy' questions.
- Less helpful questions include:
  - leading questions;
  - multiple choice questions;
  - embroidered questions;
  - unanswerable questions;
  - statements posing as questions.
- Providing feedback is a crucial phase in the consulting process, and is essential for development and progress.
- Both positive and negative feedback are of value but must always be constructive.
- Feedback should be given as an assignment is progressing as well as at the end. Saving all the feedback for a final feedback meeting is a recipe for disaster.
- Personal feedback needs to be given with care and in an environment where the recipient feels valued.
- Remember, feedback is never 'the truth', it is simply your perception.

Exercise Using Your Intuition as a Source of Data

You can often collect a lot of data about a new client group simply by being aware of your own feelings and reactions. This can tell you a lot about what it's like to work in the group. Earlier in the chapter we asked you to generate a list of questions you might ask yourself in order to draw on intuitive data. Below is our list – once again it is not meant to be definitive.

- How do I feel? Comfortable? Uncomfortable? Threatened? etc.
- What is the atmosphere like? Polite? Friendly? Strained?
- Is there an air of formality or informality?

- How welcome do I feel?
- Who talks to me?
- Who ignores me?
- How am I treated?
- How is the boss treated? With deference? As an equal? With respect?
- How inhibited do I feel about raising the possibility of human process issues?
- Do I feel listened to or not listened to?
- Who talks to whom?
- Who gets ignored?
- What kind of humour prevails? Is it sarcastic? Are there lots of in-jokes? Are there lots of put-downs? Is it gentle humour? Is it supportive?
- Do I feel comfortable or uncomfortable with the humour?
- Are women treated differently from men? Women consultants can often get an enormous amount of data about gender issues which is less obvious or unavailable to men.
- How open or closed are people with the information they give me?

Checklist 10.1 Gathering Organizational and Exotic Data

When gathering data you might ask the following questions:

- What is the presenting problem?
- How clear are different members of this client system about the common objective to which they all contribute?
- How do they get agreement on resources needed to achieve their objective?
- What are the formal organizational relationships between members of the system?
- What are the formal communication channels? How effective are they?
- What do your own feelings tell you about what it might be like to work here?
- What kind of humour is prevalent? Is it supportive? Is it ritualistic? Are there a lot of put-downs?
- How does the boss operate? How do people behave when the boss is around?
- What are people open about and what doesn't get talked about?
- How are decisions made?
- Who participates in decisions? Who gets listened to? Who gets ignored?
- How is disagreement managed?
- How empowered or powerless do people feel?
- Are feelings discussed openly?

Checklist 10.2 Managing the Feedback Meeting

Some ideas on what data to use and what not to use:

- The clients have a right to all the information you have collected.
- You probably will not use all the data you have collected so trust your intuition and provide enough to give a clear picture of the situation as you found it.

- Include data which confirms success not just failure.
- Remember which information was provided on a confidential basis, which has to be reported anonymously and which may be freely and openly discussed.
- Include data that calls attention to the real problem as well as the presenting problem where you see these as different.
- Don't hide data which may be uncomfortable for the client to face.
- Highlight data which refers to what the client has authority and responsibility to change.
- Use data to highlight a manageable number of problems or aspects of a problem.
- Include data which is likely to be seen as important and calls attention to problems where there is commitment to change.

Some ideas on how to present the data and how not to do it:

- Don't overload the client with detail. Consign as much of it as possible to an appendix if you must put it somewhere.
- Go easy on historical data – the client will most certainly know more about it than you do.
- Support the client while you are giving feedback by emphasizing what is going well and being encouraging about the future.
- Be prepared to confront the client. Reactions may be uncomfortable but they are part of your job. If you are not prepared to confront, why have you been hired?
- Be aware of the limits of what your *client* can accept – don't let your own feelings be projected onto the client. Don't leave out data because you wouldn't like to hear it.
- Don't collude by allowing the client to put the blame on others or on circumstances beyond his or her control.
- Remember the guidelines for effective feedback. Feedback is about 'what is', not 'what should be'. Feedback which the client receives as aggressive or non-assertive is likely to raise resistance or be ignored.
- Say clearly and concisely what problems you see without implying that the management is at fault – don't judge or evaluate.
- Be aware of the human process issues during the meeting – deal with resistance as it happens and share your own feelings when appropriate.
- Feedback doesn't need to be one-way – from consultant to client. If you have been working well together, the client will have some idea of what the problems are and what to do about them.

Some ideas on how to structure the feedback meeting to achieve results:

- However much data you present and however many recommendations you make nothing will happen without client commitment.
- Your recommendations need to be tied to some aspect or aspects of the problem and point to some expected benefits.
- You need the client to take responsibility for the recommendations and own them – ensure that they are manageable and achievable.

- Try to ensure that all those involved in implementation receive the feedback. (Remember the definition of a client system – 'Who knows, Who can, Who cares'.)
- The following structure might help with the meeting:
  - restate the original contract;
  - state purpose and structure of the meeting;
  - agree the agenda;
  - present the data in simple form;
  - present the diagnosis of the problem;
  - get reactions to diagnosis;
  - present recommendations, implications and benefits;
  - get reactions to recommendations;
  - get decision to implement.
- Finally, stay in control of the meeting, keep the client focused on action to deal with the problem and keep most of the time for discussion.

Checklist 10.3 Giving Personal Feedback

Effective feedback is:

- given in a climate in which people value each other;
- balanced between positive points and negative points;
- for the benefit of the recipient, not the giver;
- honest;
- given close to the event;
- clearly expressed in language the recipient can understand;
- non-judgemental;
- a description of the recipient's behaviour and the emotion of the giver;
- requested by the recipient;
- constructive;
- checked out with others;
- given in a way that leaves the recipient free to choose whether or not to take it on board;
- timely.

11 Making Sense of the Data, Problem Diagnosis and Decision Making

Who Needs to Clarify the Data

The first thing we need to ask when discussing this phase in the consulting process is: who is it that is making sense of the data. It is very tempting for consultants to work hard applying lots of different analytical techniques so that they better understand their clients' problems. However, you must always remember that you are endeavouring to help your clients to make sense of their data and clarify their understanding of the issues involved. They will then be in a position to start making decisions which will improve the situation.

It is at this stage that clients often start to realize that the problem they started with is actually more complex than they first thought. The presenting problem may look simple. It is often expressed in terms of a need to improve some element of the systems and procedures or a frustration that the current system isn't working. As we discovered in Chapter 1 however, problems are rarely simple. The presenting problem may be a symptom of ineffective or inappropriate systems and procedures but there are likely to be attendant human process issues that will also be important.

If you are to help your clients make effective decisions, then you will need a number of models which have been developed to help us make sense of complex situations. We briefly describe some of these models later in this chapter, although you are likely to be aware of many more which you use on a daily basis to help you understand and deal with the problems that you meet. The dilemma is whether to use the model to help the client structure the data in a way they can understand, or to teach the client the theory or model so that not only can they deal more effectively with the current issues but will be able to apply the model themselves to future problems. But more of that later in the chapter.

The Nature of Problems

Before we examine the issues of problem diagnosis it is important to acknowledge, at the outset, that the word 'problem' can create difficulties. It is hard to think of an alternative word – 'issue', perhaps, although it sounds rather like jargon. So why is 'problem' such an inappropriate word? People often find it difficult to acknowledge that they have problems. The word can suggest that the individuals are in some way inadequate, ineffective and unable to cope. To 'have a problem' suggests that the owners are powerless to solve it themselves and are therefore dependent on someone else. This kind of thinking leads us to assume that there is something wrong with needing help, and makes it less likely that we will ask for help when we need it.

It may be something of a platitude now to think in terms of opportunities rather than problems. But if you are to be effective it is probably best to help the client define the problem in optimistic rather than pessimistic terms. After all, we need help with the good things in life as well as the bad. If we are planning a holiday we need help to decide on the best place to go, and when, where to stay and how to get there. If we have spare money we don't shrink from seeking help from a financial adviser to help us decide where to invest it. So the word 'problem' doesn't have to have negative connotations.

If clients want to improve it doesn't mean that what they were doing was wrong, just that they want their operation to be even more effective and run more smoothly than it does at present. The other disadvantage of the word 'problem' is that people often imagine that for every problem there must be a solution or a correct answer. This kind of thinking probably has its roots in traditional education where students did indeed deal with correct answers. We all learned how to add two and two, the date of the Battle of Hastings, the capital of Australia and the chemical formula for water. It comes as a shock to find that when we leave the confines of academia the problems we face in the rest of our lives are rarely as neat as these. It is useful to distinguish between *puzzles*, which have a best answer, and *problems*, for which there are lots of alternative courses of action, none of which will 'solve' the problem in the sense of it going away. Education usually presents us with puzzles while life confronts us with problems which are messy and ambiguous and where there is never a right answer. Getting through a maze, solving a Rubik cube or doing a jigsaw are all puzzles, while 'how to motivate the sales force' or 'how to balance the budget' are problems. When dealing with problems there is never a ten-out-of-ten solution. Rather you may be trying to help your clients choose between several four-out-of-ten options. Having decided on the option to take there will be no way of knowing for sure if it was better or worse than any of the others we didn't choose.

When you are working with clients there may well be aspects of the assignment which are indeed puzzles. The OR consultant can use mathematical models which can help a manager decide on the most cost-effective course of action. However, when it comes to selling the consequent changes to the work force so that they are committed to them, you are firmly in the realms of problems to which there can never be a perfect solution. When helping clients to examine the data that has been collected and make decisions about the way forward it is important to differentiate between the presenting problem and the underlying real problem. Often the problem may appear to be concerned with systems and procedures but so often the real problem, or at least part of the real problem, is to do with human process issues.

For example, on one occasion we were involved in what looked on the surface like a straightforward office reorganization problem. A department of about thirty people was divided into two groups. The operational group was responsible for working on a number of projects with their clients, mostly in other organizations. This role was subject to a lot of pressure and instant decisions, and members of this group were frequently out of the office. The other group provided a research and information service to the operational people. The quality of this service was crucial to the success of the department as a whole. The large open-plan office contained the whole department but the operational people occupied one half and the research people the other. Between them had been erected a wall of filing cabinets and cupboards which contributed to the isolation of the two groups. So the presenting problem seemed to be how to rearrange the office to maximize contact between the two groups. Further research revealed, however, that this was only part of the problem. The department had undergone a period of very rapid growth and had taken on new responsibilities which had led to a lack of clarity about individual responsibilities. The research group tended to recruit people who had an eye for detail, rational analysis and caution, while the operational group was largely composed of extroverts, who enjoyed managing crises and making instant decisions. Both sides consequently tended to devalue the other's strengths rather than recognize that they were complementary. They tended to blame each other rather than collaborate. The operational group would fail to involve the research group early enough in a project, and would request urgent information in a piecemeal way, leading to frustration on both sides.

The erection of the barrier between the two groups exacerbated the problem but it seemed to be rather more a symptom of an underlying problem of two groups of very different people trying (or perhaps not trying) to work together. The problem was redefined as one of helping people in the group to value each other's contribution, recognize how their strengths complemented each other and work together in a more collaborative way.

So you need to remember to help your clients look at problems in a positive way while at the same time discouraging them from expecting you to wave a magic wand. Real problems rarely lend themselves to perfect solutions. However, it will help if you can try to identify the real problem rather than simply working with the apparent problem.

Making Sense of Human Process Data

Sometimes teams are unable to complete their task because they have inadequate resources or do not have the required skills. There are also situations where the task does not get done because of inadequate policies and procedures, poor organization or lack of a proper definition of roles and responsibilities. However, it is often more likely that the real reason for not getting the task done is a human process one, such as poor power/authority relationships, lack of understanding about goals and objectives, inappropriate norms and standards, or strong feelings about the organization or its management which are producing severe morale/cohesion problems. Such process issues are hard to surface and difficult to deal with for a variety of reasons which were discussed in Chapter 3.

A frequent dilemma faced by change agents is: 'Do I stay at the felt-needs level or take a more direct line?' Often the client will be aware of the real needs and may take a poor view of a consultant who doesn't identify them. You may need to work hard to surface and clarify the underlying human process issues so that your clients are better able to understand the real needs.

With some understanding of what is likely to happen in groups at a human process level it is possible for a skilled person to observe what is going on and feed back the observations to the group. Such observations can alert group members to what they are doing or not doing which is preventing them from getting their task done satisfactorily.

These include:

Participation Who are high participators, who are low? How are silent people treated? Who talks to whom? Who leads? Who keeps the ball rolling?

Influence Who is high in influence, who is low? Is there any rivalry in the group? Is the boss more influential than the team members?

Styles of influence How do people influence others? Do they use rewards and punishments, common vision, assertive persuasion or participation and trust?

Sensitivity to feelings Do members of the group notice when people are ignored, interrupted or talked over? Do they do anything about it or merely ignore it? Do they ask each other how they are feeling?

Dealing with issues as they arise Does the group recognize when members are upset, in difficulty or not saying what they feel?

Conflict handling How does the group handle differences of opinion? Do they avoid all conflict, handle it to reach agreement collaboratively, constantly compromise or end up with a slanging match?

Group atmosphere What is it like? Friendly and cosy, quiet and demotivating, noisy and argumentative? Do you get the feeling that there are hidden agendas around? Do you get the impression that the trust level is low? These are some of the many aspects of group process which you can help group members to look at with a view to improving their relationships and therefore the way they work together. So how do you go about helping a client group to identify human process issues which are blocking the effectiveness of the group?

First of all, it is important to have a high level of trust and a clear contract with the group. Group members are unlikely to open up and discuss difficult, perhaps painful issues with someone who is not equally open and whom they do not trust. Equally, it is important that group members are involved in the diagnosis of the human process problem(s) and explicitly contract to explore the issues and deal with them.

The role of the consultant is to help clients find techniques for identifying and surfacing human process issues and then help them to decide what group actions and behaviours need to be improved. Clients will be much more committed to improving the way they work together if they decide themselves what needs to be done.

A prescriptive approach to dealing with human process issues is unlikely to be successful. If you simply observe the group, and identify what you see as the problem, you are likely to miss all the significant things that are happening in the group which simply can't be seen: the issues that are being avoided, for example, or how people are feeling about the way the group works. In addition, if you feed back your observations to the group and prescribe what must be done to improve, the people in the group are likely to feel criticized and become defensive. They will reject the feedback and you may find yourself under attack.

A more appropriate style for process interventions is catalytic. It is much more effective to ask questions that help members of the client group explore their own perceptions of what is happening in the group and listen to the perceptions of others. There are two ways of helping with this exploration. One is simply to put questions to the group and help them deal with the issues that surface. Appropriate questions might include:

- How are decisions made in this group?
- Who are the high and low participators in this group?
- How did group members feel when a specific event occurred?
- What are the major areas of conflict in the group?

A second way is to ask group members to complete questionnaires or feedback instruments about group effectiveness and then share the results of such surveys. You need to help the group deal with similarities and differences in the way the instruments are completed.

At the end of the chapter you will find a number of feedback instruments which can be used to help clients focus on human process data.

Whatever method of process intervention you use it is important to remember that the purpose is to help the clients identify and diagnose the problem and then make decisions about what they want to do about it.

As an outsider you have several advantages over the group members:

- You do not share the same pressures felt by ordinary members to be loyal to the group and stay the same.
- You can more easily focus attention on procedures, processes and relationships.
- You are not likely to be involved in power, leadership or formal authority relationships as members of the group often are.
- You are not likely to be party to participant-centred frictions, antagonisms and cliques.
- Consultants, by virtue of their interventionist role, are membership free.

However, this may put the internal consultant under even more pressure if he or she tries to give feedback to the group which they perceive as critical, evaluative or judgemental. So if you want the group to use the feedback – prescription should only be used with very great care.

Decision Making

We often think that an absence of information prevents us from making decisions. This may be true but in organizations the opposite can also be the case. A manager may well feel impotent simply because there is too much data about the problem. The most helpful thing that you can do in this situation is provide ways of clarifying, simplifying or restructuring the data so that the clients are able to understand the dimensions of the problem more clearly and can decide what they want to do about it. If you are going to help your clients in this way it is important that you have access to a few decision-making models which are designed to clarify the problem and what needs to be done. You may have such models as part of your normal technical expertise, like, for example, discounted cash flow, cost benefit analysis, critical examination, variation analysis or control charts. Indeed, all consulting professions have their own techniques for making decisions. These can be used prescriptively to solve clients' problems or catalytically to help them make sense of their own data and make their own decisions. As we will also see later in this chapter we may wish to teach our clients these models so that they are equipped to deal with other such problems in the future.

Two simple but very useful models which can help clients clarify their understanding of problems and make decisions are decision trees and force field analysis. The decision tree method is a way of helping clients look at all the data about the problem systematically, clarify its nature and then identify possible options and examine them objectively. The force field method can be used with any situation of change, from one facing an individual to a complex organizational problem where there are lots of human process issues which can't be controlled directly but which need to be worked on over a period of time.

Decision trees

There are many forms of decision trees which can be used for problem solving. The approach we prefer was developed by Paul Sargent, *A Decision Tree Approach to Case Study Solution*, NEBSM (1979) as a means of imposing structure and logic on what is often a sea of ambiguity. It is called a decision 'tree' simply because when it is complete its shape bears a strong resemblance to a tree with a trunk, roots, branches, twigs and fruit (see Figure 11.1).

Statement of the problem

A crucial stage in problem solving is defining the problem and it may be necessary to go back to this point several times before progress can be made. It

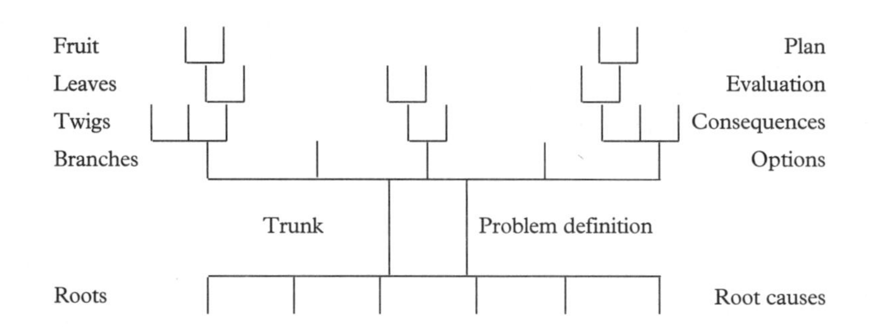

Figure 11.1 Schematic diagram of a decision tree
Source: Paul B. Sargent, **A Decision Tree Approach to Case Study Solution**, NEBSM, 1979, Reproduced by permission of the publisher.

is important at this stage to differentiate:

- the presenting problem;
- the symptoms;
- the real problem.

It is important to ensure that the clients are actually tackling the real problem, otherwise they will find that an excellent solution is being produced for the wrong problem. Clients will begin with the presenting problem and this will often be described in terms of systems and procedures: 'We're not reaching targets', 'We're not keeping to budgets', 'Quality is falling', etc.

The danger is always to rush into possible solutions immediately without clarifying and redefining the problem. The best thing at this stage is to go back to examine the background and root causes.

Root causes of the problem An examination of the background to the problem is likely to expose the fact that at least part of the problem is caused by human process factors as well as technical, systems and procedures factors. A fall in quality may be caused by a lowering of morale due to an inappropriate management style or to an inability to communicate effectively with suppliers. Failure to meet sales targets might owe as much to poor training as to the low quality of the product.

An exploration of the root causes of the problem will give clues to the appropriate definition of the real problem as well as possible solutions.

Redefining the problem Having explored the background to the problem you will be in a better position to redefine the problem and crystallize the real problem (or problems). The important thing at this stage is to make certain that the problem is redefined in such a way as to ensure that the clients own the problem and are prepared to take responsibility for it. You should discourage clients from defining the problem in a way that places blame and responsibility on other people.

'The problem is that people just aren't interested.'
'My boss is incompetent.'
'The department is just too big.'
'The sales territory is too small.'

As long as clients persist in defining the problem in a way that creates distance from themselves, it will be difficult to get commitment. One way of ensuring client ownership is to ask them to define the problem in a short phrase or sentence starting with the words 'how to'. Instead of talking about how incompetent the boss is, ask clients to redefine the problem starting with the words 'how to'. A few redefinitions might include:

'How to give my boss some feedback.'
'How to persuade my boss that I want to be involved in decisions which affect my job.'
'How to help my boss to delegate better.'
'How to arrange a meeting where my boss and I can discuss the way we work together in an open way.'
'How to get another job.'

Redefining the problem in this way ensures that when you start generating possible solutions you will at least be trying to solve the problem that the clients want to work on.

At this stage it is quite likely that what appeared to be a single problem may actually turn out to be a number of separate but inter-related problems. Helping your clients to acknowledge that there are a number of separate problems can be very helpful. What previously appeared to be an overwhelming problem, can suddenly become manageable. So confronted with the fact that there are a number of separate issues you need to help your client to decide which one to continue to work on. At this stage you should encourage them to work on the most important, or the one with the greatest pay-off rather than least difficult.

Generating alternative solutions Having clearly defined the problem or problems the next step is to explore any options that may be available. Try to generate as many options as possible without considering the arguments for or against. Also ensure that no option is rejected at this stage. If several 'real' problems are identified, you may need to produce a separate list of options for each problem.

Evaluating the options The next stage is to evaluate each option in turn. To do this means asking such questions as:

- Would this option help to solve the problem as it has been redefined?
- What would be the consequences of taking this option?
- What are the costs and benefits?
- What are the advantages and disadvantages?
- How do you feel about that option? Often an option can look like the logical thing to do, but there may be lots of emotional barriers.

By evaluating all the options in this way it will become evident that some options can be rejected while others might point the way forward. Furthermore, it is important to recognize at this stage that there is rarely a simple neat solution that will 'solve' the problem. More likely you will be looking at a combination of options which are likely to improve the situation rather than provide an everlasting solution.

Taking action Identifying the option or options which seem to be appropriate is not the end of the line. It is now necessary to work out a detailed action plan of what needs to be done in order to implement the selected option(s). To do this you need to ask questions like these:

- What do you need to do first?
- Then what needs to happen?
- How do you need to prepare for that?
- When does that need to happen by?
- What reactions might you get?

By doing this you are increasing client commitment to implementing the action plan.

Using a decision tree approach It is possible to use the decision tree approach in two ways:

- as a way of exploring a problem with clients (Figure 11.1 on page 186);
- as a way of presenting clients with the content of a complex investigation (Figure 11.2).

The decision tree can be used as a framework for asking questions to help clients explore the problem, define it and generate possible solutions. By asking a series of structured questions clients are enabled to structure their own decision tree and work from confusion to a degree of clarity. Let us see how this works in practice. Choose a problem you have at the moment and try to answer the following questions:

1 *The trunk*
Give a brief description of the problem as you see it now (trunk).
2 *The roots*
Who else is involved in the problem?
How do you feel about the other people involved in the problem?
What are the technical aspects of the problem?
How is the problem being managed at the moment?
What do you see as the symptoms of the problem?
What difficulties does the problem cause you?
How important is it to you to solve the problem?
What do you see as the root causes of the problem?
3 *Back to the trunk*
Can you now redefine your problem in a single sentence starting with the words 'how to . . . '?

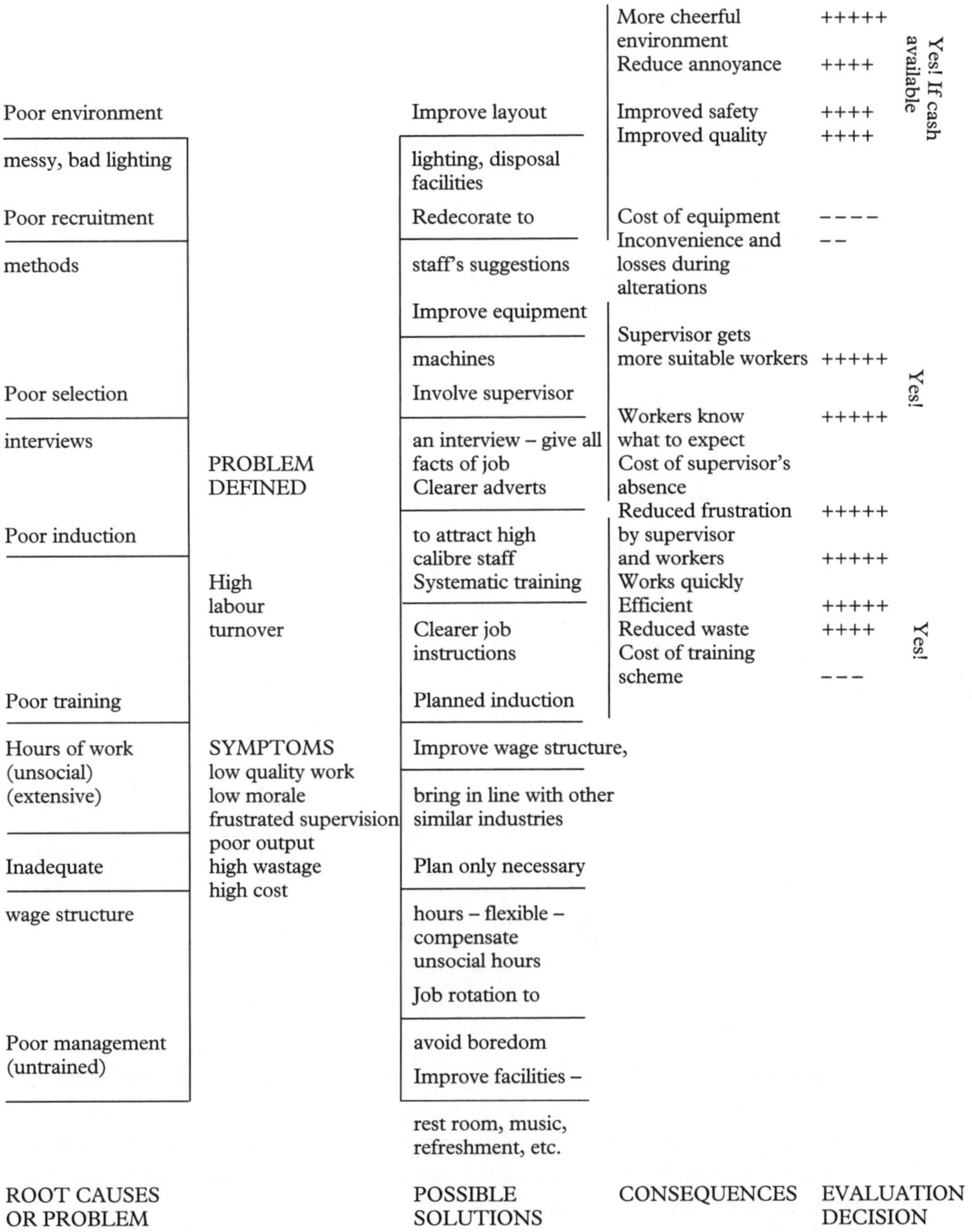

ROOT CAUSES OR PROBLEM

- Poor environment messy, bad lighting
- Poor recruitment methods
- Poor selection interviews
- Poor induction
- Poor training
- Hours of work (unsocial) (extensive)
- Inadequate wage structure
- Poor management (untrained)

PROBLEM DEFINED

High labour turnover

SYMPTOMS

low quality work
low morale
frustrated supervision
poor output
high wastage
high cost

POSSIBLE SOLUTIONS

- Improve layout lighting, disposal facilities
- Redecorate to staff's suggestions
- Improve equipment machines
- Involve supervisor an interview – give all facts of job
- Clearer adverts to attract high calibre staff
- Systematic training
- Clearer job instructions
- Planned induction
- Improve wage structure, bring in line with other similar industries
- Plan only necessary hours – flexible – compensate unsocial hours
- Job rotation to avoid boredom
- Improve facilities – rest room, music, refreshment, etc.

CONSEQUENCES		EVALUATION DECISION
More cheerful environment	+++++	Yes! If cash available
Reduce annoyance	++++	
Improved safety	++++	
Improved quality	++++	
Cost of equipment	----	
Inconvenience and losses during alterations	--	
Supervisor gets more suitable workers	+++++	Yes!
Workers know what to expect	+++++	
Cost of supervisor's absence		
Reduced frustration by supervisor and workers	+++++	Yes!
Works quickly	+++++	
Efficient	+++++	
Reduced waste	++++	
Cost of training scheme	---	

Figure 11.2 Example of a decision tree

4 *The branches*
What options are available to you? Write down as many options as you can think of. Don't evaluate any of them.
5 *The twigs*
Now take each of the options you have identified and answer the following questions:
- What are the advantages and benefits?
- What are the disadvantages and costs?
- What will be the other likely consequences?
- How do you feel about this option?
- To what extent does this option solve the problem redefined by you?

6 *The fruit*
Which option or options seem to have the greatest chance of success? Now plan how you will implement the option. First write down all the actions you need to carry out in the order you need to do them. Then write dates against each one to indicate when you intend to have it completed.

We believe this exercise indicates that it is possible to help clients construct their own decision tree even though you have very little understanding of the technicalities or details of the problem. The purpose of the technique is to help the clients understand the problem rather than to understand it yourself. Having clarified the problem in this way, clients are better able to move into decision making with confidence.

Presenting data to the client Sometimes, having completed a detailed investigation for a client, you may need to present the results in report form. If the report is long or complex, then using a decision tree is a very effective way of presenting the dimensions of the investigation in a way which is readily understood. Figure 11.2 gives an example.

Force field analysis

Some years ago Kurt Lewin developed a set of ideas in sociology called 'field theory' (1951). One of his ideas, the force field analysis, is a simple but extremely useful technique for exploring problems and developing strategies for change. His ideas have been modified and developed over the years but the basic framework has stood the test of time.

The first step in the force field process is to describe the problem as it is now, and then describe how you would like the situation to be in the future. For example, someone exploring the problem of morale might describe the present and future situations in the manner shown in Table 11.1.

Force field analysis suggests there are two sets of forces working in the system. One set of forces is driving towards the desired goal while the other set is pushing in the opposite direction (Table 11.2). When these forces are in equilibrium then no change will occur.

Table 11.1

Present situation *Low morale*	**Desired future situation** *High morale*
• high absence • people unconcerned about quality • resentment of managers • 'us' and 'them' outlook • low cooperation • work needs to be closely inspected • few ideas from staff • poor communication between sections	• low absence • people concerned about quality • collaborative relationship between staff and manager • lots of ideas coming from the staff • staff take responsibility for discussing and working on problems with colleagues

Table 11.2

low morale	high morale
Driving forces → → →	*Restraining forces* ← ← ←
• desire for job satisfaction • desire for long-term security • intelligence of the staff • desire of managers and staff to work more harmoniously • pride in their skills • managers committed to change • products well regarded by customers • need for long-term survival in a competitive industry	• history and culture has led to mutual suspicion between managers and staff • autocratic management style • people are not encouraged to generate ideas • communication systems tend to be bureaucratic • reward systems reward quantity not quality

The advantage of using a 'force field' on a problem is that it now becomes more manageable. If we simply describe the current situation and the desired future situation then the gulf between them appears huge. There is no simple solution and no clear way to manage the change. However, when we list the driving forces and restraining forces we begin to clarify ways in which we can actually influence the system and facilitate the change. We can take positive action either to strengthen the driving forces or reduce the restraining forces. However, there is a danger in expending too much energy trying to reduce the power of the restraining forces. You are likely to get more effective change by working with the people who want it rather than the people who don't.

In the example cited in Table 11.3 we can pick out some of the drivers and restrainers that can be influenced.

Table 11.3

Driving/restraining forces	*What can be done*
• desire for long-term security	• communicate long- and short-term plans to the workforce
• desire for job satisfaction	• communicate past and current successes • encourage staff to generate ideas for improvement. Make sure ideas are listened to and acted upon • involve staff in making decisions • work on ways of delegating more responsibility • introduce a system of briefing groups • introduce quality circles, problem-solving groups or task forces
• desire of managers and staff to work more harmoniously	• team building • give the team opportunities to talk through the way they work together • group to work on clear department and individual goals and objectives
• autocratic management style	• organization development programme during which managers examine their management style and the implications for the business

Force field analysis is a very effective model to use with clients when they are facing change which seems too large, unmanageable and difficult to control. In this situation clients can feel powerless because they can't see the 'solution' to the problem. However, using a force field can bring the problem into focus and help them to recognize that, while there may not be a simple solution, there are actions they can take which can influence the problem. So you end up with empowered clients.

Using Theories and Models

As we have already seen there are many ways of organizing complex data so that it becomes manageable. Using a decision tree and a force field are two ways of doing this. Another way is to use theories and models as a means of helping clients to understand the nature of the problem. This is, after all, how we make sense of the world around us and make decisions on a daily basis. If I throw a ball in the air and watch it fall to the ground I can understand, describe and predict what will happen on future occasions through the theory of gravity. When driving a car, the decisions we make are based on a number of theories and models – relative speed, for example, and the convention that everyone will drive on the correct side of the road.

All consultants have available to them a range of theories, models and conventions which are part of their technical expertise. Consultants may use these theories and models to identify clients' problems and solve them. They see their superior knowledge as a guarantee of future employment. However, the danger of this approach is that it creates client dependence. We often hear stories about consultants who introduce a new system and them stick around for months or even years because they are the only ones who know how the system works.

It is easy to fall into the trap of jealously guarding this expertise as a source of power. In contrast, client-centred change agents try to empower their clients by sharing their knowledge and expertise. When you are working on a problem with clients you can share some of your expertise so that your clients are enabled to make the decisions. In this way your clients can not only only decide what to do about the current problem but will be able to tackle future problems themselves. The old adage is certainly true: if you give a starving man a fish you feed him for a day; if you teach him to fish you feed him for life.

Soon after establishing his business one of the authors went to see his accountant with a pile of receipts, invoice copies and VAT demands, in a state of general confusion. It would have been possible (and lucrative) for the accountant simply to ask the author to send all future invoices and statements to him so that he could prepare the accounts. Instead, a thirty-minute lesson in basic double entry book-keeping meant the author was henceforth able to handle that side of the business himself. It was not necessary for the accountant to provide a lot of theory. The author certainly did not need to be turned into an accountant, he just needed enough theory to help him become more organized and keep his own basic books.

What then is the best way of enabling clients to learn and use theories and models that will help them to become more effective? Traditional educationalists have often used the 'mug and jug' approach to learning. They see learning as merely passing on knowledge from the expert (the jug) into the brain of the learner (the mug). The assumption is that learning can be passed from one person to another. This often results in classrooms of unenthusiastic pupils being lectured on theories which they are expected to learn and then implement. Unfortunately, this approach is also quite common among trainers in organizations, who develop courses that involve 'teaching' participants a number of theories chosen by the trainer which the participants are then expected to take back to the workplace and use. In our experience this transfer of learning rarely takes place.

In order to recognize why this approach fails, we need to understand what differentiates a useful theory from one that is not so useful. At this stage it might help to identify two theories that you have been taught at some time in your life. Choose one that you still understand and is clear to you and one which remains only a hazy memory, the detail forgotten. Write in Table 11.4 why you remembered one and forgot the other.

Table 11.4

A theory that remains clear *Characteristics*	A theory that has become hazy *Characteristics*

When describing theories they have found useful, people often make statements like these:

- It was well taught in the first place
- I could see its relevance when I learnt it.
- It helped me understand my own behaviour/failures/successes/difficulties, etc.
- I have been able to convert the theory into practice and use it.
- I feel confident in using the theory.
- It has stood the test of time.

We can conclude that in order to be useful a theory must help the client understand the problem and make effective decisions both now and in the future.

Learning cycle

As we saw in Chapter 1, Kolb recognized that the learning process can be developed into a cyclical model of learning, and suggested that internalizing new learning requires the learner to engage in all stages of the learning cycle (see Figure 11.3).

Concrete experience The learning process usually starts with the learner's own experience. The learner becomes involved in an activity, acts or behaves in some way, performs, observes, says something. This experience is the basis for the entire learning process.

Reflective observation The experience itself generates a lot of data. The learner or learners will be left with a variety of feelings and memories of the event. The learner now needs to reflect on the experience in order to make sense of it, to understand what happened and why, and to come to terms with his or her own feelings about the event. To do this it is necessary to answer questions like these:

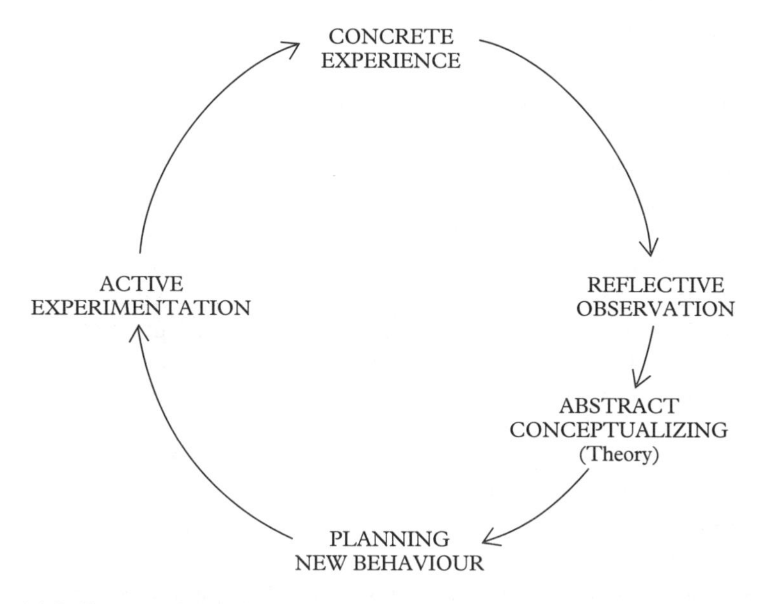

Figure 11.3 The experiential learning cycle

- What happened and in what sequence?
- How did it feel?
- What did the learner do?
- What did the other people involved do?
- What was said?
- How did others react?
- What worked? Why?
- What didn't work? Why?
- How could the situation have been handled differently?

The process of reflection helps the individual understand events that have taken place and increases the possibility of learning from them.

Abstract conceptualization This is the stage of conceptualizing and theorizing when the learner develops general principles from the experience which are applicable to other situations. In other words, the learner starts to develop his or her own theory which can be used to make decisions in the future.

Planning new behaviour The next step is to plan new behaviour based on the theory which has been developed. This is a crucial phase in the cycle because it is not until this stage that the learner begins to think in terms of changing and actually doing things differently.

Active experimentation Kolb's model is cyclical so that as soon as the learner moves to active experimentation to put the plan into action and try out new behaviour, then he or she moves quickly back into the experiencing phase.

This leads to reflecting on the success of the new behaviour, modifying the theory if necessary and then deciding if further change in behaviour is required. Eventually, after several trips round the cycle, the theory and the behaviour become internalized. This means that they become part of the individual and can be accessed at an automatic or unconscious level.

A good example of the learning cycle in action is learning to drive a car. Learning to drive is a continuous process of experimentation with attendant successes and failures, followed by gradually increasing understanding and skill. At first all the actions involved are done at a very conscious, usually uncomfortable, level. Gradually, however, the driver internalizes all the behaviour until eventually most drivers operate their cars at an unconscious level.

As we saw in Chapter 1, it is important to acknowledge at this point that different people have different learning styles. This means that we all have a preference for the activities associated with one or more phases of the learning cycle; it could also mean that we underutilize the others.

So how can you use this learning cycle to help someone to learn? It is possible to break into the cycle with either the experience or the theory. Let us look at an example. If you are a sales manager helping a sales executive to build skills in closing the sale, you can do this in several ways. The first way is to accompany the sales executive on a number of calls on customers (the experience). After the calls you could spend some time discussing them and how the sales executive operated, why some sales were successful and some weren't (reflection). At this point you could introduce a theory of closing the sale. This can be done in two ways. One is to explain the sales executive's success and failures in terms of your theory of closing the sale. The other option is to help the sales executive generate his or her own theory. This can be done by asking such questions as: 'So what do you think is important when closing the sale?'

Finally, you would need to help the sales executive think through how to close the sale on the next call. At this point the whole process starts all over again until eventually the theories and skills become internalized and automatic (see Figure 11.4).

The second option is to start with the theory. This would involve introducing the salesperson to the theory of closing the sale and ensuring a good level of intellectual understanding (theory). You would then need to help your client to plan how he or she can implement the theory when calling on customers (planning new behaviour). Next you accompany the salesperson while he or she calls on customers and practises the new behaviour (experience) and afterwards you discuss the calls with the salesperson (reflection). During this discussion you help the client identify how successful he or she was in doing what was intended and how it felt, while also giving additional feedback. Again it will be necessary to continue round the learning cycle until theory and behaviour have been internalized (see Figure 11.5).

While acknowledging that there are times when you have no option but to start with the theory, we strongly believe that the most effective theories and models interventions are firmly rooted in the client's data. If the theory makes sense of the client's experience and helps to explain and clarify why they are

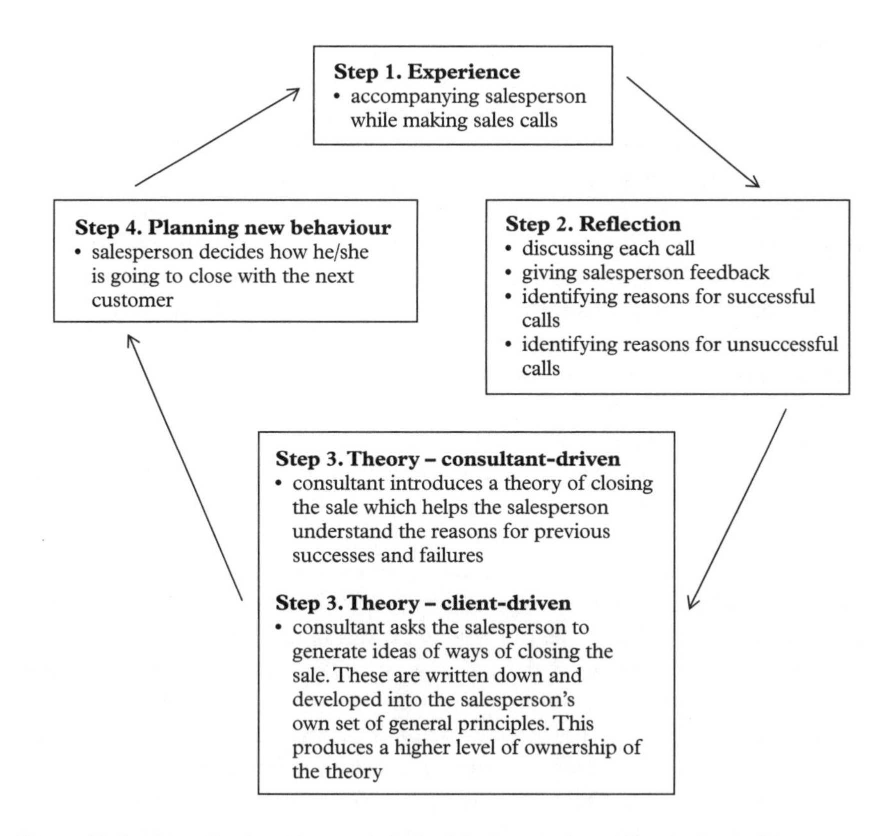

Figure 11.4 Using the learning cycle to build sales closing skills: starting with the client's data

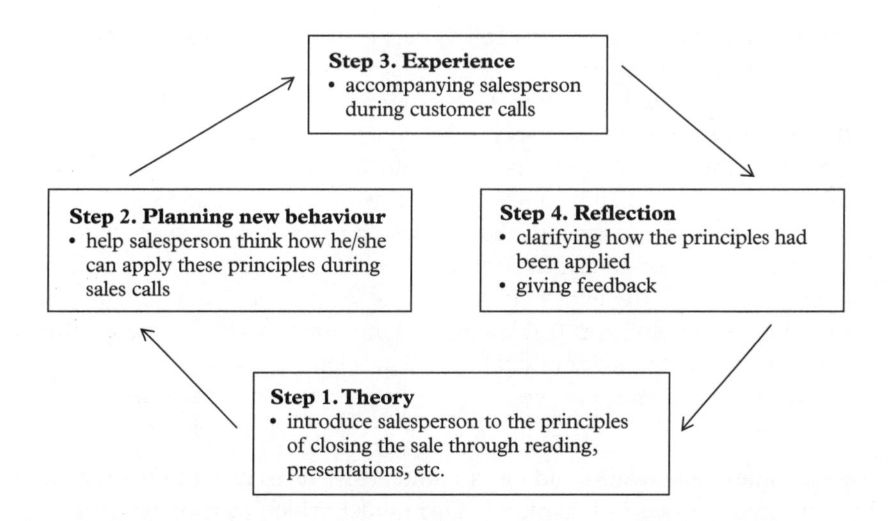

Figure 11.5 Using the learning cycle to build sales closing skills: starting with the theory

having difficulties then they are much more likely to take it on board and use it. Thus the approach outlined in Figure 11.4 is likely to be more successful. Here the starting point is the salesperson's own experiences, successes and difficulties when working with customers and closing sales. The manager spends time exploring with the salesperson why they are sometimes successful and sometimes not. The salesperson is likely to be involved right from the start, discussing a real issue that is important rather than what might at first appear to be an abstract theory. We would also suggest that the salesperson already has a perfectly valid theory of closing the sale, although they may be unaware of it. By working in a client-driven way the manager can, at the next stage, ask the client for any ideas they may have on closing the sale. Working catalytically the manager is able to help the salesperson develop their own theory or model for which he or she feels significant ownership.

So when making a theories and models intervention it is not always necessary to prepare long and complicated lectures. By working with your clients catalytically and acceptantly you can help them explore and clarify how they are managing the problem now and then help them to develop their own model or general principles that they can apply in the future. You may wish to add something of your own to the model but it remains fundamentally theirs.

In Chapter 1 we discussed the striking similarity between Kolb's learning styles model and the consulting cycle. This is not surprising because, as a consultant, you are in the business of helping people change their behaviour, that is, helping them to learn. Figure 11.6 shows that the introduction of theories and models can help the client to make sense of the data and make decisions. It also indicates that the best time to introduce theories and models is when you're helping clients to make sense of their data, and not before.

We believe there are five stages when using a theories and models approach. These are:

1 Help the client or client-system collect data to explore how they are managing the situation at the moment.
2 Give the clients an opportunity to start to discuss and clarify for themselves the data they are being presented with.
3 Introduce the clients to the theory or model. Make this as participative as possible. It is often better to help the clients to build the model in their own words, rather than giving long lectures which reduces them to spectators.
4 Go back to the original problem, and the data which was surfaced. Help your clients make the links between the theory or model and how they were managing their problem. If it has been done successfully, the theory should shed a significant amount of light on the problem.
5 Work with the clients, catalytically, to generate options, make decisions and plan how they will deal with the issue more effectively in the future.

An example: On team-building assignments we often use the Organizational Life model described in Chapter 3. This model, which categorizes all activity into Task, Systems, procedures and processes and Human process, is very useful in helping a team identify where it focuses most of its energy and where

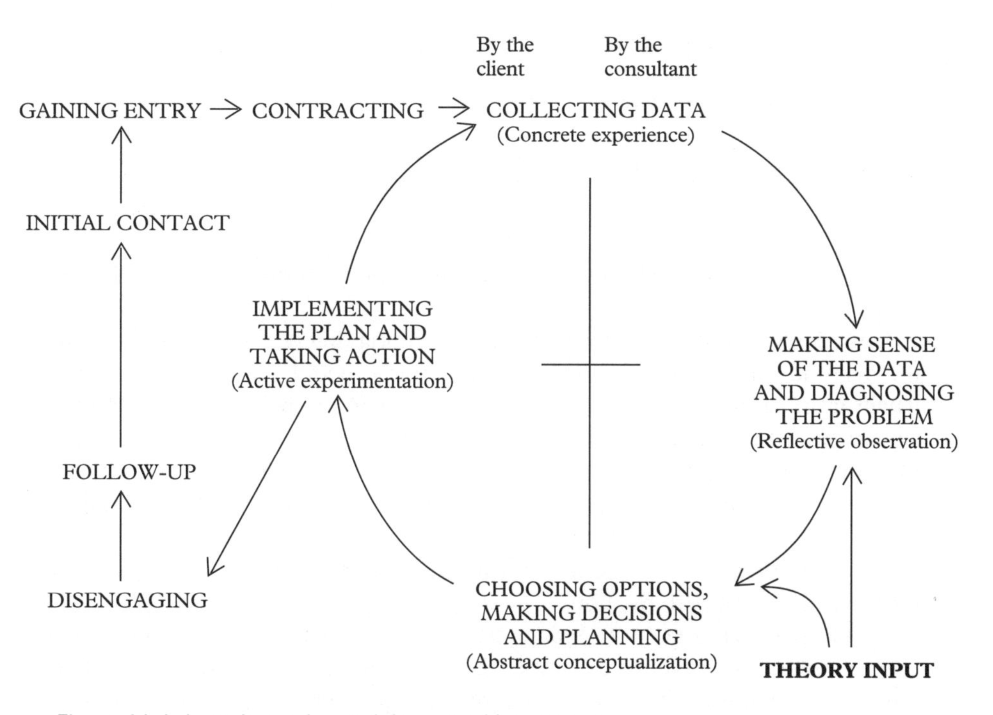

Figure 11.6 Learning styles and the consulting process

any blockages exist. Rather than simply introducing the model cold, we ask members to write down individually the answers to two questions:

- What behaviours, events or activities give you satisfaction and make you feel good about working in this team?
- What behaviours, events, activities, etc. frustrate you, make you dissatisfied or angry in this group?

This is the data-collection phase.

The next phase is to ask each member of the team to share his or her own list (data sharing) and these are written on a flip chart. Usually there is a huge list of events and activities. This in itself often leads to a great deal of useful discussion and insight.

The model is then introduced in a way that helps the team to classify its own data in terms of the three categories. This helps them understand how their team operates. Very often they begin to recognize that many of the difficulties stem from human process issues which are rarely addressed. Finally they can work on ways of improving their team effectiveness in all three aspects of the model.

Helping Clients to Plan

Having helped clients to make a decision, it is very tempting to rest on one's laurels. But making the decision is often the easy part. Clients will probably need

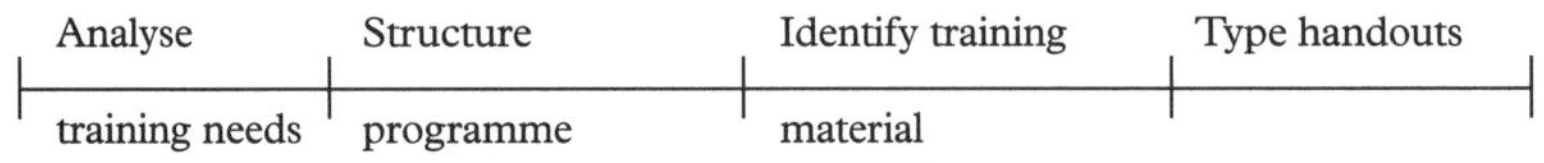

Analyse training needs	Structure programme	Identify training material	Type handouts

Figure 11.7 The critical path

help to think through the best way to implement the decision, and to do this they need to develop a plan.

A good plan should describe, in detail, everything that needs to be done to put the decision into action. It should include timing, people and other resources which must be marshalled and co-ordinated. It should include clear performance standards, production, service and quality targets. It will also include ways of monitoring progress and taking necessary corrective action.

There are many sophisticated planning and scheduling techniques available, often based on complex computer programmes. This is not the place to describe those techniques. However, one very simple technique which can be used for planning is critical path method.

Critical path is based on the recognition that any project, no matter how complex, consists of completing a number of individual activities in such a way that they all fit together neatly. Thus, when preparing to run a training programme, the trainer may need to:

- do a training needs analysis by interviewing managers and potential trainees;
- design the structure of the training programme;
- choose appropriate training materials;
- type and duplicate handouts, exercises, etc.;
- identify managers who will run specialist sessions;
- brief managers running specialist sessions on what will be expected of them;
- arrange accommodation;
- send out joining instructions to participants.

Unfortunately, many of these individual activities cannot be started until other activities have been completed. For example, nothing can be done until the training needs analysis is complete. Some activities will take longer to complete than others and there will also be some sequences in which several activities follow each other. In fact, there is almost certain to be one sequence that takes so long that it predetermines the length of the whole project. For the trainer with the job of preparing the programme, this sequence might be as shown in Figure 11.7. This is known as the critical path: if the time to complete this sequence could be shortened, the whole project could be completed earlier, while if it took longer the project would be extended. All other activities can be scheduled around those included in the critical path as illustrated in Figure 11.8.

In our experience this technique can be of value as an adjunct to the planning process. However, we suspect you will also need an array of questions to help

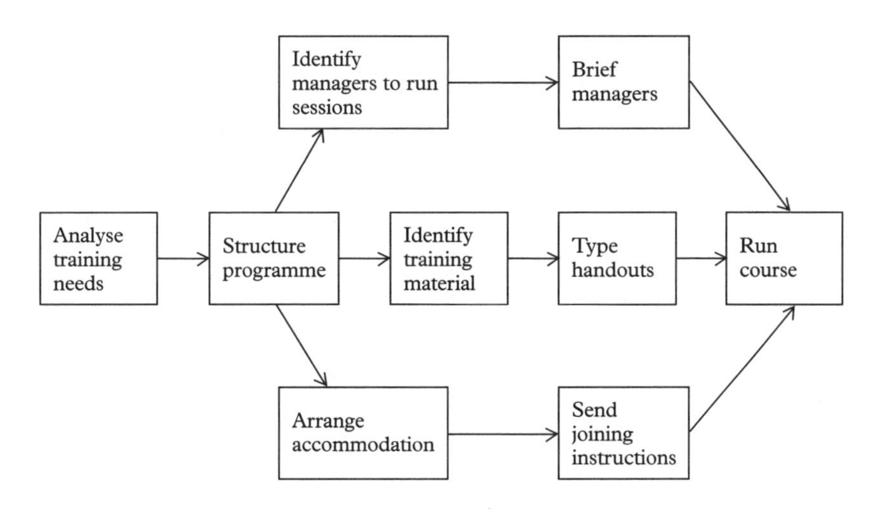

Figure 11.8 A critical path analysis

clients clarify the way forward. Such questions could include:

- What objectives are you trying to achieve?
- When does it need to be completed?
- How will you know when you have been successful?
- What activities need to be carried out along the way?
- In what order do any activities need to be done?
- By when does each activity need to be completed?
- Who should do what?
- What are the budget limits?
- What other resources are available?
- How will you monitor progress?
- How will you communicate the plan to other people?
- How are they likely to react?
- What are the likely barriers to success?
- How do you feel about these barriers?
- How can the barriers be overcome?
- What can possibly go wrong with this plan?
- Who will this plan affect and how will it affect them?
- How will you ensure completion?
- How do you feel about this plan?

This list is by no means exhaustive. No doubt you can think of other items. Of course, the questions you ask will depend on the nature of the decision. What is important is that you move the clients on from decision making and galvanize them into action, so increasing commitment to the decision and the plan of action. To help you document and structure the planning process we have included a simple planning form (see Figure 11.9).

<table>
<tr><td colspan="7">Goal</td></tr>
<tr><td colspan="7">Standards</td></tr>
<tr><td colspan="7">Deadlines</td></tr>
<tr><td>Action steps</td><td>Who</td><td>When</td><td>Standard</td><td>Help needed</td><td>Resources needed</td><td>Monitoring</td></tr>
<tr><td></td><td></td><td></td><td></td><td></td><td></td><td></td></tr>
</table>

Figure 11.9 Action planning form

Summary

- Difficulties in organizations are not usually puzzles – they are problems and they rarely have a one-hundred-per-cent solution. Hence, helping clients could involve choosing between several forty-per-cent options.
- Organizational problems are usually much more complex than they initially appear. The presenting problem may be defined in terms of task or systems and procedures issues, but there are usually much more complex human process issues which need to be acknowledged.
- Helping clients to diagnose problems is often about clarifying, simplifying or restructuring the data. This can be facilitated by using data presentation models such as decision trees or force field analysis.
- It is vital that you help the client focus on the problem, explore symptoms, clarify the inter-related issues and redefine the problem before moving into decision making.
- Theories and models can be a powerful way of helping clients make sense of the data which they have collected. To be successful the theory should be introduced late in the intervention when it can be used to help clients make sense of their problem and to make decisions about changes that they wish to make.
- Moving from problem diagnosis to action involves generating and evaluating options and planning. A good plan will describe in detail everything that has to be done to put the decision into action.

Feedback Instruments

The following are examples of feedback instruments that you can use to provide feedback to the group or to help them give feedback to themselves.

1 The *communication pattern worksheet* is useful to record the frequency and direction of comments in a group. It can often illustrate quite graphically the differences between high and low contributors and the patterns of interactions.
2 The *group behaviour questionnaire* is useful to get group members to give feedback to themselves without your having to tell them what you observed. You can supply evidence to confirm or deny their assumptions about what actually happened.
3 *'What happened in the group?'* is a variation of the group behaviour questionnaire which focuses on different dimensions or aspects of group behaviour.
4 The *personal reactions questionnaire* can be used to help individual group members explore their relationships with others. Where the human process issues are not being dealt with, this form can help you to bring them to the surface. Take care, it can be confrontational.
5 The *group systems and procedures questionnaire* might be useful if the group doesn't seem to have an appropriate set of systems and procedures.

Don't feel restricted by any of these instruments – process consultation and observation is a very individual affair. Do what you feel is right – and if all else fails, tell the group how you feel!

Instrument 1
Communication pattern – Observer worksheet
Frequency and direction of comments

Individuals being spoken to

		John	Mary	Jane	Simon	Bill	Peter	Joan	Alice	Group	*Total made*
	John		✓✓✓✓✓								
	Mary				✓✓						
	Jane										
Individuals making comments	Simon										
	Bill										
	Peter										
	Joan									✓✓✓✓✓	
	Alice										
	Total received										

The purpose of this observation sheet is to record the quantity of participation by each person and who speaks to whom. For example, in the simplified illustration above, after a few minutes of interaction we can see that John has spoken directly to Mary five times. Interestingly, Mary has not directed any comments back to John but has spoken to Simon twice. In the meantime Joan has made several comments but directed them to the group as a whole.

Instrument 2

Group behaviour questionnaire

This form is designed to help you think about behaviour in your group. First read the questions, then on each scale circle the number that typifies the behaviour of your group.

Write your reasons for your rating in the space provided after each scale.

1 How well did we clarify and set objectives?

0 1 2 3 4 5 6 7

LOW HIGH

2 How well did we clarify and agree a plan of action?

0 1 2 3 4 5 6 7

LOW HIGH

3 How well did we manage our time?

0 1 2 3 4 5 6 7

LOW HIGH

4 How well did we listen to each other?

0 1 2 3 4 5 6 7

LOW HIGH

5 How well did we keep the discussion focused?

0 1 2 3 4 5 6 7

LOW HIGH

6 The degree to which members participated equally

0 1 2 3 4 5 6 7

LOW HIGH

7 The degree to which decisions were made by consensus

0 1 2 3 4 5 6 7

LOW HIGH

8 The degree to which disagreements were acknowledged and managed productively

0 1 2 3 4 5 6 7

LOW HIGH

9 The degree to which feelings were asked for, acknowledged and shared

0 1 2 3 4 5 6 7

LOW HIGH

10 The degree to which members gave each other feedback about their behaviour

0 1 2 3 4 5 6 7

LOW HIGH

Instrument 3
'What happened in the group?'

Consider the behaviour of the members of the group and answer the following questions by ticking a point on the scale for each question.

1 How far were the objectives clearly agreed?
Not at all 0 . . . 1 . . . 2 . . . 3 . . . 4 . . . 5 . . . Clear and agreed

2 How far did members of the group generally agree with each other in order to reduce tension?
Rarely 0 . . . 1 . . . 2 . . . 3 . . . 4 . . . 5 . . . Most of the time

3 How far did members of the group give each other information, opinions or suggestions?
Rarely 0 . . . 1 . . . 2 . . . 3 . . . 4 . . . 5 . . . Most of the time

4 How far did members of the group ask each other questions?
Rarely 0 . . . 1 . . . 2 . . . 3 . . . 4 . . . 5 . . . Most of the time

5 Conflict was apparent in the group:
Rarely 0 . . . 1 . . . 2 . . . 3 . . . 4 . . . 5 . . . Most of the time

6 How would you rate the level of trust and openness in the group?
Very low 0 . . . 1 . . . 2 . . . 3 . . . 4 . . . 5 . . . Very high

7 To what extent were decisions made by consensus?

Not at all 0 . . . 1 . . . 2 . . . 3 . . . 4 . . . 5 . . . Completely

8 How far did the group use the knowledge, skills, expertise and resources of all the members?

Not at all 0 . . . 1 . . . 2 . . . 3 . . . 4 . . . 5 . . . Completely

Instrument 4

Personal reactions questionnaire

Answer all questions with the *first name* of a group member. Base your nominations on your experience in the group. You don't have to answer all the questions.

1 Who influences me most in this group? ______________

2 Who is least able to influence me in this group? ______________

3 Who do I have most conflict with in this group? ______________

4 Who supports me most? ______________

5 Who seems to take up most group time? ______________

6 Who appears to lead this group? ______________

7 Whose contributions do I find most helpful? ______________

8 Whose contributions do I find least helpful? ______________

9 Who do I feel closest to in this group? ______________

10 Who avoids discussion with me? ______________

11 Who can I be most open with? ______________

12 Who am I least open with? ______________

13 Whose humour is helpful in the group? ______________

14 Whose humour gets in the way in this group? ______________

15 Who would I choose to work with? ______________

16 Who have I talked to least? ______________

Instrument 5

Group systems and procedures questionnaire

Make notes in the blank spaces provided. Record what happened.

Planning	How did the group start?
	How did they agree objectives?
	How did they identify the resources available?
	What procedures did they develop?

Generating ideas	How did the group identify the information available?
	What ideas were generated/rejected?
	How were the ideas developed?
Control	How did the group stay on track?
	How were decisions made?
	What norms were evident?
Reviewing performance	How did the group review its own performance?
	What ideas emerged to improve future performance?

12 Implementation – How to Help Your Client Take Action

Why do Clients Fail to Implement?

Implementation is the key phase in the consulting cycle. This is the time when the change starts to take place and people do things differently. The success of any consulting assignment hinges on the way it is implemented. Yet so often consultants' reports simply gather dust and are never acted upon, or implementation takes place in the teeth of severe opposition. So why do clients fail to implement?

To answer this question we must clarify what needs to be in place before implementation is likely to be successful. We feel that successful implementation depends on four factors:

Ownership the degree to which all the people responsible for implementing the change own it and are committed to it.

Leadership the degree to which senior managers are seen to be committed to the change.

Capability the degree to which people have the necessary skills to carry out implementation properly.

Organization the way the implementation phase is actually organized.

Ownership

The implementation phase of an assignment is likely to be uncomfortable for all those who are affected. This is because people are now required to make actual changes to the way they work. How they feel about the change is crucial and those feelings will be rooted, often, in the way decisions about the changes were made.

We often assume that 'change is uncomfortable' or that 'people resist change'. But is this always true? It is true that sometimes we feel threatened, uncomfortable, or even angry at the prospect of change. But there are other times when we feel excited by change, we welcome it and feel very positive about it. So what factors affect our feelings towards change? To explore this you might like to write a list of significant changes which have taken place in your own working (or non-working) life. Identify the ones you felt positive about and the ones you felt negative about. Use the chart below.

Changes I felt positive about	Reasons
Changes I felt negative about	**Reasons**

The factors that affect the way we feel about change can be placed in six categories:

- The amount of information we have about the change.
- The extent to which we participate in the change decision.
- The degree of trust we have in the initiator of the change.
- What kind of previous experience we have with similar changes.
- The impact the change is likely to have on our relationships with other people.
- Our individual personalities.

As an example, consider how you would feel if a senior manager brought in a systems auditor to check the efficiency of your department with the brief that his report will go direct to that senior manager without being seen by yourself. Our hunch is that you would feel pretty uncomfortable at this prospect. This is because the change has been managed in a way that scored very low on many of the factors we have listed. You have been given very little information about the reason for the audit, what the auditor is looking for or what will happen as a result of the report. You weren't allowed to participate in the decision to bring in the auditor. The initiator of the change was a senior manager and it is in the nature of organizations that the further apart people are in the hierarchy, the lower the trust between them.

Imagine, on the other hand, that your manager asks you to take on a project but offers to talk through the background and purpose of the project with you, how you intend to go about it and the help you need. This time you're likely to feel much less threatened because you have more information, you have participated in the decision and are likely to have more trust in your manager.

If you want to ensure a high level of ownership and commitment when your project is implemented then it is important that decisions which affect people are made appropriately. It may be necessary to discuss with the manager or management team the degree of involvement that their people will need in the decision-making process.

There are a number of styles available to the manager when undertaking a change programme. These styles are ranged along a continuum. At one end of the continuum the manager, together with the consultant, retains the responsibility for diagnosing the problem and making decisions which are then imposed on the rest of the group. At the other end of the continuum the people who will be affected by and required to implement the change are involved in both the diagnosis and decision making.

It is easy to assume that you, the consultant, would always encourage the manager to adopt a style of decision making which is high in involvement, because this will increase the level of ownership and commitment when it comes to implementation. But it is important to recognize that there is no right or wrong decision-making style. Sometimes it is appropriate to have a high level of group involvement in decision making and sometimes it is more appropriate for the manager to decide alone (see Figure 12.1). However, if we want people to feel positive about a decision which affects them but in which they have not participated, it is necessary that:

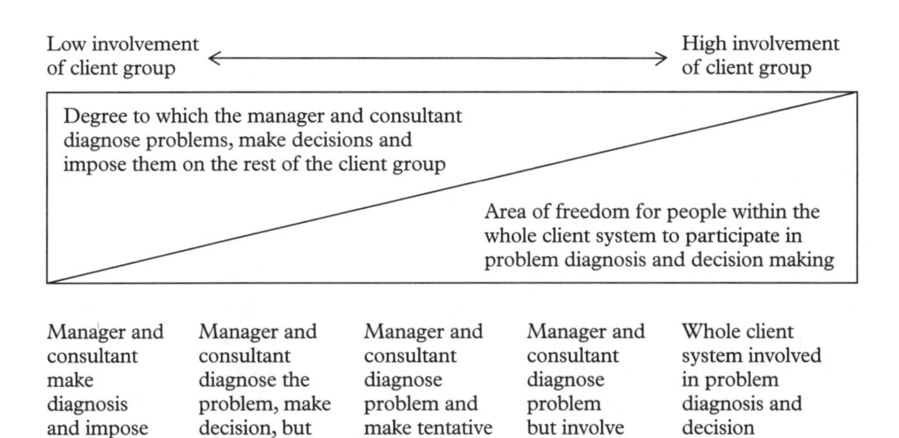

Figure 12.1 Involvement of client group

- They have a high degree of trust in the person making the decision.
- They are informed as soon as possible about the decision and the rationale behind it.

So what are the factors that will determine an appropriate decision-making style?

The **degree of emotional investment of the group**. If the group members have a very high level of emotional investment in the decision, a redundancy, promotion or a reorganization, for example, it may be appropriate for the manager to retain a high degree of responsibility for making the decision.

The **time available**. Sometimes there genuinely is no time to involve everyone in the decision. If this is the case, however, it is important that client group members are told the reasons for the decision and helped to work through their feelings about it.

The **size of the client system**. If the client system is very large then it may be impossible to involve everyone in every decision. In this case it may be necessary to help managers and supervisors brief people in small groups, tell them the reasons for the decision, allow them to think through how they can implement their part of the change, the advantages and disadvantages for them, and how they feel about the decision.

The **degree of secrecy required**. There are some decisions which, for commercial reasons, need to be kept secret, so only a limited number of people can be involved. But these decisions are few and far between. Some organizations, and some people, treat decisions as though they are state secrets, when this really is not necessary. When it is necessary, the decision (and the need for secrecy) should be fully explained afterwards.

The **maturity of the group**. There are some occasions when it is difficult to get a client group to participate in the decision-making process. It may be that they are accustomed to an autocratic style and are unable to cope with being more involved. It may be that this reluctance is simply a symptom of some underlying discontent – about the organization, the manager, the consultant or the proposed changes. Either way, this situation should be treated as exotic data which is likely to have a huge impact on the implementation of the project. You may find it necessary to confront this reluctance to become involved in decision making and explore it more deeply until the real issues become apparent and can be dealt with. You may often be involved in helping managers to identify an appropriate decision-making style which will maximize the degree of ownership that people have. You may well find it necessary to confront the manager and/or the group where the approach being adopted is inappropriate. This can obviously be a difficult and uncomfortable confrontation and needs to be handled very gently. Managers may find it painful to have to acknowledge that their behaviour is much more autocratic than they had believed.

Leadership

Leadership is another factor which is crucial to successful implementation. So often major organizational initiatives fail because key members of the management team simply do not believe in them. Organization development projects are doomed to failure, for example, if the chief executive makes it clear that he or she intends to remain aloof and unaffected by the whole process. What incentive is there for someone lower down the organization to be committed to change when the boss simply isn't interested?

As the consultant you need to talk through with managers how they are going to demonstrate commitment to a project. Whenever we embark on a total quality management (TQM) project, for example, we ask the senior management team to work on a number of questions:

- What do we want to achieve with TQM?
- What is a TQM employee? How does a TQM employee behave? How is this different from the way our employees behave at the moment?
- If employees are to behave in a TQM way what sort of management style is appropriate? How does this differ from the way our managers operate now?
- What are the implications of this for the board of directors, or senior management team? How do they need to operate differently if they are to support this change?

By answering these questions the senior management team begins to recognize that successful implementation of TQM depends on them as individuals and as a group being prepared to examine the way they manage the business and their relationships. Only when they accept the necessity to make changes in the way they operate can they reasonably expect the same from others.

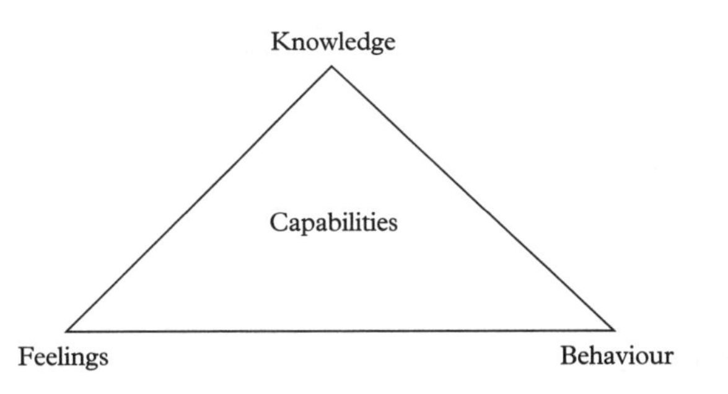

Figure 12.2 The capability triangle

Capability

An assignment will fail if people lack the skills and competence needed to implement the change. Hence an important reason for failure is lack of capability. So what can you do if your clients are incapable of making the necessary change?

First, let us clarify what we mean by capability. Capability is the ability to do something well. This can be divided into three separate components (see Figure 12.2).

- a cognitive or *knowledge* level
- a doing or *behaviour* level
- an affective or *feelings* level.

If I am to acquire a new skill I shall need a degree of knowledge. When learning to drive a car I need to know where the controls are, on which side of the road to drive, what various traffic signs mean and many other things. However, this knowledge alone will not make me a capable driver. I can never learn to drive unless I actually want to do so and feel confident about my ability. So to be competent in any new skill clients need the appropriate knowledge, an opportunity to practise the behaviour – to do it – and also the opportunity to work through their feelings about the need to change, abut their level of knowledge and about their success or failure in practising the skill, i.e. in actually doing it.

This model is very useful when you are confronted with a client group that seems incapable of implementing agreed recommendations. It is helpful to find answers to the following questions:

- Do the clients simply lack the knowledge to carry out the implementation?
- Have the clients had sufficient practice with the new system?
- Is it people's attitudes and feelings which prevent them from being committed?

We have already seen that it is often the feelings component which is the most significant blockage to successful implementation. The clients might understand the new procedure, might even have the skills to carry it out, but if they feel resentful about being excluded from the decision-making process, or feel de-skilled by the new procedure, they are unlikely to give the change whole-hearted support.

Organization

Projects will not be implemented successfully unless they are properly organized. Of course, the organization depends on ensuring that the implementation is properly planned.

The first thing to remember is that the people involved in the implementation of a project might come from different functions, different locations, different technical disciplines and perhaps even from different companies. If this is so they may bring past departmental conflicts to the project. They may be used to working with different procedures and rules. If the implementation team is very big there are likely to be communication difficulties. Imagine, for example, the organization required in a large construction project which may involve people in several different geographical locations coming from a large variety of technical disciplines.

It is important, then, when planning for project implementation, that attention is given to issues of teamwork, conflict and co-operation, communication, and the rules and procedures.

Low Client Commitment

We have already established that the commitment of the whole client system is crucial to successful implementation. You need to look for signs that will indicate whether your clients are really committed to change. Before looking at our suggestions, write down your own ideas on how you would recognize low commitment among your clients. Clients who are not committed to the change are likely to behave in any of the following ways:

Anger and hostility Sometimes clients show signs of strong antipathy towards you and the project. Their hostility may stem from many sources: fears of inadequacy; frustration at lack of consultation; their anger may be rooted in some previous grievance and may simply come to the surface as a result of the project.

Objections Often clients are able to identify many disadvantages to the project and are able to put forward objections without acknowledging any advantages. They may bring in previously undisclosed objections and appear to be moving the goalposts.

Unwillingness to look at the options Sometimes clients are prepared to define and clarify the problem but are unwilling or unable to identify any possible courses of action. This may be due to a lack of ownership of the problem or a lack of commitment to doing anything about it.

Unwillingness to look at the human process issues Sometimes a client group is willing to acknowledge and work on systems and procedural issues but unwilling to confront the human process issues which get in the way of successful implementation of change.

Hidden agendas Where there is an unwillingness on the part of the client group to acknowledge human process issues these may well emerge as hidden agendas. People may be trying to score points, settle scores or withhold information, all of which indicate that at least part of the problem is to do with such process issues. Real success is unlikely unless there is commitment to dealing with them.

Delaying tactics When the implementation plan has been agreed, clients may find many reasons for delaying tactics: the time is not quite right; the priorities have changed; we need to respond to an emergency situation; we need to wait until after a reorganization, etc. Sometimes the reasons are genuine but often they are signs of low client commitment.

Failure to implement The ultimate sign of absence of commitment is where the agreed action plan is simply not implemented by the clients.

There are many other signs that clients are low in commitment and no doubt you have identified some of them for yourself. However, the important question now is what you can do when you recognize low client commitment.

Dealing with low client commitment

It is very tempting, when confronted with clients who are not committed to a project, simply to collude with them. Collusion happens when there is an unspoken agreement to avoid certain issues, or to take the clients' objections at face value without risking the discomfort of challenging them and exploring more deeply. You may find yourself, for example, joining in with humour which is aimed at the project, the consulting team or management rather than confronting and exploring what lies behind the humour. It is important that you do not collude when clients display low commitment. Instead you need to explore the reasons that such barriers exist. This can be difficult for clients as the barriers may be deep-seated and clients may feel vulnerable in exposing them.

When exploring low commitment you will need to use a range of intervention styles as described in Section II. One option is to use a confrontational style. This is particularly useful where clients have agreed to take some action but have simply failed to do so for some reason. In this case you may be able to confront in a classic way by using words like: 'On the one hand you said that this project was important to you and you said you would take the action we agreed, but on the other hand you don't seem to be committed to actually taking action.' By confronting inconsistencies between clients' stated intentions and actual behaviour you will help them to acknowledge any barriers to commitment and make it possible to explore them further.

Often the causes of low commitment are deeply rooted in the clients' feelings, so you will need to use an acceptant style to help clients really examine their feelings about any future change, and start to deal with those feelings. Often, by acceptantly exploring the issues, you find that for the first time there is acknowledgement of the real problem or a dimension of the problem which has not yet been disclosed.

When dealing with objections to the proposals it may be useful to work catalytically with your clients. You can ask them to identify the advantages and disadvantages of the new system. This may help them to acknowledge that, while the system may not be perfect and could have disadvantages and potential pitfalls, these are outweighed by its potential advantages.

Change Agent's Role in Implementation

Implementation is quite a difficult time for the change agent, with many attendant ambiguities and dilemmas. The first dilemma is whether to stick around for implementation or disengage as soon as you have helped the client to make decisions about what to do next. This will depend on the original contract which may have been simply to help the client identify the problem, to gather data and make recommendations, and then to help the client plan the implementation of any recommendations. The advantages and disadvantages of staying out of implementation are outlined below:

Advantages

- Ownership of implementation stays firmly with the client.
- It maximizes opportunities for the client to learn and develop through taking responsibility for the agreed action.
- It reduces dependency.
- It frees the consultant for other projects.

Disadvantages

- It is possible that nothing will be done.
- The client may feel that there is no support
- Implementation may be carried out ineffectively or incompletely.
- The client may not have as much expertise as the consultant.

Sometimes it is impossible for the consultant to remain involved throughout implementation. The trainer, for example, may contract to carry out an agreed off-job training programme but may find it impossible to follow everyone back to the workplace. If this is the case it is important that there is a strong contract with the line manager which ensures that he/she accepts responsibility for debriefing, following up and offering support while the client works on implementing the learning back at work. So if you can't (or decide not to) be involved in implementation, before you disengage you need to ensure that:

- there is a solid plan for implementation;
- thcrc is a high level of management support;
- there is a high level of client commitment;
- everyone has the appropriate skills;
- clients are clear about the circumstances in which they should contact you.

If you are to be involved in the implementation then the problem of the nature of your involvement still remains. Essentially, you now have two choices. You can take a hands-on role, carrying out the implementation yourself; or you can take a more facilitating and supporting role.

There may be times when it is appropriate to carry out the implementation yourself. There may simply not be anyone else with the time or the expertise. However, there are some important implications in doing this. The primary task is that you are denying your clients an opportunity to learn how to solve problems for themselves. The other factor is the issue of control. By taking responsibility for implementation you are taking on the role of manager and taking control away from the real manager. By doing this you are actually reinforcing one of their suspicions about consultants – that they undermine the role of managers and take away authority and control. By reinforcing this suspicion you may well be creating barriers to gaining entry for other projects. So if you are taking a hands-on approach to implementation at least try to negotiate a contract in which you are responsible for no more than 50 per cent of the actual work and the client is responsible for the other 50 per cent.

The advantages and disadvantages of taking a hands-on approach to implementation are outlined below:

Advantages
- It gets done properly.
- It saves time
- The extra skills of the consultant are available.
- Low risk for the client.
- High level of satisfaction for the consultant.

Disadvantages
- Denies the client a significant learning opportunity.
- Engenders client dependence.
- Low level of client ownership.
- Takes control and responsibility away from the manager.
- The change may not survive the departure of the consultant.

Perhaps the best role for the change agent during implementation is one of supporter and facilitator. When you are fulfilling this role, you are there to support and help but you never take over from the clients. In effect, implementation is treated as a second data-gathering activity during which you gather data about the changed behaviour within the client system and offer feedback to your clients. The facilitating role is that of observer, supporter, listener, coach and helper to the whole client system. You are there to check people's feelings about the new way of working, explore difficulties they are having, help them identify ways in which the plan might be modified and improved, surface any barriers that are still around, bring together parts of the client system that are still having difficulty working together and confront people who fail to implement their part of the new system. Acting as a facilitator rather than a doer at this stage is an empowering role that makes you available when needed, while freeing you to work in other parts of the organization. A checklist for carrying out this role is given at the end of this chapter.

The advantages and disadvantages of the facilitator's role are listed below:

Advantages
- Empowers client.
- Maximizes opportunities for learning.
- Client can modify the plan with consultant's help.
- Client feels supported.
- Reduces dependency.
- Consultant is able to oversee the project and bring the client's attention to any major difficulties.
- Frees consultant for other projects.

Disadvantages
- This is a more difficult role for the consultant.
- The implementation may take longer.

You have, then, a choice of three approaches when entering the implementation phase of an assignment. You can:

- disengage when the client has a clear plan of action and not get involved in implementation;
- take a hands-on approach in which you take responsibility for implementation yourself;
- take a facilitating and supporting role in which you act as an observer and coach to help the client come to terms with organizational or technological change.

All three approaches are used by change agents and can be adopted as appropriate. Generally speaking, however, the facilitating role is likely to be the one that empowers clients, increases their involvement and ensures that the change sticks.

Summary

- Successful implementation depends on:
  - ownership;
  - leadership;
  - capability;
  - organization.
- The degree to which we accept ownership of change depends on:
  - information about the change;
  - participation in the change decision;
  - trust in the initiator;
  - previous experience of change;
  - the impact of change on our relationships;
  - individual personality.
- The appropriateness of decision-making style during implementation depends on:
  - emotional investment of the group;
  - time available;
  - size of the client system;

  - degree of secrecy required;
  - maturity of the group.
- Successful implementation of change demands both commitment and leadership from the top.
- Successful implementation requires individual competence. Competence or capability is the ability to do something well and involves knowledge, behaviour, and feelings.
- Successful implementation also requires adequate organization.
- Clients who are not committed to the change may:
  - show anger and hostility;
  - raise objections;
  - be unwilling to look at the options;
  - be unwilling to look at human process issues;
  - use hidden agendas;
  - use delaying tactics;
  - fail to implement.
- If clients demonstrate low commitment it is important to explore the reasons why.
- During implementation, the change agent may:
  - stay out of the implementation altogether;
  - adopt a 'hands-on' approach;
  - adopt a facilitating role.

  However, of the three, the facilitating role is likely to be the one which empowers clients, increases their involvement and ensures that the change is permanent.

Checklist 12.1 Implementation – taking the role of facilitator consultant

If you want to take a facilitating and supporting role during implementation these are some of the things you might do.

- Provide support and encouragement.
- Observe and give feedback.
- Listen and offer counselling when things go wrong.
- Help clients plan modifications and fine tuning.
- Identify human process issues which are getting in the way of successful implementation.
- Bring together parts of the client system to work on human process issues, e.g. unresolved conflict, communication breakdown, etc.
- Help people from different disciplines, or from different parts of the organization, to work together.
- Prepare groups for change.
- Carry out training and education sessions with individuals or groups.
- Work with managers and help them as they support the change process.
- Open doors to other departments where their involvement might be helpful.
- Confront inconsistencies between the plan and what actually happens.

13 Disengagement and Follow-up

What is Disengaging?

Disengaging and where necessary, arranging appropriate follow-up is the acid test of whether your activities have been effective. If the main purpose of your intervention has been abut initiating change then it is imperative that change is achieved and is not allowed to degenerate into a repetition of old patterns of behaviour. In this sense disengaging is the pinnacle of your efforts. It is though, inevitably, a bitter-sweet experience. On the one hand it is the culmination of previous work, but at the same time it is the moment to start saying goodbye. Occasionally, you may be involved in follow-up activities to ensure that the change is consolidated. In other cases you may be engaged in constructing effective support systems but, in either case, disengaging is about completion and ending. Nevertheless, you are likely to find that the process has just as many pitfalls as any of the previous phases of the assignment and it is all too easy to stumble and fall at the final hurdle. For this reason the process of disengaging needs to be thought about just as carefully as initial contact.

Lippitt and Lippitt (1978) argue that 'a professional responsibility and goal of most consultants is to become progressively unnecessary'. This is the intention of disengagement. Although in some cases follow-up may be required, you should always aim to become redundant. However, this should be carried out in such a way that the organization or group is not left with a gaping hole which you previously filled. Ideally, disengagement should be a gradual process rather than an abrupt end. The only way you can ensure this is by raising the issue early in the relationship and then designing your intervention with disengagement in mind. This could include a number of options:

1 Involving and developing members of the client department to take over a similar role to the one you filled.
2 Agreeing during contracting a sequentially reducing time frame or budget for using your help.
3 Planning at the outset some form of terminal collaborative effort such as a report, article or publication to celebrate the end.
4 Agreeing a minimal support or maintenance plan – perhaps an annual or quarterly 'review of progress' meeting.
5 Agreeing an 'end point' celebration of what you and your client have achieved.

The central idea in this whole process is that every intervention must include some plan for the termination of the relationship between consultants and clients. Furthermore, the sooner this is acknowledged and planned, the easier it makes the actual process.

If you are a line manager the idea of disengagement may seem inappropriate. After all the relationship you have with your people is a much more permanent one. Indeed in Chapter 2 on Client-centred Leadership, we refer to this phase as celebration – formally acknowledging the completion of a successful project. However, managing change as a line manager is not dissimilar to working as a consultant. Whether everyone in your department is affected by some significant organizational upheaval or whether you are involved in personal mentoring or coaching, you need to reach a point where the group or the individual becomes self-sustaining. This is the point at which they have acquired all the necessary understanding and knowledge, where they have experienced the changed situation and now feel confident to handle any new problems on their own without your support. If this is to happen then every empowering manager must have acquired the skills of disengaging effectively. Indeed it might be argued that if an organization is to be a learning organization then the process of letting go and helping people to take more and more responsibility is fundamental to the empowerment process.

Timing

Judging when to start disengaging is an important part of the consulting skill. To help us make this decision we need to review the overall model of consulting introduced in Chapter 1 (see Figure 13.1). In this model we can see that under ideal circumstances disengagement should follow implementation. However, in theory, it is possible to disengage at any point after initial contact. This leads to several disengagement scenarios:

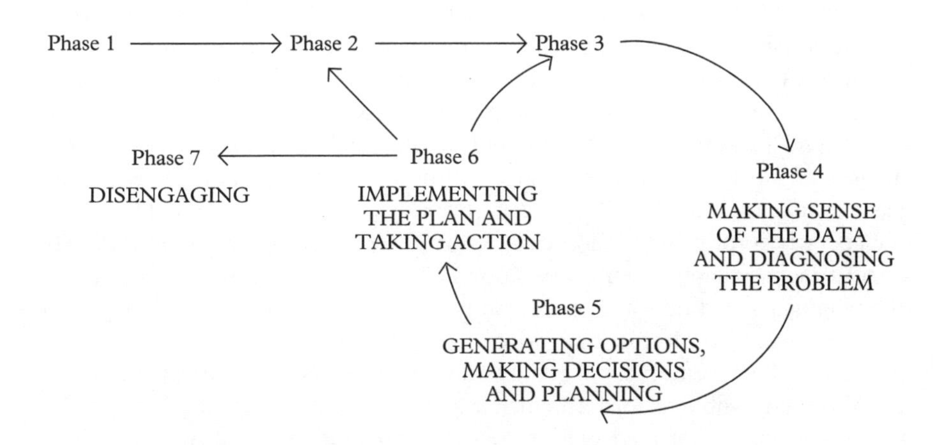

Figure 13.1 The seven phases of consultation

- If, after initial contact with a client, you find you are unable to gain entry, it could make sense to disengage from the assignment without going any further.
- Similarly, disengagement may be necessary as a consequence of being unable to agree a satisfactory contract.
- Your contract with the client could be simply to gather relevant data and then disengage – the client being left to make sense of the data and decide what to do.
- In other cases, your contract could involve helping the client to make sense of the data and diagnose the problem, but then leaving the client to make any decisions about what to do and to plan further action.
- Yet another option could be to help the client consider options, make decisions and plan what to do, and then leave, allowing the client to turn the decisions into action.
- Finally, the most satisfactory option (from the consultant's point of view) is when you agree to disengage after implementation of any decisions about action. Only after implementation can you be sure that any agreed action has been effective. Disengaging prior to implementation runs the risk that any change will not be maintained after your departure. However, staying beyond implementation runs the risk that you will overstay your welcome and as a consequence your relationship with the client will deteriorate.

When assessing the time to close an assignment (at whatever point in the consulting process) it is important to question whether you are avoiding anything by terminating at this point. For example, it is not unusual during decision making, or when you are trying to make sense of the data, for line managers to want to end a project if the focus moves from business or technical concerns to more personal issues (in other words, from the presenting to the real problem). There is a point in many projects where clients begin to recognize that their own style of management may be contributing to the problem. Furthermore, they may be reluctant to address the need for change in themselves. One way of avoiding personal change is to end the project prematurely. For example, during consulting assignments concerning total quality or customer care, data collection may lead to examining and modifying patterns of operation for the workforce. However, these are unlikely to be sustained without commensurate changes in management style and management philosophy. In both total quality and customer care assignments it is usually impossible to institute changes in how a workforce behaves without examining and changing the existing management style. It is not surprising therefore to find that some managers become fearful and seek to terminate the assignment prematurely without facing change themselves. Your task at this point is not to collude by disengaging but to find some way of supporting the managers and helping them face the discomfort, despite their wish to run away.

Similarly, if an assignment is going badly you may wish to terminate early and flee. Yet it is possible to turn a failure into an opportunity for development by asking your clients for feedback on how they see you contributing to the difficulty. Paradoxically, the more that you as the consultant, are able to acknowledge openly any mistakes you may have made, the more your clients will feel able to trust you.

Having looked at some of the difficulties surrounding disengagement, it is important to return to the original question and examine how you know when to initiate the process. Essentially, this decision has two parts: the first sets up an expectation of disengagement, the second marks the actual start of the process.

We believe that the expectation of an ending should be raised as early as possible with the client – and never any later than during contracting. The second decision, 'when to start', is more subtle. Fortunately, there are a few signals that legitimately indicate the need and these include:

- Recognizing that the contract has been fulfilled and needs reviewing.
- A reduction in the level of your direct action.
- Both you and your client recognizing that little more can be achieved and/or a mutual recognition that the client system needs to continue on its own.
- Your relationship with the client has developed to the point where you can leave the door open for further work as and when needed.

As soon as you are satisfied that these criteria are highly likely to be met you should start to move towards a close. If you expect to stay with the assignment until it is absolutely complete it is likely you will never leave (and as a consequence overstay your welcome).

How do I Disengage?

Disengagement is initiated by raising and discussing with the client how you can withdraw from the assignment responsibly. As stated in the previous section we believe the time to raise this expectation is as early as possible in the consulting relationship. An illustration of how this can work in practice occurred for us some years ago. All three of us were involved in setting up a professional and personal development group for trainers within a large commercial organization. In order to get the project rolling we decided to use the services of David Casey, an external consultant, to help accelerate the group through some of the early difficulties in forming a new group. Before the start of the first meeting David wrote to each of the prospective group members. Among other things in his letter, he raised the issue of his own withdrawal from the group. He chose to do this in the following way:

> Another issue I want to table now is withdrawal – my own withdrawal. I know I haven't started yet but that's when I like to talk about withdrawal: I would like the right to manage my own withdrawal, working jointly with the group, to get me out of your system as soon as we can, consistent with discharging my responsibility to help us all learn as much as we can. I know from Peter Cockman that your present commitment is to some sort of extended period of about a year, but that doesn't mean you have to have me around right up to the end. In fact the word 'end' may not be the right concept either.

This seems to us an ideal way of opening the discussion about disengagement and has influenced our own behaviour as consultants ever since. In effect it raised the issue of ending before the project had really started. However, in retrospect, it also highlighted a number of other points:

- It emphasized that the relationship with the consultant was finite – in some cases it could be for a fixed number of days, in others it could be until the implementation of some change.
- It immediately started to counteract any possibility of client dependency.
- It gave the consultant the opportunity to state clearly and assertively how he wanted to withdraw.
- It facilitated open and honest negotiation of any differences in expectations.

If you raise the issue of ending early in the assignment the actual start of your disengagement is inevitably less abrupt. Also it then become possible for both you and the client to use the process as a further opportunity for learning. This learning could involve:

- Checking out with the client the actual termination plan.
- Requesting an opportunity for both you and the client to give one another feedback on how the project was managed.
- Agreeing any end-point celebration/publication, etc.
- Contracting with the client about what may be required in the future.

The final closure of an assignment is also very important – particularly for internal consultants who may work in the same building as their clients and hence feel no need to close assignments formally. It is worth recalling the illustration we used in Chapter 1 where an internal consultant had been working with a client group over a number of months. As the clients' office was only down the corridor from the consultant's, she felt no need to close the assignment formally. On the Monday following, the manager of the client group protested – in essence claiming that the consultant had not said 'goodbye'. Endings are as important as beginnings; saying 'goodbye' and 'thank you' is always vital (even when the client works next door).

Feedback

With all assignments, whatever point you select to disengage, it is important for you to obtain feedback, both as the assignment is unfolding and at the end. This is just as important with assignments that went well as with those that were not as successful; there is as much to learn from success as from failure. Given the importance of feedback it is essential it is planned as early as possible. Ideally, it should be included as a contract provision. This sets up the expectation with the client that you will be seeking feedback along the way and towards the end of the assignment. It then comes as no great surprise when you request it.

The feedback sessions are an opportunity for you and your client to learn from one another. Each of you needs to give the other feedback on your perceived strengths and weaknesses. It is important though, particularly when discussing weaknesses, that this is done constructively. Disengagement is not a time for airing grudges. If you and the client have been giving each other constructive feedback throughout the assignments neither of you should get any surprises at the end.

Is Disengagement the End?

This is a particularly important question for internal consultants whose very existence relies on their being needed by other departments in an organization. It follows therefore that one of the objectives for internal consultants is to demonstrate their value to client departments such that they are invited back to do other work. Needless to say, all consultants experience some anxiety around disengagement (particularly if no further work is planned).Yet, paradoxically, we believe that the best way to ensure further work is, from the outset, to aim to become redundant. This means working to reduce client dependency to the point where you are no longer needed. Hence, our rationale for invitations for further work is based on a mature relationship that does not foster client dependency. On past experience as both internal and external consultants, we have come to recognize that this kind of approach is the best way of ensuring that clients feel comfortable about making requests for further work. This, we believe, is the essence of client-centred consulting.

Follow-up

Regardless of whether you are directly involved, some form of support or follow-up structure may be required to ensure that changes brought about during the consultation are maintained. Obviously, the precise nature of any structure will vary from one assignment to the next, but it is important that you have an overview of the types of structures which are feasible. These include:

- Planning for ongoing reviews of progress – if possible involving a wide range of staff from within the client system.
- Formation of support pairs or small groups which meet or keep in touch with one another on a regular basis.
- Documenting or reporting successful innovations through publications or professional meetings.
- Planning ongoing training designed to support change and/or introduce new staff.

It is worth noting that the internal consultant is in a very powerful position to provide follow-up support. By being present within the organization on an ongoing basis, you may be able to observe where further help is needed. However, while being more easily available, you do need to guard against engendering client dependency. Disengaging from an assignment with solid back-up and support structures in place is probably the best form of advertising for future work.

Transfer of Training

Many consulting assignments for trainers involve running one or more off-the-job training courses for groups of staff. During these courses participants may be expected to learn about new or different methods of working which are to be implemented when they return to work. This transfer of learning from off-the-job settings to the workplace is always a problem in training. In many cases the transfer simply does not happen. Organizations spend vast sums of money providing training for employees, yet the changes intended are rarely fulfilled. This is particularly true in the case of management and supervisory training.

Over the years numerous courses have included sessions on leadership, management style, motivation, delegation, etc. yet their impact is often minimal. To understand why this has been the case we need to look at how many trainers choose to work. Usually the need, theme and content of training courses are agreed with senior management. From a consultancy point of view the contract is made with only a small fraction of the total client system. The groups who are to be trained are rarely consulted beforehand about intended changes. However, once the course has been agreed, the training department steps in and senior management usually have no further involvement until their staff return from the training. In effect the training department takes over the problem from management (see Chapter 17, page 280). Although the actual training may be sound, the difficulty is that the environment and culture to which the staff return has not changed. Furthermore, it is highly unlikely that it will support the changes which the training course was intended to initiate. Not surprisingly, within a short period of time staff return to their old ways of working.

Although the case described may be oversimplified, the theme of the argument is accurate in many training settings. To overcome the difficulty we would urge anyone involved with training to behave more as a consultant: instead of taking problems *from* management, involve management in a more collaborative effort to carry through change. This will include working through what needs to be done to support the change when trainees return to the workplace. If necessary you may need to confront more senor management on how they also need to change the culture to allow the new behaviour to take place and not be sabotaged by people who don't want it to happen.

Summary

- Disengagement and (if necessary) follow-up is about ending an assignment responsibly.
- The main goal of a consultant is to become redundant – paradoxically this is probably the most effective way of ensuring further work.
- Ideally, disengagement should be a gradual process.
- All consultations need a disengagement plan – this means raising the issue of disengagement early (and no later than contracting).
- In theory disengagement can take place at any point in the consulting process

after initial contact. However, to ensure that decisions about action are carried out, it is better to disengage after implementation.
- Beware of managers wanting to end a project prematurely if the focus shifts to involve them in any change.
- If an assignment is going badly, ask for feedback – this will probably lead to greater trust from the client.
- The disengagement can be split into two stages:
  - raising the expectation;
  - carrying out the process.
- Formally acknowledging the end of an assignment is very important for both clients and consultants.
- Plan for feedback – both as the project progresses and at the end.
- Internal consultants are in a powerful position to provide ongoing support.
- For trainers – problems with transfer of training can be tackled more effectively by adopting a consultancy approach and by being prepared to confront difficulties of implementation.

Checklist 13.1 Successful Disengagement

- Is there a clear contract about when and how disengagement will take place?
- Is everyone clear about the plan for disengagement?
- Has the original contract been fulfilled?
- Is there a plan for ensuring how the client-system will become and remain self-sustaining?
- Is there a contract for any further support that might be required by the client?
- Are you satisfied that the reasons for disengagement are legitimate and not simply a way of avoiding difficult issues for you or the client?
- Has your relationship with the client developed to the point where you can leave the door open for further work as and when needed in the future?
- How will the learning from the project be recorded, documented and made available to others?
- Is there an opportunity for both you and the client to give one another feedback on how the project was managed?
- How will the end point be formally acknowledged and celebrated by everyone involved?

14 Evaluating the Assignment

What is Evaluation?

It is tempting at the end of an assignment to rush straight on to the next one. However, it is important to stand back and assess how effective your intervention has been. No doubt the assignment has involved a cost to the organization which could be measured in money, time or technology. There needs to be some way of measuring the degree to which the organization has gained a return on its investment.

Evaluation is the process of measuring how effective your intervention has been. This may sound simple but in reality it can be a complex business. One pitfall is that evaluation is carried out from the perspective of the consultant's professional discipline. For example, a training consultant may measure success in terms of a training programme, how well it was delivered and how much participants had learned. An IT consultant may measure success in terms of the elegance of the new system. A recruitment consultant may only be interested in the number of candidates that were attracted and whether an appointment was made. The danger in this type of evaluation is that there is no account taken of the needs of the organization and the client system. Client-centred evaluation asks whether the client's needs have been satisfied and whether the problem has been reduced or eliminated. Was the problem that was identified the real problem or a symptom? Was the solution that was agreed the most effective solution? Has the solution been successfully implemented?

No matter how professional a training programme, how well qualified a new appointee or how 'state of the art' a new piece of technology, no such measures will be effective if they are solutions to problems that were wrongly diagnosed.

Hence, evaluation is a process which ensures that:

- The diagnosis of the problem was valid.
- The methods used for tackling the problem were appropriate.
- The methods used have actually made an impact on the original problem.

In addition it is also important to review how effectively you managed the relationship with the client, how each phase of the consulting process was managed and how skilful you were in the intervention. By doing this kind of review it is possible to learn and develop your client-centred skills.

Purpose

The main purpose of any evaluation is to maximize learning. Effective organizations are those which provide frequent opportunities for their people to learn, develop and grow. A consulting project will be a time of change, stress and challenge for everyone in the client system. By reviewing how the change was managed by all concerned it is possible to:

- Identify ways in which changes in the client system might be handled better in the future.
- Examine human process issues that are affecting the client system.
- Clarify related problems which haven't yet been dealt with.
- Help the consultant examine areas for improvement when handling future projects.

It should always be remembered that, in a learning organization, people learn from their successes as well as their failures. They take time out to identify best practice, by the consultant and within the client system, so that this can be repeated or passed on to others.

Evaluating Success

Often consultants, and their clients, start to think about evaluation at the end of the project. We have heard of organizations deciding to evaluate training programmes which have been running for some time. The difficulty with this is that there may be nothing to evaluate against. There may not be any record of the original organizational problem that the training programme was meant to alleviate.

The time to consider evaluation is at the beginning of the assignment, not at the end. It is crucial at the contracting stage to identify and agree what the real problem is, what are its causes and its dimensions, and how things will be when the problem has been overcome. Only when these kinds of questions are answered at the beginning of an assignment can it be properly evaluated at the end.

When you are assessing your effectiveness as a consultant, you need to be able to answer two questions:

- To what extent have we (you and your clients) made an impact on the original problem? (the problem and technology dimension).
- How well have you managed your relationship with your clients? (the consulting dimension).

As far as the clients are concerned, they want the problem solved, and they want it to stay solved. This is the ultimate 'proof of the pudding'. It is vital that a project is evaluated against the original objectives. In fact, you may argue that this is sufficient. We believe, however, that it is also important to review how effectively you have managed each stage of the consulting cycle, and how successful you have been at managing your relationship with your clients.

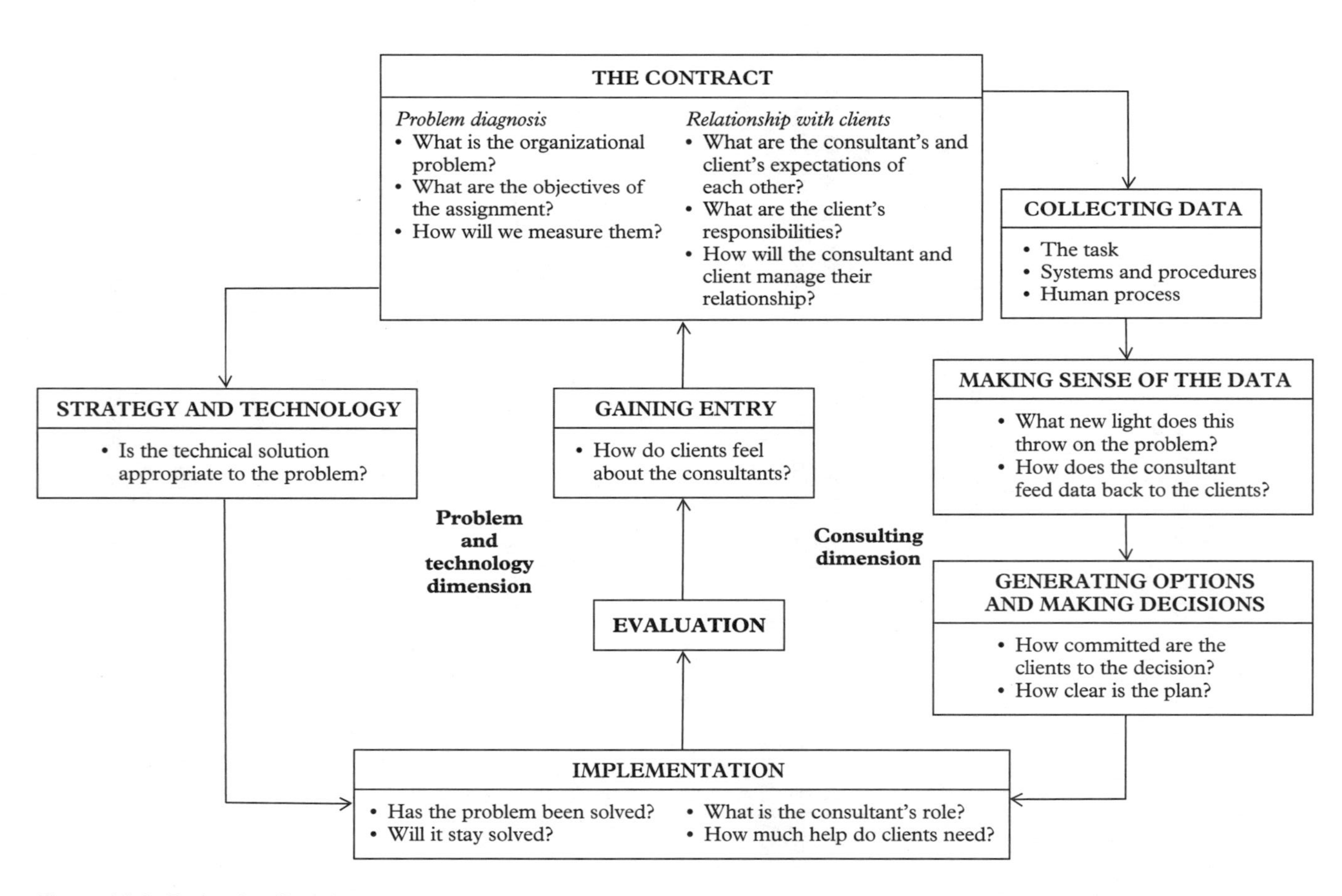

Figure 14.1 Evaluation flowchart

The flowchart in Figure 14.1 outlines the various parts of the consulting process against which an evaluation can be carried out. In reality, the 'problem and technology dimension' and the 'consulting dimension' are inseparable; they can't exist independently. However, if we are to evaluate every part of the system it is useful to review them separately.

Gaining entry It is tempting to see gaining entry as a discreet first stage in the consulting cycle. However, an effective consultant continues to gain entry with members of the client system. So if you are reviewing your effectiveness in gaining entry you should ask yourself not only about the barriers to gaining entry at the outset of the assignment, but also how your clients felt about you and the project throughout its life. The willingness of clients to accept feedback about the problem, their willingness to deal with human process issues, the energy put into decision making and the commitment to implementation are a function of the degree of entry you have made with everyone in the client system throughout the project.

The contract – problem diagnosis There are two elements to contracting. The first is the way the problem is identified, diagnosed and agreed – the terms of reference of the project. The second element is the working relationship agreed between clients and consultant. Although in reality they are linked, we propose to deal with them separately as the first leads into the problem and technology dimension and the other into the consulting dimension.

The 'problem diagnosis' element of the contract should contain a clear definition of the problem in organizational terms. It should be a statement about the organizational pain or the improvement that is required. It should be stated in terms such as 'how to reduce the scrap rate' (not 'how to introduce better quality control') or 'how to project a better image and improve service to our customers' (not 'how to introduce total quality management'). A good problem diagnosis will include a statement of the objectives of the assignment, a picture of how things will look when the problem is 'solved', and some means of measuring success.

The contract – relationship with clients This element of the contract prescribes the responsibilities of clients and consultant. This contracting was successful if all parties were clear about their responsibilities, were committed to them and subsequently behaved in a way that was consistent with what was agreed.

Strategy and technology Having identified the problem the consultant and client will determine the overall strategy or technology needed. If the problem is one of failure to meet a customer's quality requirements then an appropriate strategy might be to introduce a new technology, a new quality control system or a total quality programme. If someone leaves a section the appropriate strategy might be to fill the vacancy with someone similar. Alternative strategies might be to restructure the department, introduce new technology, or buy in expertise. The question to be asked at evaluation is whether the overall strategy was appropriate to the problem.

Collecting data When evaluating the data collection you need to check the degree to which you stayed within the boundaries of the task and systems and procedures; to what extent you were prepared to surface human process data about the way relationships were handled within the client system; and how you fed this back and helped your clients to deal with human process issues.

Making sense of the data, problem diagnosis and decision making You should help the clients to use appropriate methods of decision making and ensure that the clients take responsibility for making the decision. It is also important that you check the degree to which people affected participated in decision making and their genuine commitment.

Implementation – problem focus At the end of the assignment you need to re-examine the situation. Has the original problem been 'solved' or has there been a measurable improvement? Has quality actually improved? Have costs been reduced? It is also necessary to ensure that the improvement is permanent.

Implementation – relationship focus If you are effective at being client-centred you will have worked hard during the implementation phase not to usurp the rightful role of the line manager. Instead you will have taken a facilitating role offering support, coaching people and giving feedback where the agreed action plans are not being met.

Evaluation To evaluate your success you must look in two directions. It is not sufficient simply to ask if the organizational objectives have been achieved; if you do this you will miss an opportunity to examine the intricacies of the consulting dimension of the project and thus to maximize the learning for you and your client system. At the same time if you simply look at the consulting dimension you could find yourself losing sight of what you were trying to achieve in the first place.

Who Should Evaluate the Project?

As a client-centred internal consultant there are a number of people who have a stake in the work you do. When evaluating a project it is important to gather data from all of them. Perhaps the easiest place to start is with yourself. You have been intimately involved in your work and your own reflections, recollections and feelings will tell you a lot about the success of the project. The questions in Checklist 14.1 at the end of this chapter will help you to evaluate every element of the project from your own perspective.

Another person with a stake in your work is your boss. As an internal consultant it is likely that the projects you are engaged in will be part of a larger departmental strategy. Your boss is likely to have a view on the way your work fits into the whole.

Your work is also likely to impact on your fellow consultants: people in your own department as well as consultants working in separate disciplines. If you have handled your project well, and created good relationships in the client departments, you will have enhanced the image of your own team and made it easier for others to follow in your wake. As part of the project you may have identified opportunities for other disciplines to help in the client department. Indeed, the most successful change agents recognize that the most effective organizational change tends to be multidisciplinary. For example, the same project may have planning, technological, human resources and training implications. Effective consultants are able to involve other specialists and work collaboratively with them.

We have left until last the people who will provide the most important source of evaluation data. This is because we felt that the last word in this book on client-centred consulting should go to the clients. Ultimately, it is on the way you manage your relationships with your clients that your success as a consultant will depend. It is important to remember that everyone who is affected at any stage of the consulting cycle is part of your client system.

So when evaluating a consulting assignment be sure to gather data about every element of the consulting process from as diverse a selection of clients as you can. Checklist 14.2 at the end of this chapter consists of a questionnaire which you may be able to use to structure information from your clients.

Summary

- Evaluation is a process which ensures that:
  - the diagnosis of the problem was valid;
  - the methods used for tackling the problem were appropriate;
  - the methods used have actually made an impact on the original problem.
- It is important to review how effectively you managed the relationship with the client and how each phase of the assignment was carried out.
- When evaluating a project it is important to gather data from all the people who have a stake in the project including:
  - members of the client system;
  - yourself;
  - your manager;
  - other change agents and consultants from your own and other departments.

Checklist 14.1 Evaluating a client-centred consulting assignment

Gaining entry

- What were the boundaries of my client system?
- What were the major barriers to gaining entry?
- What strategies were used to gain entry?
- Which member of the client system was I most successful with in gaining entry? Why?
- Which member of the client system was I least successful with in gaining entry? Why?
- How much commitment was there to implementing the project?

- How do members of the client system feel about the new system now – at the end of the project?
- How do members of the client system feel about me now that the project is over?
- Who are the people in the client system with whom I feel most comfortable now?
- Who are the people in the client system with whom I feel least comfortable now?

The contract – problem diagnosis

- Did we identify the underlying organizational problem?
- Did our definition of the problem change as more data was collected?
- What were the stated organizational objectives of the assignment?
- What measures were used to indicate success?

The contract – relationship with clients

- How clear were my clients at the outset of the project about who was responsible for which elements of the project?
- How clear were my clients about how we would work together?
- Which elements of the contract did I fail to deliver?
- Which elements of the contract did my clients fail to deliver?
- Which elements of the contract needed to be renegotiated?
- Was there any element of my relationship with my clients that I was uncertain or uncomfortable about but which was not surfaced and discussed?

Strategy and technology

- What technological or organizational strategies were used to overcome the problem?
- To what extent were the technological or organizational change strategies appropriate to the diagnosed problem?

Collecting data

- How involved were my clients in data collection?
- How much of the significant data collected was to do with:
  - the task?
  - the systems, procedures and processes?
  - the human process?
- How was the data fed back to my clients?
- Did the clients accept the data that was presented?

Making sense of the data, making decisions and planning

- What models were useful in helping the clients understand the dimensions of the problem?
- How committed were senior managers to the decisions made?
- To what extent were more junior members of the client system involved in the decision-making process?
- How were decisions communicated throughout the client system?
- How committed to the decision were people throughout the client system?
- How detailed was the planning for implementing decisions?

Implementation – problem focus

- To what extent have the objectives of the project been met?
- To what extent were the measures I chose appropriate?
- Has the organizational problem been solved?
- Will it stay that way?

Implementation – relationship focus

- What role did I take during implementation?
- How much help did clients need?
- How much responsibility for success did clients take?
- Will the new system outlast my disengagement?

Checklist 14.2 Getting feedback from your clients – a questionnaire

Consultant's name:
Your name:

What is your position and role within the department in which the consultant was working?
What was your involvement in the project the consultant was engaged in?
When did you first meet the consultant? What were your first impressions?
Was the consultant the type of person you had been led to expect? How was he or she the same or different?
Was the consultant the type of person you could trust? Why?
Did you feel that the consultant listened sympathetically to your point of view? Why?
How clear were you about what the project would entail, what your involvement would be and how you would be affected?
How much influence did you have on the decisions which affected you?
Do you think that the consultant was expressing his or her true feelings when consulting with you and your colleagues? Please give reasons.
Do you think you could rely on the consultant to act in a consistent manner?
How clear were you about your own role when the new technology or system was actually introduced?
How committed will you be to the outcome of the project when the consultant leaves?

Section IV
Client-centredness – Being Different, Not Just Doing Things Differently

Introduction to Section IV

We have written at great length in this book about the reality of the modern world being one of continuous change. We are all being asked to do things differently and to do different things. Much of this book has encouraged you to re-examine what you do when you consult with your clients and reconsider the way that you do it.

We would suggest that it is not enough to merely do things differently, or change actions and behaviours. Becoming a client-centred change agent or empowering manager involves actually *being* different.

While doing things differently is about changing actions and behaviours, being different involves change at a much more fundamental level. Being different means re-examining your fundamental beliefs, your attitudes, your values, your self-image and how you relate to other people. The questionnaires at the end of Chapters 1 and 2, should have helped you examine some of the barriers you may have to overcome to work in a client-centred way or to empower your people. These barriers are all about values and attitudes rather than behaviours. If you have a high need to be in control; have low self-esteem, feel that you're not being helpful unless you're giving advice; feel superior or inferior to other people or see your profession as being central to who you are, then you're unlikely to be able to change the way you do things to become more client-centred, without a significant change in your attitude. Client-centredness then, is as much a way of being as what you actually do.

In Chapter 15 we look at the basic skills you need to be an effective change agent. These are the micro-skills required if you are to use any of the styles described in Section II. In our experience, being influential depends much more on how you demonstrate these behaviours on an ongoing basis than on adopting a role (be it consultant, manager or leader) in specific situations.

If you are to work in a way that empowers other people then you need to start empowering yourself. Chapter 16 explores sources of personal power which enable you to work effectively and professionally with little or no formal authority, in situations which are ambiguous and uncomfortable.

Finally, in Chapter 17, we turn our attention to the development of client-centred change agents. We believe passionately that if you are responsible for helping change agents to acquire the principles and practices described in this book and to reassess their current attitudes, then it is essential that you work with them in a client-centred way. That is consistent with the values and attitudes you want them to adopt. This means that you should:

Always find out where your students are and start from there.
Work with them as a consultant using all styles as appropriate.
Allow them to test their skills with real clients rather than using role-plays.
Encourage them to experiment with new ways of working with clients.
Understand that the locus of control must remain with the students rather than with you.
Help them deal with the feelings involved in learning to be different and trying out new behaviour.
Encourage them to use the here and now behaviour as useful information on what is happening to themselves and their clients.
Encourage them to give each other constructive feedback about behaviour and their feelings engendered by it.
Always allow them to make their own decisions about what they want or need to do to improve their effectiveness.
Help them to put together realistic action plans for transfer of learning back to work.
Be prepared to be a client by asking for help, admitting that you are stuck, don't know or made a mistake and sharing your feelings.

Essential Skills for Client-centred Change Agents 15

What Skills do I Need?

Most consultants spend years developing the technical skills required to do their jobs. Yet often very little attention is paid to the skills they require to become successful change agents. Perhaps the reason for this is that these are exactly the same skills we require for everyday social intercourse. We tend to take them for granted, assuming that they are common sense. Unfortunately, the one certain thing we can say about common sense is that it isn't very common.

Talking of the skills that underlie effective consulting reminds me of the professional golfer who demonstrated his skill by doing trick shots. He could pile three balls on top of each other and hit the middle one; hitting the ball so that it swung round and came back to him; then twisting it in a circle. He could do anything with the ball, he would say, but make it talk. Yet when asked if he could hit six balls out of six straight down the middle of the fairway, he would always say that he couldn't guarantee that. What seems simple is often the most difficult to do. The same is true of consulting.

Client-centred consulting involves managing relationships with your clients and often involves you in helping them to manage relationships with each other. If you are to do this effectively you need to follow the phases of the consulting cycle and you need facility in a range of consulting styles. All this requires a range of basic skills. We have grouped these skills into seven separate categories:

1 **Knowing yourself** Successful client-centred consultants are aware of their strengths and weaknesses and how they impact on others, and have a strategy for their self-development.
2 **Communication skills** If you are a change agent you are a professional communicator. It is important that you are able to express your ideas clearly. However, if you want to work in a client-centred way and successfully use a combination of all four consulting styles, then an ability to express your ideas is not enough. In addition you need a set of communication skills which underlie acceptant, catalytic and confrontational styles. These are the skills of helping others to express their: confusions; feelings; difficulties; concerns; ideas; visions and goals. The skills of, listening; asking questions; summarizing; reflecting and drawing out others are all essential if you are to work in a client-centred way.

3 **Observation and feedback skills** Whenever you are working with a client group, whatever the issue, you need to be aware of how relationships and behaviour in the group are affecting the problem. You need a high level of observation skills to enable you to be aware of what is happening in the group and to feed it back to them.
4 **Problem-solving skills** You are likely to have knowledge of a number of problem-solving techniques as part of your technical expertise. However, the more client-centred you are the more you will need to involve your clients and client groups in the problem-solving and decision-making process. You need skills in helping groups to look at problems together, generate creative ideas, examine the options and finally make decisions to which they are all committed.
5 **Team building** Organizational change always has an impact on the way people work together. Often part of your role as a consultant is to assist your client group to be a strong and effective team. This means you will be involved in helping team members to listen to each other and value each other; take a flexible approach to problem solving; deal with uncomfortable and risky interpersonal issues; confront issues to do with leadership style; and deal with each other's feelings.
6 **Dealing with people's feelings** It may be stating the glaringly obvious to say that change agents are in the business of change. But it is our experience that consultants often try to drive through changes in technology, procedures or structure without recognizing the impact these changes will have on people in the organization. Those who are in the throes of change inevitably experience feelings, even when they themselves have chosen to make that change. These feelings can range from anxiety, anger and threat at one extreme to excitement, satisfaction and happiness at the other. One thing is certain, if you ignore people's feelings about any change required by an assignment, you do so at your own peril. To handle this you need a number of skills related to helping people acknowledge, explore and come to terms with their feelings.
7 **Dealing with your own feelings** You will not be able to help other people deal with their feelings if you find it difficult to deal with your own. You need to be in touch with your own feelings because those feelings can tell you a lot about what is going on around you. If you are uncomfortable and anxious it is likely that others will be too. If you can talk about your feelings it makes it more legitimate for others to share theirs.

So what skills do you require if you are to operate effectively in each of these seven areas? We have listed all those we think are important in each category as Checklist 15.1 at the end of the chapter. Before turning to our checklist, write down all the skills you think are important in each category, then compare your list with ours.

Skills I require to know myself adequately

-
-
-
-
-
-

Skills I need to communicate with groups and individuals

-
-
-
-
-
-

Observation and feedback skills I require

-
-
-
-
-
-

Skills I need to help groups solve problems and make decisions

-
-
-
-
-
-

Skills I require to facilitate team building

-
-
-
-
-
-

Skills I need to help people deal with their feelings

-
-
-
-
-
-

Skills I need to deal with my own feelings

-
-
-
-
-
-

When you compare your checklist with ours, add any of your own items that you feel we have missed. Then examine yourself critically against each item on the checklist and identify which skills you feel proficient in, which you should work on and develop and which you overuse and could use less often.

It is impossible to go into detail here about all the individual interpersonal skills noted in the checklist. That would be the subject of a complete book in itself.

To develop skills there is no substitute for practice followed by honest, constructive feedback. No matter how experienced we are, there is always benefit to be gained from feedback about our impact on others. This feedback can come as part of ongoing training sessions or during peer group meetings with other consultants; feedback can come also (perhaps most valuable of all) from clients themselves. But feedback cannot take place in a vacuum, it has to be based on practice. Obviously, as responsible consultants, our practice when dealing with clients will be directed by their needs and it will range across most styles. However, we also believe there is much to be gained from participating in situations (such as ongoing training), where we can force ourselves to remain with one style well beyond the point where we feel comfortable. Not only does this teach us about the limitations of any particular style, we also often find that our clients report feeling genuinely helped despite our discomfort. Furthermore, on each occasion that we step outside our comfort zone we become a fraction more skilled and our degree of discomfort becomes a fraction less.

Exercises

1 Consulting trios

Purpose To practise acceptant and catalytic styles.

We find the best way of practising and developing acceptant and catalytic styles is to use real problems and issues. This gives the consultant an opportunity to work with a real client and receive genuine feedback. The client has the opportunity to experience each style from this perspective. Each practice lasts for 15 to 20 minutes followed by 10 to 15 minutes review.

For each practice allocate the following roles:

- client;
- consultant;
- observer.

The client should choose a genuine current issue or problem which they are prepared to work on with the help of a consultant. It is important to use a real issue, it shouldn't be a role play.

The consultant should stay 100 per cent within the acceptant (or catalytic) style throughout the consultation. Resist the temptation to move into a different style no matter how difficult you find it.

The observer should observe the consultation and record examples of when the consultation stays within the style and when they move out of it. You should keep the time and gently signal when there is a minute to go.

As a general rule you should manage the feedback session so that:
(a) The consultant and client, in that order, say immediately how they feel.
(b) You and the client help the consultant identify whether or not he/she stayed in the style and what went well.
(c) The consultant has some ideas about how to effect an improvement.

NB Try to avoid continuing to discuss the client's problem. Deal with the human process and the method of consultation.

2 Our gift to you

Purpose To give and receive feedback on consulting skills within a group of consultants.

This exercise is designed to help consultants get feedback from other members of a team within which they have been working. This could be a group of people who work together, or have worked together on an assignment or training programme. It is an exercise which must be handled with care and requires a skilled facilitator to ensure that the following prerequisites are met:

- There must be an open, trusting climate within the group.
- There should be a high level of care and desire to help each other.
- People must feel valued by other group members.
- Group members should already have started to give each other some feedback.
- Everyone should want to do the exercise.
- A high level of honesty is essential.

The way in which to do the exercise is as follows:

(a) Each person spends 15–20 minutes alone thinking about the members of the team and how each behaves as a consultant.
(b) The team re-forms, without the facilitator, and all the names are put in the pot. They take out one at a time to determine the order in which feedback will be given. They should not pull all the names out at the beginning or the pressure on the last person becomes a form of 'creeping death'. The Russian roulette method is good – someone selects the first name and that person, after receiving feedback, pulls out the next name, and so on.

(c) For 10 minutes (no more/no less) the person receiving the feedback stands at the flip chart ready to write. The rest of the group provide feedback by giving adjectives – words or phrases – that describe that person. Recipients can divide the sheet into plus and minus columns and decide on which side to put the words, but they may not comment – only write.

(d) The recipient leaves the words on the flip chart so that the group can see them and hands in their Personal Feedback Sheet to a member of the group, who will coordinate its completion. This sheet has several sections. They overlap to some extent but all are important and all should be completed.

Our gift to you
Personal Feedback Sheet

To ______________________

The things we have found most valuable about you are:

Your major strengths as a consultant are:

Your most helpful actions in this group have been:

Your principal weaknesses as a consultant are:

The types of behaviour you might think of changing are:

From ______________________ Date ______________________

The person receiving the feedback now sits outside the group but inside the room listening to the discussion as the group decides what to write. The recipient may find it useful to make notes on the discussion while listening. This discussion and completion of the 'gift' should take 20 minutes – any shorter time is likely to lead to superficiality; any longer and the group could be 'sawing sawdust'.

When members of the group have agreed what they want to say, their comments are written on the feedback sheet. All members sign it (very important) and it is given to the person concerned. (NB This is not a consensus exercise – if one or two group members think an aspect is important, it should be put down.)

(e) The person receiving the feedback then has up to 10 minutes to ask for clarification or explanation of either the adjectives on the flip chart, or the feedback sheet. Recipients should use this time to make sure they really understand the feedback given – especially behaviour they might think of changing.

3 A letter to myself

Purpose Planning for increased personal effectiveness.

This exercise is long term and is a variation of one used by the Brontë sisters. Most organizations now have some form of annual appraisal. Why not use a variation of this purely for yourself? At the time of your appraisal (or new year, or your birthday) write a letter to yourself describing:

- your strengths;
- your weaknesses;
- your hopes and fears;
- areas you wish to develop over the next year (most important of all).

As the letter will only be read by you, you can afford to be really honest. When complete, seal it in an envelope and file it away until next year. When the next year comes around (and that will be quicker than you think) don't start your next personal appraisal until you have read what you wrote last year. We suspect you will be amazed how much you have changed.

4 Listening and summarizing

Purpose To practise listening and summarizing styles.

If you have a TV and video recorder then try listening to, and recording, the evening news broadcast. Most stations now adopt a three-part pattern:

i They announce the headlines.
ii They give you the news.
iii Finally, they summarize the main points of the news once again.

You can use this to develop your listening and summarizing skills. Switch on your TV and video at the start of the news. Listen to, and record the programme. As they start the summary at the end, switch off the TV and make your own summary of what has been said. Try to summarize the points you have heard. In the meantime your video will have captured the summary announced on TV. Finally, rewind your video and replay the recording. At the same time check the TV summary against your own. It will highlight what you listened to and remembered, measured against the main points that the broadcasters felt were important.

5 Asking questions

Purpose To practise asking open questions.

This exercise requires the help of a colleague. It is competitive and should be treated as fun. Each of you will take turns at being a speaker or a questioner for a fixed period of time in each role (say 5 minutes). Instructions for what to do in each role are given below.

Speaker
When you are the speaker, choose a topic to talk about (e.g. a holiday, film, favourite interest, sport) and tell your questioner your chosen topic. Your questioner will then ask you questions on the topic. If he or she asks an open question (i.e. beginning with who, what, why, where, when or how) give some information. If he or she asks a closed question, answer with yes or no (do be quite ruthless where you can answer yes or no). You score a point whenever you answer yes or no.

Questioner
When you are the questioner it is your job to ask questions. If you ask an open question and receive a piece of information, you score a point. If you ask a closed question and receive a yes or not, the speaker scores a point.

Example
Questioner: Where did you go on holiday?
Speaker: Spain (Questioner scores a point)
Questioner: Did you like it?
Speaker: Yes (Speaker scores a point)
Questioner: How did you get there?
Speaker: By plane (Questioner scores a point).

And so on for 5 minutes.

When you have both had a go at each role, total up your points. Whoever scores the most wins the round.

6 Identifying feelings

Purpose To extend the vocabulary people have to describe feelings.

Working individually or as a group write down as many words to describe feelings and emotions as you can. Ensure that every word is a genuine feeling. It should be possible to generate a list of over 100 words.

7 Exploring feelings

Purpose To practise exploring other people's feelings.

Working as a pair, one person volunteers to be the client and the other the consultant. The client should choose a real problem that he or she has at present. It can be from work or outside work; the only prerequisite is that it is genuine.

The client should talk about the problem. The consultant should listen and help the client explore his or her feelings about the problem. The consultant can only ask questions about the client's feelings. It may be necessary to ask a 'feelings' question more than once if the client gives a thought or opinion as an answer. (See Chapter 10, Asking about feelings.) The consultation should last for about 15 minutes. At the end of this time client and consultant should discuss fully how they both felt during the exercise.

Repeat the exercise so that each person is able to experience both roles.

Checklist 15.1 Consulting skills – a checklist for individual development

This checklist is designed to help you identify the skills you require to be a successful client-centred consultant. It is intended to help you recognize the range of skills you require and identify those which you need to work on.

Read through the list of skills and for each one identify whether:

- You are already competent in this activity and use the skill appropriately.
- This is a skill that you need to develop or one you underuse at the moment.
- This is a skill you are competent in but actually overuse at the moment so that you become less effective. You need to work on doing less of this activity.

	Competent	*Need to develop*	*Need to do less*
Knowing myself			
1 Understanding how I am seen by others	....	....	....
2 Being aware of how my personal style differs from others	....	....	....
3 Being able to ask others to comment on my behaviour	....	....	....
4 Being able to assess my own strengths and weaknesses	....	....	....
5 Being able to set goals for personal change	....	....	....
6 Being able to work on improving personal effectiveness	....	....	....
7	....	....	....
8	....	....	....
9	....	....	....
10	....	....	....
Communication skills			
11 Talking in small groups	....	....	....
12 Talking in large groups	....	....	....
13 Asking questions	....	....	....
14 Drawing others out	....	....	....
15 Summarizing and clarifying others' ideas	....	....	....
16 Building on others' contributions	....	....	....
17 Listening	....	....	....
18 Keeping to the topic	....	....	....
19 Summarizing the discussion	....	....	....
20 Showing interest	....	....	....
21 Dealing with more senior people	....	....	....
22 Asserting my own rights	....	....	....
23 Stating my own needs	....	....	....
24	....	....	....
25	....	....	....
Observation and feedback skills			
26 Being aware of high and low participators	....	....	....
27 Noting if people are excluded	....	....	....
28 Recognizing who talks to whom	....	....	....
29 Noting how decisions are made	....	....	....

30 Being aware of who takes on leadership roles	....	....	....
31 Being sensitive to how people in the group are feeling	....	....	....
32 Sensing tension in the group	....	....	....
33 Being aware of how open or closed the group is	....	....	....
34 Identifying those issues which are avoided	....	....	....
35 Giving feedback on behaviour in the group	....	....	....
36 Giving feedback to individuals	....	....	....
37	....	....	....
38	....	....	....
39	....	....	....
40	....	....	....

Helping client groups solve problems and make decisions

41 Identifying and clarifying goals and objectives	....	....	....
42 Clearly defining the problem under discussion	....	....	....
43 Examining all facets of the problem	....	....	....
44 Exploring human aspects of the problem	....	....	....
45 Surfacing vested interests and feelings about the problem	....	....	....
46 Encouraging others to generate ideas	....	....	....
47 Creativity – developing new ideas	....	....	....
48 Evaluating options	....	....	....
49 Helping groups make decisions	....	....	....
50 Helping groups explore their commitment to decisions made	....	....	....
51 Encouraging groups to develop action plans	....	....	....
52	....	....	....
53	....	....	....
54	....	....	....
55	....	....	....

Team building

56 Helping the team to confront difficult issues	....	....	....
57 Drawing attention to unhelpful behaviour	....	....	....
58 Dealing with tension	....	....	....
59 Helping the team deal with conflict	....	....	....
60 Giving praise and appreciation	....	....	....

61 Supporting individuals against group pressure	....	....	....
62 Helping team members acknowledge each other's strengths	....	....	....
63 Helping team members give each other feedback	....	....	....
64 Facilitating team review and critique	....	....	....
65	....	....	....
Dealing with people's feelings			
66 Being sensitive to others' feelings	....	....	....
67 Asking people how they feel	....	....	....
68 Acknowledging people's feelings	....	....	....
69 Helping others express their feelings	....	....	....
70 Being comfortable with closeness and affection	....	....	....
71 Facing conflict and anger	....	....	....
72 Dealing with hostility and suspicion	....	....	....
73 Withstanding silences	....	....	....
74	....	....	....
75	....	....	....
Dealing with my own feelings			
76 Being aware of my own feelings	....	....	....
77 Being able to identify my feelings	....	....	....
78 Expressing my feelings to others	....	....	....
79 Expressing the following feelings:			
• Warmth	....	....	....
• Affection	....	....	....
• Comfort	....	....	....
• Discomfort	....	....	....
• Anxiety	....	....	....
• Frustration	....	....	....
• Fear	....	....	....
• Confidence	....	....	....
• Uncertainty	....	....	....
• Irritation	....	....	....
• Annoyance	....	....	....
• Anger	....	....	....
• Gratitude	....	....	....
• Satisfaction	....	....	....
• Excitement	....	....	....
• Determination	....	....	....
• others	....	....	....
•	....	....	....
•	....	....	....
•	....	....	....

Checklist 15.2 Planning new behaviour

1. What new behaviour or new skill do I want to work on?
2. What precisely will I be doing when I am using that skill effectively?
3. How does that differ from the way I operate now?
4. What barriers to changed behaviour will I need to overcome?
5. How long will it take me to become proficient?
6. What are the steps along the way?
7. What situations will be available to practise?
8. What help do I need from other people? Who?
9. How will I ask for that help?
10. How will I know if I am succeeding?
11. How will I get feedback?
12. Where and when am I going to start?

Personal Power In Action 16

Why Do Change Agents Need to be Powerful?

During the 1990s the word 'consultant' has come to be widely used as a way of describing the people who work as helpers and change agents within organizations. Look in any situations vacant column and you will find organizations seeking to recruit legal consultants, financial consultants, marketing consultants, human resources consultants, the list is endless. If you are reading this book you may well have the word consultant in your own job title. Yet it was not always so. When we started working on training and developing people who worked in these functions in the early 1980s, they tended to be called advisers, officers, executives or assistants. The title 'consultant' was reserved for those highly paid, high powered people who came in from outside to correct the company's ills. When we announced that we were in the business of training and developing consultants we were often met with the response of 'we don't use outside consultants here'. Yet we decided to persevere with the use of the description 'consultant' long before it started to become fashionable. The reason for this lies at the heart of one of the most serious issues for many consultants: from where do they derive their power?

Traditionally, those departments we now refer to as consulting departments had very little real power or influence in their organizations. They were often referred to as 'staff' departments; with the insinuation that they were less important than the 'line' departments where the real power lay. Titles such as adviser or staff officer simply served to underline the lower status of their functions. The people within such functions saw themselves as less important, less influential, less powerful than those they were asked to serve. Worse still, less effective managers were often given these, less important, advisory roles.

We persevered with the title 'internal consultant' because it seemed to convey a more powerful image, and a high level of authority. Perhaps this is because of its association with the medical profession where the word consultant infers a high level of status, knowledge and skills. We felt that internal consultants should be powerful people, not powerless ones. They should have a high level of confidence and self esteem and feel themselves to be equal to the managers who are their clients. They should be valued as having an important contribution to make, not seen as lower level advisers.

So why do consultants need to be powerful? This really takes us back to the opening lines of the book. As a consultant you are often responsible for facilitating large scale organizational change. This means that you need to deal with a significant degree of ambiguity, uncertainty and unpredictability. How often have you done two similar projects in two parts of the organization? The problems have been similar, the technology the same, the methods and procedures identical yet the outcomes have been totally different. One project went smoothly while the other was beset by disagreements, obstacles, politics and delays. This is because, as a consultant, you are no longer cocooned within your technical or professional discipline but must work with human aspects of organizational change. You need to be skilful in dealing with people with all their foibles, feelings and emotions. When experiencing change, people are likely to feel uncomfortable, anxious, suspicious or angry; and that suspicion and anger may well be directed towards you – the perceived initiator of their discomfort. Hostility and suspicion are difficult to deal with when they come from an individual, but when you are dealing with emotional issues concerning large groups of people, it can become quite intimidating. Added to all this you may be working away from the familiarity of your office, on the clients' territory. Many of your clients are likely to be more senior in the organization than you and you may be expected to operate with little if any formal authority. Little wonder then that consultants need to possess significant personal power.

What is Power?

When we (the authors) work with groups on issues regarding power, we often start by asking them to brainstorm words which they associate with power. You may wish to do this yourself before reading on. The words which usually come up include: force; status; strength; seniority; threats; being intimidating; domineering; dictatorial; autocratic; power dressing; telling people what to do etc.

It's interesting how often we associate 'power' with having 'power over' someone else. Most people immediately think of power in terms of being in a position of authority, being able to deliver orders and tell people what to do and control them. Usually we envisage the person with this power as being someone other than ourselves. We tend to disapprove of people who seek power or positions of authority. Power then is often seen in a negative light.

Perhaps it is more helpful to see power not in the sense of having 'power over' power to control others, but rather as feeling 'powerful' or 'powerless' within any relationship. It is possible to still feel powerful when working with someone in a more senior position. The authors have also met many people who had what seemed to be quite powerful positions yet felt powerless to really influence what was going on in their organization. Better questions might be, 'what is it like to feel powerful?' and what is it like to feel powerless? You may like to answer these questions for yourself before reading on.

If you are feeling powerful (as opposed to having power over) in a relationship, you are likely to feel valued and respected with a significant contribution to make. You are likely to feel confident, articulate, influential, equal, creative and intelligent. You will feel that you are able to make choices about how you behave, what you do, what you say, even how you feel. You will assume that people will listen to you and take your ideas seriously, even if they disagree. There is an element of mutuality in a relationship where people feel powerful. There is mutual respect and a willingness to build on each other's ideas and make joint decisions.

The feeling of 'powerlessness' is very different. If you have a sense of powerlessness you are likely to feel undervalued, and lacking in self-confidence. You may imagine that you won't be listened to, your opinions won't be valued and you will be unable to influence others. You are likely to assume that you have very little choice about what you do. When people feel powerless they often use the words 'have to' work in the way they do and they 'can't' work in any other way. They don't recognize that when they say this they are really making choices, although it may not feel like that.

It is important that consultants feel powerful when working with their clients without feeling they need to have power over them. Yet this can be very difficult if there are no obvious sources of power or authority. It is tempting therefore to operate firmly out of your own technical or professional expertise; after all this is where you feel safe and at home. Unfortunately this can be more a source of 'power over' the client. Working from the solid foundation of our expertise we are able to tell the client what they ought to do, what is right and what is wrong. The result can be a very disempowered client. So if we are to feel powerful in our relationships with our clients, without using our technical or professional expertise to control them, then we need to be aware of sources of powerfulness available to us.

Sources of Power

Powerfulness can be described as having a strong sense of well being – a solid feeling of who you are, what your values are, what you stand for, what you are able to contribute and that you are valued by yourself and others. When we feel powerful we are able to get things done and make things happen.

It is a commonly held belief that personal power is directly related to formal organizational power and therefore stems from formal authority and position in the organization's hierarchy. Yet it is possible to find people in quite senior positions who feel powerless to change things while others (client-centred consultants perhaps) who feel empowered and able to exert significant influence on what goes on around them. So what other sources of power are available to us at work?

The power of information

Access to information is crucial if we are to feel empowered when working in any organization. We need information about the goals of the organization, its norms and standards, how it is organized, why certain decisions are made and who is responsible for what. We have probably all felt powerless at some time in our lives, when we haven't had sufficient information to do our jobs properly. We have probably complained about 'not being informed', or 'lack of communication', or that 'I'm always the last to know' or 'nobody tells me anything'. We often feel that it is someone else's responsibility to keep up informed and simply complain about the absence of information. When we do this, however, we are simply disempowering ourselves. If we turn the problem around and see it as our responsibility to 'keep informed' and 'get communicated with' then we empower ourselves.

The power of asking questions and listening

The ability to ask questions seems to be much less widespread amongst the human race than one would think. If you tune in to many conversations or meetings, you will find that most people are in 'transmit' mode, determined to get across their own views, opinions and ideas. Very few invest energy in asking questions, clarifying, probing, checking and really trying to understand someone else's perceptions and ideas. Yet the best way of keeping informed and getting communicated with is by asking appropriate questions.

The ability to listen and ask questions, however, not only increases the information available to us but it can also increase our ability to help people re-evaluate the way they do things and make decisions to do them differently. We have all seen people engage in verbal combat, each trying to influence the other or get them to change their mind. They work on the assumption that those who shout loudest win the argument. They are so intent on expressing their own views that no-one listens to the other. Yet if, instead of trying to prove someone wrong, we listen to them and ask them why they do it that way, what assumptions they made when making that decision, what other options were available, then the other person may find some flaw in their argument and choose to change their mind for themselves.

The power of expertise

Having knowledge, skills and expertise can be a very important source of power. Each activity in an organization requires the possession of knowledge or specialist skills and the more limited the expertise then the more powerful are the people who have acquired it. When the central heating breaks down, the most powerful person in the company is the maintenance engineer who has the expertise to get it going again. However, it is very easy to use your expertise to have power over people who don't have any.

The power of options

Anyone who has a problem and is unable to find a way out is powerless. The person who has one solution feels a little powerful, although of course, that solution may not be the best one. Even then, if the person perceives one option they often feel forced to take it and powerless to do otherwise. We often find people justify decisions they make by saying they 'had to' do it that way. They felt in fact that they had no option.

Where two possible options are perceived, then more power is available, although the direct choice of 'either–or' may sometimes present a dilemma which is difficult to deal with. The people with the real power are those who are able to think creatively, who are not constrained by how things have always been, and who are able to identify a range of options and give themselves a real choice.

Power to think

It would be difficult to generate options without the ability to think. This is a power that everyone has but which unfortunately many people choose either not to use, to give away, or to feel that others have taken from them. Everyone has the capacity and the right to have ideas, opinions, values and perceptions. Yet it is very easy to deny ourselves this right on the assumption that someone else's ideas will be better than ours, that we only speak when we have something worth saying (the assumption here is that all the other things we think but don't express are not worth saying) or that we won't be listened to.

The power of where you are

In some organizations to be geographically situated in one place rather than another may imply power. The visitor from head office, or someone from a high profile organization may be perceived as being more powerful or more important by virtue of their location. For consultants, being based at a distant location can be a disadvantage. If you are not located close to your clients you may not be involved when important decisions are made and may be perceived as being out of touch and on the periphery of the action.

The power of who you know

It is an old cliché, often used by those who see themselves as being powerless, that 'it's not what you know but who you know' that is important. Indeed people who know others who do have formal authority are often perceived as themselves having significant power. This would certainly be so in the case of many senior managers' secretaries, for whilst they have no formal authority, they are usually very powerful people in the organization. This source of power can of course be used in a way that may be less than legitimate. Many people have learned the importance of having a mentor who is senior in the organization and is a significant source of coaching, guidance and empowerment. Effective consultants take care to build relationships at every level in the organization, especially those with the authority to get things done and those who hold the purse strings.

The power of collaboration

It is very difficult for anyone alone to achieve anything of lasting significance. Most human activity is collaborative in nature. People work best when they are members of effective, cohesive teams which work together towards common goals. People who are able to work collaboratively with others and foster relationships of mutual support and respect are often powerful, influential and able to get things done. This power base is at work when there is a high level of rapport, co-operation, good working relationships or mutual friendship.

The power of having rights

The concept of rights lies at the heart of Assertion Theory which is a set of solid ideas designed to help people deal effectively with difficult, uncomfortable or stressful situations. Assertion is based on the premise that all human beings need certain basic rights in order to live well together. Assertive rights are anything one feels no human-being should be deprived of. Because there isn't any 'declaration of basic assertive rights' like that embodied in the United Nations Charter, each person needs to develop their own. These are rights one is entitled to oneself which one is also willing to accord to everyone else. Such rights are likely to include:

- The right to be treated with respect and dignity.
- The right to ask for what you want.
- The right to make mistakes (and be responsible for them).
- The right to be listened to.
- The right to have and express your own feelings, opinions and ideas.
- The right to refuse requests without feeling guilty (while giving an explanation to the other person).

These might seem quite obvious yet they are frequently violated in work and social situations and we often find it difficult to assert such rights – especially if we have low self-esteem.

Take for example a situation in which you are in a meeting of senior managers where your ideas are continually being ignored, or where an important client asks you to do some urgent, unscheduled work for tomorrow when you already have a full diary today and a social occasion you're looking forward to tonight. Both these situations can be quite uncomfortable. When your ideas are being ignored you may feel angry and react by shouting and demanding to be heard. On the other hand you may feel intimidated by the seniority of the group, perhaps tell yourself that your ideas weren't as important as theirs anyway and simply let it go. Similarly when confronted with the request to do some unscheduled work you may feel guilty about letting the client down, that he or she will feel disappointed in you or may not use you again in the future. You begin to think that tonight's social engagement is not so important after all and agree to do the work which will take up your whole evening. Quite possibly, at the end of it you feel quite resentful.

In both these scenarios the person involved feels powerless. They have had their rights infringed or have failed to assert them. However, if the person had been able to identify their rights in this situation, they may have found a form of words which asserted their own rights without infringing other people's. At the meeting with senior managers, the individual might have recognized that they have rights:

- to have and express my feelings, opinions and ideas;
- to be listened to.

They might then have said quite reasonably:

> I'm feeling quite frustrated here because I've expressed several ideas and haven't had any response. I wonder why that is?

When asked to do the urgent unscheduled work the individual might remember their right to refuse requests without feeling guilty and respond by saying:

> I'm afraid I'm not able to take on any more work today, my diary's full, but if you'd be happy with a deadline of the day after tomorrow, I'll be able to fit it in.

The concept of rights is very important for consultants. You are often working in difficult, ambiguous situations without formal power or authority. People often, perhaps not deliberately infringe your rights. This can be uncomfortable and disempowering. If you are clear what your rights are, that's the first step in developing a strategy for asserting them.

It is important to remember that the concept of having rights is not designed to give you *carte blanche* to do as you please. Having rights carries responsibilities to accord the same rights to others.

Professional and Technical Expertise

When talking to managers of consulting departments we, the authors, often feel seduced into arguments about the relative importance of consulting skill vs. professional and technical expertise. Because we emphasize the importance of client-centredness people often interpret this as undervaluing professional and technical expertise. Nothing could be further from the truth. Professional and technical skills are an important part of the holistic pyramid model of change agent development described in Chapter 13. Indeed this element is one of the pillars which underpin the rest of the skills and without which the whole model will collapse.

It is crucial that consultants have a high level of professional or technical skills. No matter how client-centred they are, no-one wants a doctor, a lawyer, an IT specialist, a marketing executive or an HR specialist without professional skills. Technical or professional competence is usually the primary reason for being invited to talk to a potential client in the first place. Having technical or professional expertise is a very important source of personal power which underpins many of those described in the previous section. It is a potential source of valuable information, which gives us significant skills and knowledge and provides many options in problem situations. If our ideas are rooted in professional or technical competence we are more likely to express them confidently and have them listened to.

Many people invest a great deal of energy and take years to acquire their professional and technical skills. We often define ourselves in terms of what we do professionally. If we are asked 'who we are' the answer often comes back in terms of what we do. I am a teacher, a salesperson, a business consultant, a personnel manager, or a doctor. Our professional expertise is an important aspect of our self-image and self-esteem.

When we use our technical expertise we are on safe and secure ground. We feel that we have something useful and concrete to offer the client and very often this is the case; the problem could not be fixed without the use of our technical expertise. While we would never suggest that technical and professional expertise is unimportant, we should recognize the dangers inherent in staying too firmly within that competence.

There would appear to be two main dangers. The first is to do with problem definition. If you stay within your technical competence you are likely to define your clients' problems in a very narrow way, strictly in terms of your technical or professional discipline. Consequently you may collect a large amount of technical data but be less likely to take account of the human aspects of the problem and the way it is being managed.

The second danger is the potential for over-use of the prescriptive style. If you see yourself as the expert, more competent than your client, it is very tempting to use that competence to take the problem away from the client, 'solve it' and hand it back. This can disempower rather than empower clients. You will find more information about the prescriptive style in Chapter 7.

Self-Image and Personal Power

As we saw in an earlier section, there are many sources of power which are external to ourselves. Real self-empowerment however, comes from within. All human beings have an image of themselves. We constantly look at ourselves in relation to the world and the other people in it. Sometimes a person will feel good about themselves and confident of their own value; at other times they will feel less confident, possibly even worthless.

At the same time we look at the people around us and may decide that in our opinion they are valuable human beings, with a right to exist and behave in the way they do. On the other hand there are times when we feel that the actions and opinions of other people are unacceptable to us and we therefore judge and devalue them.

At one level our self-image and our image of others is adopted in childhood and tends to stay fairly constant throughout our lives. This is described as a life position by Thomas A. Harris in *I'm OK – You're OK* (1973). At another level, our view of ourselves and our view of others varies from situation to situation, even from minute to minute.

So how does one's self-image develop? Generally, we all acquire a self-image from what other people tell us about ourselves and our observations of our behaviour and its consequences. For example if children are ridiculed and frequently called stupid they are likely to come to believe that and behave accordingly. If on the other hand they are told how clever or good they are, then they are likely to develop a high level of self-esteem. We continue receiving such negative and positive messages throughout our lives, at school, in social situations and at work. So when taking positions about ourselves we may conclude:

I do many things right *or* I always make mistakes
I have interesting and valuable things to say *or* What I have to say is boring and not worth listening to
I am able to think for myself *or* I don't trust myself to make decisions.

As we develop we also formulate ideas about the value of other people. We can do this through favourable or unfavourable comparisons with ourselves. We may be told that others are more or less intelligent, more or less athletic, more or less attractive than ourselves. We also formulate ideas about others through experiences of being supported or let down, valued or devalued, rewarded or punished by them.

When taking positions about others, we may conclude:

People are wonderful *or* People are worthless
People will help me *or* People are out to get me
People are basically honest *or* People can't be trusted.

The decisions we make about ourselves and those around us offer four alternative ways of relating to the world. These are called *life positions* which express in some way, just how we relate to others in terms of thinking, feeling and behaving. These are illustrated in Figure 16.1 – Life positions model.

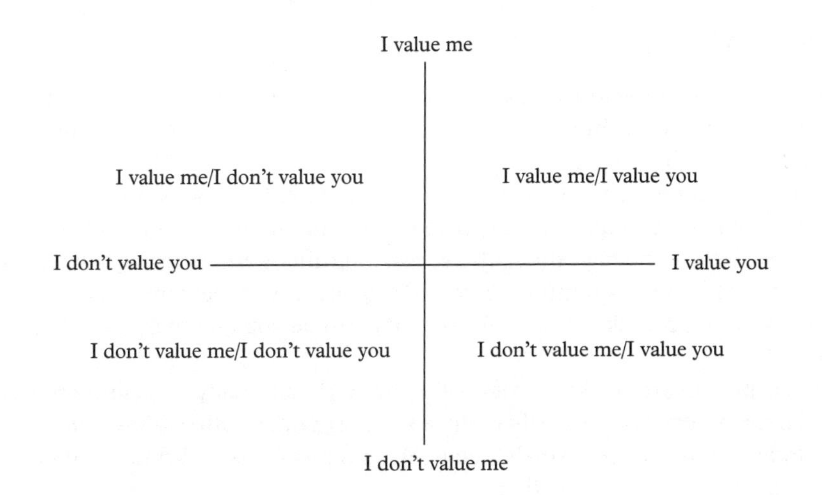

Figure 16.1 Life positions model

In reality no-one spends their whole time in one life position. Rather we tend to move from position to position according to the situation we are in. People vary considerably in terms of their 'mobility' through the life positions. One individual may move rapidly through all four within the space of a few hours with a range of mild experiences (some satisfaction, some frustration, some anger and some sense of futility). They are not prevented from functioning in society or at work, although at times their job effectiveness may suffer.

On the other hand, another individual may spend their life in 'severe' circumstances in one life position. For example someone who eventually commits suicide may have experienced an extreme degree of depression and spent most of their time in 'I don't value me – I don't value you'. While 'I value me – I value you' as a fundamental life view is worthy of attainment, it does seem something of an ideal on a twenty-four hours a day, seven days a week basis. However, it is certainly a valid, if implicit, aim of good approaches to education, training, organization development, change management and indeed, of good business practice. People can move to a predominantly 'I value me – I value you position', even late in life.

When working in organizations, it can be seen that people feel and behave differently depending on their assumptions and attitudes about the situation and the people with whom they are interacting. For example, in a team meeting a manager might feel confident and self assured with colleagues and work from an 'I value me – I value you' position. He or she might then be invited to attend a board meeting and the feelings of confidence might be replaced with awkwardness, inferiority and diffidence – a movement to 'I don't value me – I value you'. He or she may then return to their own department and feel angry and scold a junior person for not achieving certain standards – 'I value me – I don't value you'. In the space of two hours this person has acted from three different psychological positions, probably with little awareness of the changes he or she has made in thinking, feeling and behaving.

I Value Me – I Don't Value You

This position is characterized by feelings of superiority. It is sometimes referred to as the 'get rid of' position. Others are seen as inferior, unworthy, incompetent, wrong or not to be trusted.

When operating from this position an individual is likely to feel angry, frustrated, blaming, superior. Surprisingly one might also feel protective when in this position – looking after others, rescuing them and offering advice and prescriptions. The assumption here is 'you are not a valuable person, you can't look after or think for yourself so I must rescue you and make decisions for you'.

When people are in this position they may intentionally or unintentionally undermine others' sense of self-worth. As well as putting others down, they may over inflate their own self worth, deny personal problems and find it difficult to give positive recognition to others.

When someone is working from this position they may be highly competitive, working hard to win arguments or take dogmatic views and be highly critical of others.

The consultant working out of this position is likely to try to maintain as much power as possible when working with clients. They may be very dismissive of their clients' capacity to solve problems and make decisions for themselves. We, the authors, are reminded of discussing with a senior IT consultant, the possibility of adopting a non-prescriptive style. Finally he said 'I have to be prescriptive with my clients. I have to take over responsibility. My clients don't even understand the problem, never mind the solution'. The clients he was talking about were very competent senior managers responsible for managing a large business. We are sure they understood the business problems much better than the consultant, even though they needed help from IT to improve their business. Our hunch is that the consultant's position of 'I value me – I don't value you' was apparent to his clients, and the implications for their long-term relationships were very significant.

Consultants who work with their clients from this position are likely to be quite prescriptive in approach, making decisions for their clients, and leaving them with very few options. The clients may be left feeling judged, incompetent, resentful and powerless.

I Don't Value Me – I Value You

When in this position a person is likely to feel inferior and powerless in relation to others. Often referred to as the 'get away from' position it is typified by feelings such as inadequacy, sadness, vulnerability or self-consciousness.

People in this position put themselves down and find it difficult to accept positive recognition, perhaps even being suspicious of it. Their fantasy is that other people are cleverer or more competent than they are themselves. They tend to lack confidence, be self conscious and accommodate others where there is conflict or disagreement. They find it very difficult to say 'no' and are consequently often overloaded at work.

For consultants coming from this position, the results can be very significant. They are likely to feel threatened and uncomfortable when working with clients – especially those who are more senior in the organization. They are likely to work hard to accommodate their clients' felt needs and may well end up acting as an extra pair of hands rather than as change agents. They may well find it difficult to challenge their clients, accepting their view of the problem at face value rather than exploring it fully. The result can be a very weak contract with a commitment to tackle the symptoms rather than the real problem with the consultant taking on much more responsibility than the clients for solving the problem.

I Don't Value Me – I Don't Value You

Known as the 'get nowhere' position in which people are likely to feel confusion, aimlessness and pointlessness. People can feel like this in situations in which they feel powerless to control events but at the same time blame others for their misfortune. At times of organizational upheaval people may very well be in this position feeling threatened and anxious, but powerless to control events. At the same time, they may see senior managers as malevolent, unethical, incompetent and to blame for all their turmoil.

Many consultants can feel quite powerless when confronted with the size and scale of an assignment. They can then be met by apathy, suspicion or hostility from the client department. In this situation one's self belief can be severely undermined while at the same time, it is very difficult to value the clients. The temptation for the consultant is to keep their head down, cling to the familiarity of the technology, stay firmly within their technical competence and only visit the client's department when absolutely necessary.

I Value Me – I Value You

Described as the 'get on with' position it is the healthiest place to be and yet often it is quite difficult to achieve and maintain. This position is based on feelings of trust and equality. Here we have a positive view of ourselves and a positive view of the people we are dealing or working with. Working from this quadrant people will be able to be genuine and honest with each other – they trust and respect each other enough not to have to hide from each other or engage in meaningless rituals. There will be a high level of feedback from both sides and a willingness to interact at an emotional as well as an intellectual level.

This position is not about being cosy, nice to each other or not rocking the boat. It can actually be quite a risky and vulnerable place to be; it is only with people you trust and feel valued by that you will be prepared to be vulnerable and open about your deficiencies and confusions. Criticism and conflict which is tackled from this position is more likely to achieve satisfactory outcomes. The underlying message would be 'I care enough about you that I am prepared to argue with you or give you negative (or positive) feedback' rather than 'I am criticizing you in order to make you feel bad or because you are inferior'.

The implications of this model for consultants are very wide reaching. It is obvious that the best client–consultant relationship is one which is firmly rooted in 'I Value Me – I Value You'. The best relationship is one in which both parties trust each other. The client is prepared to be open about their problems and difficulties while the consultant respects the client's ability to work on the problem and make decisions. However, in times of change and uncertainty, clients may well feel threatened, powerless and suspicious. The existence of problems may either be denied or blamed on someone else, senior management perhaps or even you, the consultant. The client in this case is coming from 'I Don't Value Me – I Don't Value You'.. If this is the case then you are likely to need to spend significant time and energy on the process of building trust and gaining entry.

An equally difficult situation is one in which the client appears to be coming from an 'I Value Me – I Don't Value You' position. This can happen if the client is more senior in the organization or is older or 'more experienced' than the consultant. Their attitude may be one of 'what can such a junior person or one so young possibly offer me?' In this situation the consultant may well respond in one of two ways; either by moving into 'I Value You – I Don't Value Me' and accommodating the senior person or moving into 'I Value Me – I Don't Value You' and competing with the client using your technical expertise as a convenient weapon. Neither of these strategies is likely to be very successful. Again working on the barriers to develop a trusting and equal relationship may be a slow but necessary process.

It seems quite important for consultants to stay in the 'I Value Me – I Value You' position as much as possible and to work hard to get clients into the same position. Even when you have a client group which is really depressed about their situation it is often possible to find something that they have done really well and to highlight that.

Another issue for consultants arises from the use of the confrontational style. This requires you to stay objective and detached while pointing out the client's inconsistency between their behaviour and their stated intentions. This can be done successfully if you stay firmly fixed in the 'I Value Me – I Value You' position.

It is probably also worth assuming that clients whose overt behaviour seems to emanate from 'I Value Me – I Don't Value You', may well have underlying feelings which are firmly rooted in 'I Don't Value Me – I Value You'. They cover these feelings of low self-esteem by aggressive behaviour.

Self Affirmation

Self belief is an important part of empowerment. If you don't believe in yourself it is very difficult to feel empowered. Yet very often we talk to ourselves in a way that we would never talk to others. We are often inwardly very critical and judgemental of ourselves. We can persuade ourselves into the most dreadful situations in advance and if we do it well enough we can almost guarantee a self-fulfilling prophecy of real disaster. If we have a difficult meeting with a client group who are much more senior than ourselves, our 'inner conversation' could go something like this:

> It's Tuesday, I'm meeting the board today, I'm sure they have more important thing to do than listen to me; they'll probably be really angry that they have to give up their valuable time to see me; and I have to ask for extra resources for the project; that won't go down well; it's all my fault; I should have made it clearer at the start that I had only budgeted for the initial phase of the project; this will give them an excuse to criticize me for all the other mistakes I've made; I know I won't get extra resources; they'll probably just cancel the whole project; I wish I was at home sick today.

This is of course very unhelpful, negative, internal dialogue and these downward spiralling thoughts are likely to leave you feeling very powerless and non-assertive when you arrive at the meeting.

The world of sports has discovered how to use this kind of internal dialogue in a much more positive way. Can you imagine an Olympic athlete standing on the track a few minutes from the 100 metres final. Is that athlete likely to be having an internal dialogue like this?

> I'm not a very good runner really . . . I don't know why I'm here . . . I can't possibly be an Olympic champion . . . I'm so lucky just to have got this far . . . wow have you seen the other finalists, I'll never keep up with them.

Of course not. The potential Olympic champion, the real winner is likely to be thinking:

> In a few minutes I'll be Olympic champion . . . these other runners don't stand a chance . . . I'm the best.

Successful athletes use positive self talk to increase their confidence and their belief in themselves. We can all use the same technique to maintain our own level of confidence and self-esteem, particularly in difficult or uncomfortable situations. By consciously changing your self-talk into a more positive dialogue you can coach yourself to feel more powerful and behave more effectively in most situations. This is not a question of thinking rosy thoughts so that with false optimism you can pretend it will be alright. It is a way of preventing yourself from giving away your power and instead focusing on positive, realistic options.

If we go back to our meeting with the Board, a much more positive train of thought would go like this:

> I'm meeting the board today to discuss the extra resources we'll need now that the project has been extended. I must make sure they are aware of how successful the first phase has been and the benefits to the company of extending it. They'll probably ask about some of the mistakes we made, but I know they were unpredictable and they gave us invaluable learning. So I'm confident I can handle anything they care to ask me.

There is of course no magic wand that you can wave which will instantly increase your self-image. Some things that will help include:

- Visualize success rather than failure.
- Cut down and hopefully eliminate the negative things you say about yourself, other people or your circumstances.
- Think of at least three good things about an idea. This makes you look at it in a more positive way.
- Consciously make internal, positive statements to yourself. Acknowledge your strengths and your talents.
- Celebrate your successes and achievements. Internally congratulate yourself as you would others when you do anything you deserve to be pleased with.
- Throw away the concept of right and wrong. In most aspects of life, and consulting is no exception, there are very few absolute right or wrong ways of doing things. Yet if we cling to this concept it leads us to judge that if we

haven't done something perfectly – then we must have got it wrong. If we avoid thinking in terms of right and wrong this makes us less judgemental of ourselves and can free our minds to be more positive.[1]

Affirming Your Clients – Positive Strokes

Whenever you are working with clients who are feeling really negative about themselves or their situation, they will inevitably be difficult to help. In this state of mind the client will find it difficult to own the problem or feel powerful enough to put energy into working on it. For the consultant there is no point doing anything until the client feels more positive.

Helping clients to feel more positive about themselves and their situations is a crucial issue for all consultants. The theory of strokes has been with us for some years now, since Amy B. Harris and Thomas Harris published *Staying OK* in 1985, and has almost become part of our language. It is a very simple but also very profound set of ideas which many of us know about but few of us apply. A brief description of the theory should be helpful when developing ways of empowering our clients and ourselves.

Our starting point is with the statement that 'we all need to be recognized and acknowledged by others'. Acknowledgement and recognition are vital components of human life. As infants this was normally in the form of touch, being held, being valued and affirmed by the way we were held by our parents and other members of the family. As we grew older no doubt touch was replaced by words, gestures, looks, affirmative phrases, praise and sometimes criticism – nevertheless they all served to recognize and acknowledge our presence in the world. Indeed it's worth reflecting on the fact that the more extreme forms of punishment used by society often attempt to deny people recognition and acknowledgement (e.g. solitary confinement – the absence of other human contact, being sent to Coventry – having people ignore you).

As infants develop, their need to be held modifies into a need for other forms of approval. As a child grows older an approving smile or frown, a word or a gesture starts to substitute for touch. Yet their purpose is the same, they acknowledge and recognize the person (though, even as adults, in times of great joy or sadness the need for a physical embrace is often overwhelming).

In 'transactional analysis' recognition and acknowledgement (both physical and verbal) are called, quite simply, 'strokes'. However, as we will see later, 'strokes' can take a variety of forms. For the present suffice it to say that people need strokes to survive. Where people are deprived of strokes they actively seek to make up the deficit. For example, children who are ignored may start to 'play up' in an effort to gain attention. In extreme cases petty crime or other anti-social behaviour may be their way of seeking recognition and acknowledgement.

Strokes can be classified into different types. The first obvious distinction is positive or negative, for example, praise or criticism; approval or disapproval. A second, perhaps less obvious, distinction can be drawn between conditional and unconditional. Strokes which are given in relation to something we have

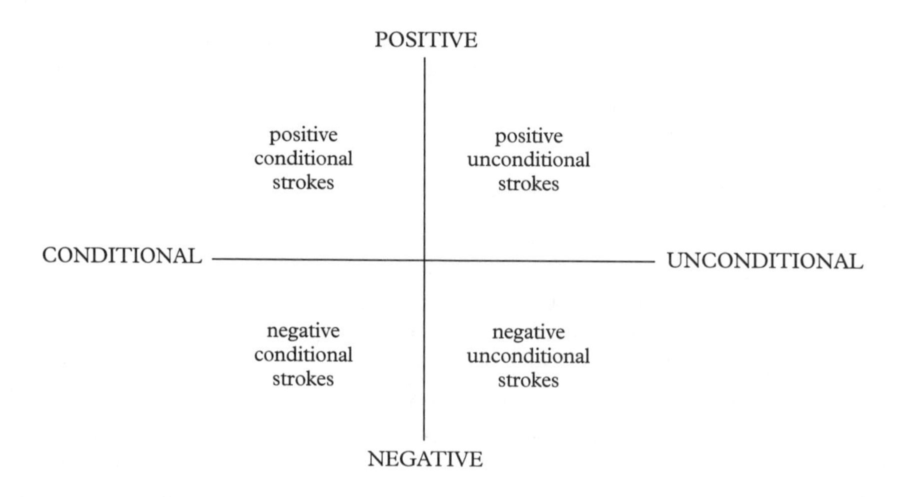

Figure 16.2 Classification of strokes

done (conditional) and strokes which are given with no qualification or strings attached, simply for who we are (unconditional).

Diagrammatically we can illustrate these distinctions in Figure 16.2 – Classification of strokes.

Perhaps this will become more meaningful if we give a few examples of each of the different types of strokes:

1 Positive unconditional: 'I really appreciate you'.
'You're always fun to be with'.
2 Positive conditional: 'This is an excellent summary of the meeting'.
'Your new hairstyle really suits you'.
3 Negative conditional: 'Your work is an untidy mess'.
'Can't you do better than this?'
4 Negative unconditional: 'You idiot! You're a waste of time'.
'You always look an absolute mess'.

As a generalization conditional strokes are about what we do whereas unconditional strokes are simply about being. However, the central point about strokes is that everyone needs them in order to stay healthy and perform effectively both at work and at home. The only way that any of us really know that others value is when they tell us what it is they value about us. However, we remember working with a client who believed that it wasn't done to show affection to his children. They went to his wife for cuddles but they knew he loved them because he bought them things. The greatest thing he learnt was to realize what they were all missing!

Unfortunately, in many organizations, there is still a culture in which it is not acceptable to give honest open feedback. One of the authors worked for a very senior officer in the Ministry of Defence who, when asked for feedback about his performance was told 'You must be doing alright. I haven't kicked you for weeks'. And what about a senior training manager who started all appraisals by

'We all know about your strengths lad, let's talk about your weaknesses'. Now that 360 degree feedback is being introduced into many organizations, such anecdotes will soon be part of history – we hope!

The culture in many organizations, unfortunately, emphasizes mutual criticisms and put downs. People often find it difficult and embarrassing to actually say what they value about their colleagues. Instead they are likely to discount each other. This includes ignoring, teasing, humiliating, laughing at, or ridiculing people. Its purpose is to treat the person on the receiving end as if they are insignificant in some way. Discounts of this type can be blatant or more subtle, however, they always involve some measure of pain for the recipient.

It is also important to remember that non-verbal signals can convey vicious discounts which are at least as powerful as words or phrases. Tone of voice, facial expression, gesture and posture can all give an impression of a discount. Furthermore, whenever there is a mismatch between a consultant's words and his/her behaviour, then generally the client will 'hear' the message conveyed by the behaviour rather than the words. For example the expression 'have a nice day' can be said with genuine sincerity, but when the same words are coupled with an incongruous facial expression or dismissive tone of voice the meaning is completely negated.

We have come across many groups where putdowns and mickey-taking, calling each other rude names and generally behaving in a disrespectful way is accepted as the norm. Groups will tell you that they understand this and 'take it in good part' or 'give as good as they get'. However, the recipient is never quite sure whether this is genuine or not. There is always the possibility that it is part of a hidden agenda. What happens is that the people on the receiving end have to desensitize themselves so that it doesn't get to them. As such it is a way of avoiding the expression of intimacy and love. How much easier it would be if we worked in a culture where it was expected that people told the truth, were genuine and felt able to say to colleagues and bosses what we really value about them.

It is vital that you always avoid disparaging your clients. It is a recipe for disaster if a client picks up the slightest hint that:

1 their problem is either not important or not significant; or
2 the consultant believes that the client is not capable of solving the problem.

As consultants, when doing a diagnosis, we often focus on the negative aspects of our clients' situations. If we're not careful we can appear to have a negative view of our clients, especially if written down in report form. The consequences can be clients who are suspicious, threatened, defensive, angry or aggressive.

Effective client-centred consultants start by taking the view that their clients are inherently competent and valuable. Carl Rogers called this 'unconditional positive regard'. If you can build up a positive relationship with your clients which includes giving positive strokes and telling them what you value about them, then they are much more likely to respond positively when you give any negative feedback. If they know that you value them (and what it is you value about them) and are on their side, then they are more likely to accept that negative feedback is given with positive intent and for their benefit.

At this stage we must include a few words on 'plastic strokes'. Typically these involve false flattery or insincere compliments which are conveyed with mock sincerity. For the receiver they are particularly distasteful and may reinforce any negative feelings which they have about themselves. For consultants the best advice when dealing with clients is

be genuine – always;
but above all
do not discount others.

One way for the consultant to encourage the client is through active listening. When someone has encountered real listening and feels 'heard' – their ideas, opinions and confusions are heard and understood, they receive a powerful stroke as a result. For the consultant, 'real' listening does not necessarily mean agreement. It means hearing, remembering, reflecting and perhaps summarizing the client's point of view. Effective consultants listen to, and understand what their clients are struggling to say. They listen and help them verbalize what they find difficult to put into words. This is positive stroking at its best.

Balancing Challenge and Support

The most effective client–consultant relationship is one in which both parties value each other and are able to give each other positive strokes. At the same time there is a high degree of feedback, genuineness and challenge.

One of the key dilemmas for consultants is striking the right balance between offering an appropriate level of support, and an appropriate level of challenge. If you offer too much challenge and too little support you can paralyse or alienate the client while too much support without challenge, simply results in giving the client an easy time. When you truly value the clients, you value them enough to challenge them, confront them, and give feedback about what is not going well. You will do this in a way that shows you value them and are willing to support them while they deal with their feelings associated with the challenge and work towards deciding on appropriate action.

The relationship between challenge and support is shown in the diagram at Figure 16.3.

Of course it is incumbent upon consultants to challenge their clients in such a way that they feel empowered to deal with their problems and support them while they muddle around with the problem and the solution. It is therefore important to get right the balance between challenge and support.

If consultants offer clients 'high challenge' with 'low support' they could well become defensive, alienated or aggressive. They could experience feelings of frustration, guilt, powerlessness or panic. They could be so overwhelmed by their problems that they do nothing but fight the consultant.

If consultants offer clients 'high support' with 'low challenge' they could well become comfortable and content and degenerate into a polite, cosy,

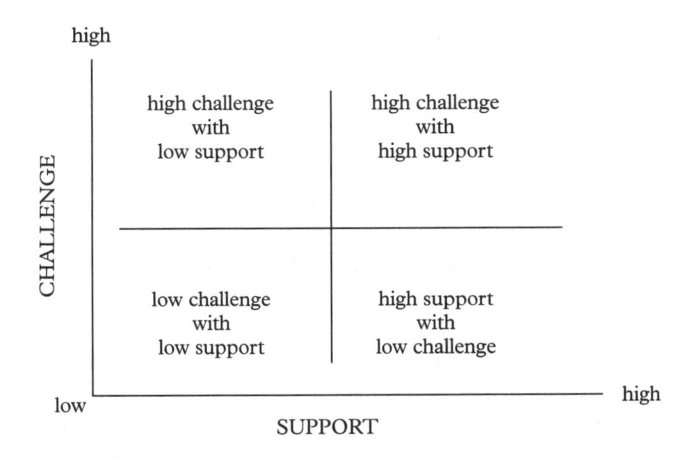

Figure 16.3 Balancing challenge and support

over-confident group. Feelings of complacency could set in and the group's creativity and ability to deal with conflict would diminish. Certainly they will have an easy time. They may accept the way they are and feel good about it. However, there is a danger that in the end they won't appreciate you colluding with them.

If consultants offer clients 'low challenge' and 'low support' there doesn't seem to be a reason to be there. However, it may be possible to recognize what you are doing when the group becomes directionless and begins to feel very sorry for itself. If they are stagnating and avoiding conflict while at the same time being manipulatively aggressive and hiding their feelings perhaps you are offering them too little challenge and too little support!

If consultants offer clients 'high challenge' and 'high support' they are likely to grow as a group, make progress towards their goals and feel a great sense of achievement. They are likely to take risks, be collaborative, deal with all issues especially human process ones, in an open way and solve their problems. But it means that consultants have to stay firmly within the 'I Value Me – I Value You' position.

The Powerful Client-centred Change Agent

Having discussed in this chapter some of the reasons why it is important for consultants to have readily available sources of internal power, it may be as well to remind ourselves at this stage, of what it means to work in a way that is fundamentally client-centred. In short it means working from a solid stance of 'I Value Me – I Value You'. Client-centred consultants then, have a high level of self-esteem and self awareness. They have a set of values and beliefs that start with the assumption that their clients are competent, intelligent and able to solve problems and make decisions for themselves – albeit with some help.

So what does it mean to work in a way that is client-centred? Obviously everyone will have their own list of client-centred values, beliefs and behaviours; you may wish to write your own list before reading ours below. We believe that working in a client-centred way means:

- Balancing a high level of support with a high level of challenge.
- Always starting where the client is – however difficult that is to determine.
- Ensuring that you spend time gaining entry and contracting even when the client sees them as wasting time and really wants to get on to solving the problem.
- Not necessarily always giving the client what they want but working hard to help them assess what they really need.
- Being prepared to speak the unspeakable rather than collude with the client.
- Being prescriptive only as a last resort and then only when the client is really at the end of their tether.
- Accepting that when you can see options for change which the client cannot see, suggesting such options may be more consultant-centred than you are prepared to admit.
- Having the courage to confront the client with inconsistencies between their stated intentions and their behaviour, which may be preventing them from being effective.
- Confronting senior managers in organizations even though you know that there is a risk that your contract may be terminated.
- Helping clients progress around the 'consulting cycle' in order from gaining entry to disengaging without reversing the order – i.e. going from data collection to implementation as many clients want to do.
- Spending as much time as it takes to look at the problem from every angle and to agree with the client what the actual problem is from their point of view.
- Staying with the client's diagnosis and frame of reference when all your instinct and intuition is telling you that the presenting problem is not the real issue.
- Being client-centred rather than problem-centred and involving the client rather than not involving the client.
- Being authentic and genuine about your own thoughts and feelings.
- Not manipulating or playing 'devil's advocate' to get the client to do what you want.
- Trying always to do what you are asking the client to do.
- Trying always to keep in mind what is in the best interests of the client.
- Being able to survive and stay with the client in situations of extreme ambiguity.
- Being very sure of yourself and what you do but very uncertain about expectations and outcomes.
- Always accepting that the client has a choice – to change or not to change.
- Working to ensure that clients retain ownership of their problem and the solution.

- Believing that clients want to solve their own problems and can do so with a little help.
- Working on tasks, systems, procedures and processes and human process issues and how people feel in the client system.

It may be appropriate to end this chapter with the words of an ancient Indian philosopher who was talking about leaders but might just as well have been talking about client-centred consultants. He remarked that people say of a good leader 'we couldn't have done without him'. He went on to say 'of a great leader, when his end is come, his aim fulfilled, they will way "we did it ourselves" '.

Summary

- Consultants and managers who are responsible for facilitating large organizational change are often required to work with very little formal authority. This means that if they are to work in a way that empowers their clients they must be able to tap into significant sources of personal power.
- Being or feeling powerful does not involve having power over other people or being able to control others. Rather it is the feeling that you are able to make choices for yourself and have control over your own decisions and behaviour. When you feel powerful you feel valued, confident, equal, creative and intelligent.
- There are a number of sources of personal power available to all of us:
  - power of information;
  - power of asking questions and listening;
  - power of expertise;
  - power of having options;
  - power to think;
  - power of where you are;
  - power of who you know;
  - power of collaboration with others;
  - power of having rights.
- Our professional or technical expertise is a very important source of personal power. It often gives us a sense of personal identity, it empowers us with options, choices, information and the ability to gather information and make decisions. Under no circumstances should we underestimate the importance of this expertise when we are working as change agents. However, if this is our sole source of personal power, then we may be tempted to use it as a way of undermining and controlling our clients, taking responsibility for their problems and making decisions that are rightfully theirs to make. This can disempower rather than empower clients.
- Our self-image will have a significant impact on our personal power. If you have a positive image and believe that you are a valuable person with something to offer, you are likely to feel more personally powerful than you would with a negative image of yourself. A positive image of yourself does not necessarily mean that you feel superior to others. Indeed the most effective

change agents have a life position in which they feel positive about themselves while at the same time they value and trust their clients.
- It is not enough just to value your clients. It is important to communicate that you value them, and what you value, in the way you work and the words you use. Giving genuine positive strokes is a very effective way of improving the self-image of others. In this sense you are your own most important client. It is important to give yourself affirmations and acknowledgement of your own successes.
- Effective change agents are able to balance the level of support they offer to their clients with the degree to which they are prepared to challenge them.

Exercises

1 Developing Self-Esteem
Write down:

- four things you like about yourself;
- four things you're good at;
- four things you're proud of.

When you have written them down try saying them out loud. Identify the one you have most difficulty with. How easy was it to identify twelve positive attributes about yourself? Would it have been easier to have identified twelve negative attributes?

It is useful to do this activity with a small group of people you trust. Each person writes down their answers to the three questions and then each person in turn should read out what they have written. This should be followed by an in depth discussion of everyone's reactions and feelings about:

- identifying positive attributes;
- writing them down;
- sharing them with others;
- listening to others.

2 Celebrating Your Own Success
Make a list of all the things you have done well and are most pleased with in the last week. Make your list as long as possible. Make a list for work and a list for non-work.

3 Strokes Questionnaire
- Think about your immediate colleagues at work (or a current client group). Think about each person in turn and think about:
  - What kinds of strokes have you been giving them?
  - What kinds of strokes they have been giving you? (Try to be as specific as possible.)
- What kinds of strokes do you feel most comfortable giving?

- What kinds of strokes do you feel most comfortable receiving?
- When you are working with a client group try to tune in to the strokes they give each other. Keep a note, for example, of positive and negative strokes that they give to each other. What do your notes tell you about your client group? You may wish to feed back your notes to the group and give them an opportunity to discuss their significance.

4 Experiencing Strokes

Invite a client group or other work group to spend a few minutes thinking about the strokes they give one another. Also invite them to think about what they have not said to one another but would like to say.

After a few minutes' reflection all members of the group take turns to give each other one or more positive strokes.

- NB **only positive strokes are allowed in this exercise** – they can be conditional or unconditional but they must be positive.
- **Everyone must be included** – do not allow any member to be missed out.

When everyone has had a turn share how everyone feels as a result.

5 Self-Image and Personal Power

Think of a current client system or change assignment you are working on. In the diagram (Figure 16.4) list situations you have experienced when you have found yourself in each of the four sectors.

Also note what happened to move you to a different quadrant.

6 Personal Power

Spend some time thinking about your own sources of personal power. Draw a picture which represents your power.

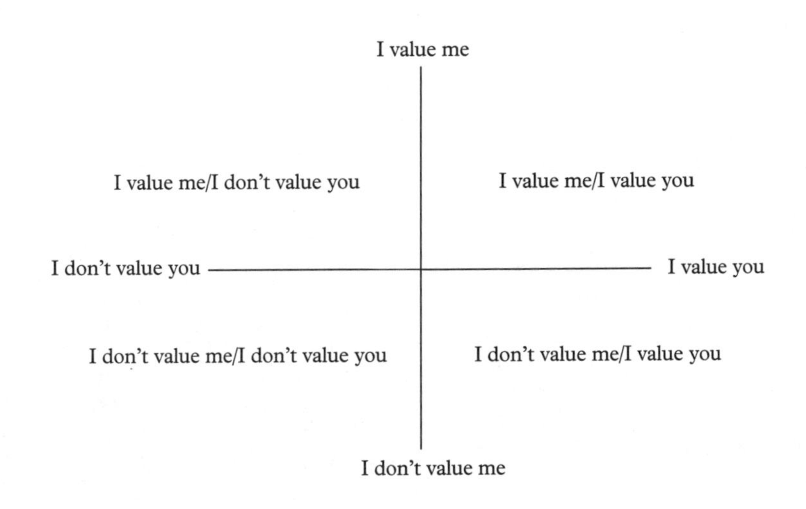

Figure 16.4 Life Positions Model

If you do this as a group each person should describe their own picture and what it symbolizes.

Note

1 Based upon the work of Thomas A. Harris in *I'm OK – You're OK* (1973), Pan Books, and Amy Bjork Harris and Thomas A. Harris in *Staying OK* (1985), Harper and Row.

17 Developing Client-centred Change Agents

This chapter is addressed particularly to those readers who have, as part of their remit, the training and development of client-centred change agents, be they managers, project managers or consultants. Our experience over many years confirms that to help people change from their often prescriptive approach, their reliance upon their power as experts or their need for control, takes a lot of hard work. We have found it useful to have, as the basis for a discussion, a model illustrating all the elements which are necessary if the change to being more client-centred is to be effective and long lasting.

A Holistic Approach

Developing client-centred change agents is rather like building a multi-layered pyramid supported on three pillars as shown in Figure 17.1 – A holistic model of change agent development.

Facilitating Organizational Change

This model is based upon the assumption that client-centred change agents will ultimately be working towards the top of the pyramid to become facilitators of organizational change. If this assumption is correct then we believe they will need some understanding of what is involved, some knowledge of how organizations work, how culture can facilitate or hinder organizational change, some ideas about what issues they might face and the difficulties faced by individuals and organizations trying to learn new attitudes, behaviour and skills.

Using a Range of Intervention Styles

It is our experience that most consultants and certainly most managers see themselves as problem-solvers and experts in a particular field. This leads to many of them being very prescriptive – telling other people what to do to solve their problems. To effect any significant change towards being client-centred requires a reappraisal of this attitude and the adoption of a wider range of approaches including the use of acceptant, catalytic and confrontational styles.

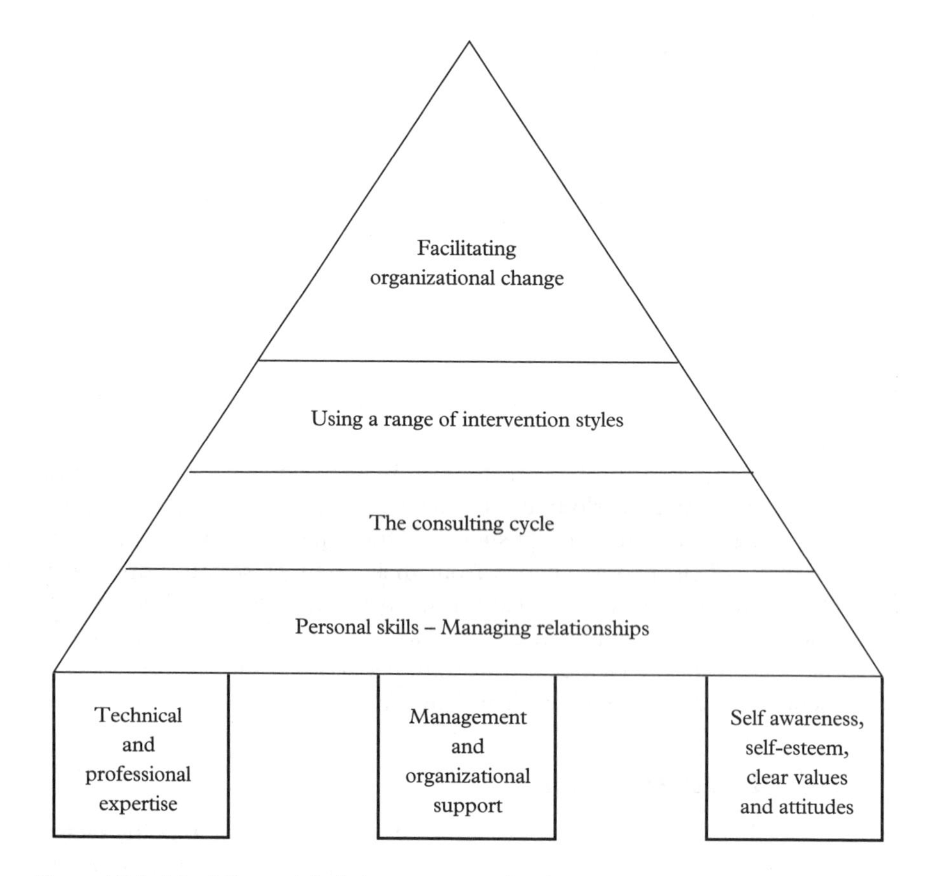

Figure 17.1 A holistic model of change agent development

The Consulting Cycle

At the next level down it is important that anyone trying to intervene in any way with clients has a plan of campaign and a map to guide them through their journey. They often have to deal with their own and their clients' feelings, with extremes of ambiguity and without control of the situation. We believe that an understanding and facility with the consulting cycle and an ability to identify where you are within it, will provide some security in otherwise confusing situations.

Managing Relationships

There seems little doubt that people only trust people they know well and that to achieve a satisfactory level of trust between client and consultant is often quite difficult. Without a fairly high level of trust the flow of information about the issue being worked on is likely to be rather low. This means that the contracting process is unsatisfactory from both points of view. To achieve a high level of openness and trust the consultant has to have a high level of interpersonal skills and ability to manage relationship within the whole client system. For many of us this is a tall order. While accepting that we can never be perfect and that the relationship between two people depends upon them both, we can nevertheless work hard to be as good as we can. How effective we are at using the consulting styles and skills depends to a large extent on how effective we are at managing relationships with our clients.

What Supports the Pyramid

Technical and Professional Expertise It is assumed that anyone aspiring to be an agent of change in an organization has a sufficiently high level of technical and professional expertise. The problem is that it is very tempting to rely on this expertise to help clients by taking ownership of both the problem and the solution. Very often, to change from this apparently helpful, prescriptive approach, requires considerable effort and acceptance that the risks involved as described in Chapter 7 – The Prescriptive Styles, are too great and not in the long-term interests of the client. It also requires acceptance of the fact that what is helpful is described by the client and not the consultant.

Self-Awareness and Self-Esteem For us this means always trying to work from a stance of feeling good about yourself while at the same time feeling good about your client. In other words working from I'm OK – You're OK. We believe that in many situations consultants are hired on the basis of the fit between their values and attitudes and those of their potential clients. It follows that when embarking on any change initiative you have to be clear about what you are setting out to do and why. What view you have of the clients – are you treating them as equals or are they getting the impression that in some way you despise them or blame them for their present problems? Do you try to hide your mistakes or imperfections from the client or are you open enough to admit that you are not perfect? Are you prepared to be open about your feelings and to help your clients express theirs? How aware are you of what is going on inside your clients as individuals and groups? These and many other issues are contained in this leg supporting the pyramid.

Management and Organizational Support Without this the whole structure becomes unstable and the likelihood of new behaviour back at work is problematic. Changes of the magnitude which are required to move from being a prescriptive expert to becoming a client-centred consultant are often quite large and are not achieved without enormous effort and determination and above all commitment. Often the culture to which trainees return is not conducive to change, their colleagues may not want them to change and their clients are also often in for a shock. So it is important for trainees and their managers to come to some agreement about what support is needed, what will be offered and what it will amount to in concrete, behavioural terms.

How Might the Training be Organized?

However well you, or someone else, do your actual training, the likelihood of it carrying over into the workplace is remote unless you get the diagnosis right and arrange for follow-up support. These aspects of training have been well researched and documented by Dr J. A. G. Jones (1985) of the Industrial Training Service Ltd. He calls these aspects of the training cycle:

Getting it right – making a good diagnosis
Doing it well – delivering effective training
Making it stick – ensuring carry-over into work.

In our experience this analysis makes good sense for all trainers and trainees alike. It is even more important when trying to develop consulting skills for the following reasons:

- The change from trainees' normal way of working to being client-centred is often dramatic and challenging.
- Such change really needs to be embedded in and integrated with organizational change. Unless there is an obvious organizational need then the individual trainee is unlikely to be helped to sustain the change.
- Change agents have to be helped to learn for themselves rather than be taught. It follows that such experiential learning has to be continued after any off-job training so that the learning is continuous.
- Any change in personal style is likely to have an impact on the clients with whom the change agent interacts. This will probably mean that there is some pressure to stay the same. They have to be confident enough to keep going in the face of such pressure.
- Unless the culture of the department or organization changes and adopts the new way of working for everyone, then the returning trainee is likely to find it difficult to sustain the new ways of operating.

Getting it Right

It seems to us that making a good diagnosis is an aspect of training and development that is often ignored or treated rather casually; or the manager's diagnosis and suggested solution is agreed without challenge. Before anyone can be trained you need to know what deficiencies or difficulties are recognized in the department or the individuals, and how the training will help. So it is with consultants. It is therefore very important for the training and development people to be very clear and firm about their diagnosis.

When doing the diagnosis it is important to ensure that you identify the complete client system or as much of it as is within your reach. This could be one individual person in need of specific consulting skills. However, it is unlikely that this individual works alone and it will be difficult for him or her to implement the learning if it is alien to the existing departmental culture.

It is probably more effective, therefore, to look at how the whole department works with its clients at present and how this might change to be more client-centred. The whole department is now your client system and you will have to work with all the staff and the manager to effect any lasting change. Even this may be too narrow a definition of the client system and you may have to look at other consulting departments within the organization. The reason we say this is that most consulting departments we encounter need help to work effectively together for the overall good of the organization. They are often very busy working from their own perspective without regard for all the other such departments who are doing the same.

Single issue initiatives

In our experience, most consulting assignments deal with what we call single issues. Generally, these are related to the main task of the client department, tend to ignore systems and procedures and human process issues, and are often dealt with by a technical specialist without regard for what other change initiatives are going on within the department.

While such technical issues are usually very important for solving the immediate, presenting problem they have serious drawbacks in terms of effectiveness. The model of organization which appeals to us is illustrated in Chapter 3. This systems models remains in balance as long as it is not interfered with. However, if even one of the facets is disturbed, by being worked on by a consultant for instance, then the whole model is affected. So if say the performance improvement department changes people's tasks and ways of working, then there is likely to be a significant impact on all the other facets. If the personnel department puts in a system of payment by results to reward individual effort, then there is likely to be an impact on everything else in the system. However hard the development department works to encourage teamwork it will fail unless both these initiatives are considered together rather than separately. Most large organizations employ a variety of consultants with different specialisms. Invariably they work from different departments and rarely integrate their work.

This results in considerable resentment from line managers who have a variety of specialists all competing for their time and physical resources. These specialists can come from anywhere within the organization and range from audit and inspection through health and safety to training and development and it is left to the manager to co-ordinate all the different ways in which they are trying to help.

It seems to us that an important role for the training and development function is to help senior managers address these issues, especially when discussing the training and development of internal change agents. Some of the questions which need to be asked within this context are:

- How can we ensure that the consulting departments don't leave it to the line manager to co-ordinate their work?
- How can we ensure that all internal consultants direct their attention to organizational and human processes in addition to their client's task?

- How can we ensure that they collaborate across departmental boundaries rather than seeing themselves in competition?
- How can we get them to take a global view of the organization rather than a narrow departmental view?

When you ask such questions, you will probably find yourself confronting all sorts of power/authority issues within the organization and you may need help. Nevertheless, we believe that such questions have to be asked and the issues have to be tackled if the whole-organization approach is to bring increased effectiveness and continuous improvement.

We are not necessarily advocating the return of the organization development (OD) department. But it does seem to us that unless the single issues initiative problems are addressed then there is likely to be little real, lasting change within the consulting departments and the organization.

Assessing the need

It is important to assess the need from both organizational and individual points of view and from all angles. So before you draw up a detailed contract you will need to collect information about:

- how the manager sees the need;
- how the change agents see the need;
- how their clients see the need.

You may also find it useful to get all three parties together to increase the manager's awareness and understanding of the real problems. In our experience, very few consulting departments have the courage to ask their clients what they think of the way consultants work.

You may also think it is important to establish whether or not there are genuine motivations for change, along the lines of Checklist 8.5, and try to assess how much commitment there is.

Contracting

Once you have established the need you can probably move into contracting with the client system. It is traditional in most training situations for the line manager – the owner of the problem – to give up all responsibility for the training and its outcome to the trainer. So the contract looks like the illustration in Figure 17.2.

The contracts between manager and trainee and between manager and trainer are either very weak *secondary* contracts or don't exist at all, while the contract between trainer and trainec is a very strong *primary* one. This has serious implications for all parties. The manager is able to abdicate and leave everything to the trainer. It also means that you are responsible for teaching and if the trainee doesn't perform better back at work you, the trainer, get the blame. The trainees can also blame you for not teaching them properly.

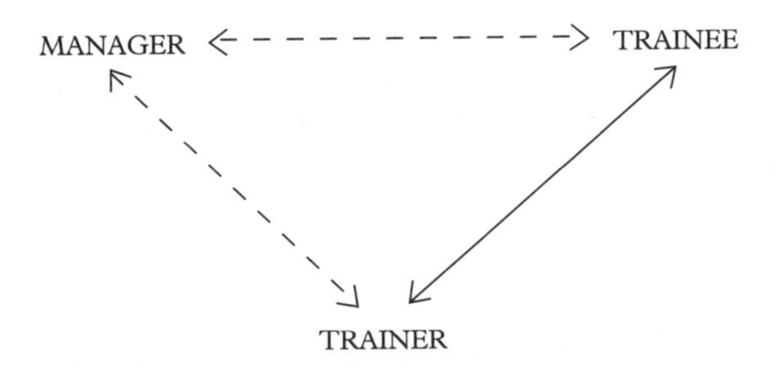

Figure 17.2 A training contract in which the manager has little responsibility

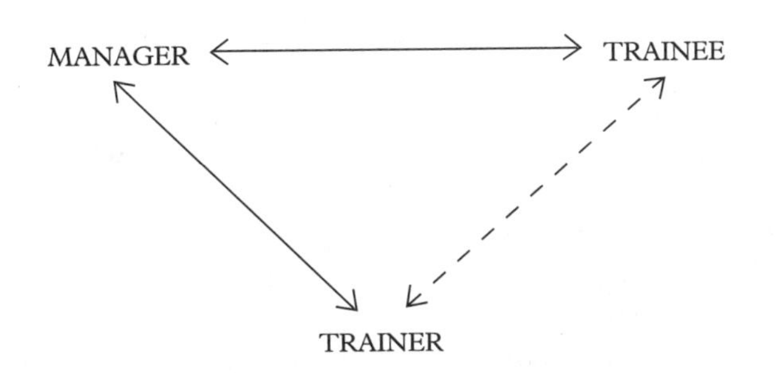

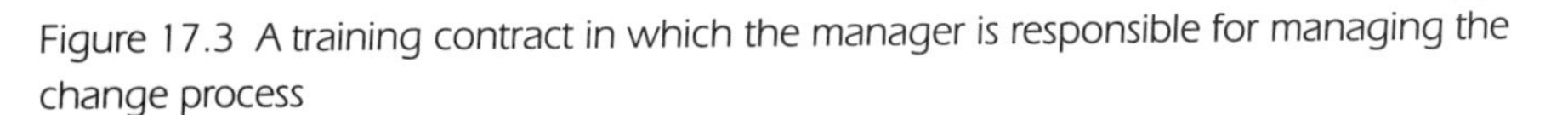
Figure 17.3 A training contract in which the manager is responsible for managing the change process

When working with a manager of a consulting department to help him or her develop the department, it is worth investing a lot of time and energy in negotiating a very strong primary contract with that manager. This should spell out the manager's responsibility for managing the change process. You may also need to help the manager agree a similar strong primary contract with the trainees. This will include the manager's expectations and the support to be offered to assist the changes, and should spell out the responsibility of the trainee for making them happen.

A better contract is shown in Figure 17.3. Now the *primary* contracts are between manager and trainee and between manager and trainer and are very strong. That between trainer and trainee is *secondary* and temporary in nature.

This means that the manager retains ownership of the change which the training is helping to bring about. The primary contract between manager and trainer ensures that it is clearly understood and agreed that the trainer's job is to help the manager rather than to take over the problem. The secondary, temporary contract between trainer and trainee means that there is no permanency in the relationship and the trainer is not there to take over the manager's authority and responsibility. Neither is a dependency relationship thought to be in the long-term interests of the client. Above all, the manager retains ownership of the diagnosis, can be encouraged to take an interest in how the training is carried out and is also committed to providing the necessary support to ensure that the training is carried over into work. Whether or not the manager actually provides the support is not your problem, although you may find it advantageous to offer your help.

Making it Stick

Making it stick is the process of ensuring that the new learning is carried over into work. At first glance this would seem to fit logically after any formal training. However, in our view, attention should be given to it before the training begins. The essential steps are:

- Helping the manager make decisions about the most effective training format options.
- Helping the manager to contract with the trainees, to agree learning objectives and to indicate an expectation that the trainees will return with an action plan for continuous improvement.
- Helping the trainees to approach the training event in the best possible frame of mind and providing any pre-work assignment.
- Structuring the training event in a way that allows the maximum amount of time for practice, so that trainees internalize the learning before returning to work.

Choice of training option

We have assumed that consulting training is likely to involve some form of off-job event. In the chart that follows, we have highlighted some of the advantages and disadvantages we see for the various options.

Option	*Advantages*	*Disadvantages*
Single participant on an external event	Allows freedom on the programme	On their own back at work
	Uses cross-company similarities and differences	Takes a long time to get significant numbers working along the same lines
Pairs of participants from same department or organization on external events	Possibility of support back at work	Slightly restricts personal freedom on the programme
	Uses cross-company similarities and differences	Takes a long time to get significant numbers working along the same lines

In-house programmes for single departments	High level of support for implementation back at work Significant numbers can be trained at a time Can confront any insularity which may exist Useful team-building bonus	May restrict personal freedom on the programme especially if relationships are not all that good Doesn't benefit from cross-company contact May confirm insularity which exists
In-house programmes for whole organizations	High level of support for implementation back at work Can confront cross-department issues Useful to enhance organization development Allows addressing of consultancy coordination issues Significant numbers can be trained at once	Some restriction of personal freedom on the programme Doesn't benefit from cross-company contact May confirm cross-departmental boundaries and antagonisms

It is also possible to train a team of consultants with their team leader either in-house or externally. This can often be useful in encouraging agreement over operating styles and enhancing team working.

We believe that when an organization has to embark on difficult cultural change it will generally need external help. Internal consultants who are locked into the existing culture are likely to find it hard to challenge without outside support.

Follow-up

Skill loss starts from the very moment the trainees leave the training environment. It is essential then that trainees go back to work with a high degree of commitment to changing the way they work with clients and begin to operate in the new way immediately. Before the end of the training event you will therefore need to encourage trainees to develop a detailed action plan which includes an assessment of the factors that will help or hinder the implementation and what can be done about them. It is similarly very important that there is adequate support back at work in terms of a manager who understands the need for changed behaviour, colleagues who will not laugh at attempts to change and clients who appreciate the new ways of working.

The next part of the follow-up must surely be to help the manager arrange for the necessary support. You may have to facilitate the negotiation between the manager and the trainees while ensuring that they all see it as their responsibility, not yours. If you go further than this and agree to arrange meetings or regular clinics you may find yourself doing what the manager should be doing. If you can help the manager to run the meetings or review sessions then that seems to us to be legitimate consultancy work for trainers. If you are an experienced consultant you could also offer supervision in the form of opportunities for people to talk over their experiences while trying to use their new skills.

Doing it Well

We have left the delivery of effective training – doing it well – until last because, in our experience, that is the easy bit. As we have said already, you need to get the diagnosis right before you start to involve both the potential participants and their manager. Participants who are well briefed about why they are being trained and what is expected of them on their return, and who understand their responsibility for making it happen, are likely to be enthusiastic about the training before they start. Having said that, the training still has to be done well or the trainees' commitment is likely to be fairly low and their involvement minimal.

As far as possible, we adhere to the following principles when training consultants.

1 We prepare them as well as we can. We try to ensure that everyone understands exactly what is expected of them by giving them a comprehensive brochure describing the experience and a personal briefing at which they can clear up any dilemmas or concerns.

2 We try to ensure that as much of the theory as possible is dealt with before the off-job event. This means that people are able to have as much practical, hands-on experience as they can get during the programme.

3 We follow the principles established by David Kolb in his work on learning styles and experiential learning, as explained in Chapters 1 and 11. We believe that most people learn best what they experience for themselves but that they need to look back at the experience critically, reflect upon it, abstract useful insights from it and put the results to work.

4 We try to ensure that people learn at three levels:

   - a cognitive or knowledge level;
   - a doing or behavioural level; and
   - an affective or feelings level.

   Virtually every problem effecting a change in life is accompanied by some form of emotional response. Changing one's attitude and learning to do things differently usually involve considerable unlearning and are likely to invoke a similar response. Working through the 'feelings' content of any difficulty is an essential prerequisite to problem solving. So we try to ensure that participants:

- Acquire new knowledge and ideas about consulting skills, styles and processes.
- Practise the behaviour to put the ideas into action and experience how it feels to use these skills as a consultant and as a client.

5 We always address all three aspects of our organizational life model: *task, systems, procedures and processes* and *human process*. This means that whenever a group runs into difficulties with its task, members are encouraged not just to put more effort or resources into it but to look for other reasons why they are having problems. The temptation to do more of the same; work harder, longer and quicker is overwhelming. In our experience the real problems or focal issues are more often than not in the human process and this is revelatory for most groups.

6 We encourage the acceptance of the event as real. In other words, it is different from their normal environment and way of working but no less real for that. The issues raised between people are real ones, the fears are real and the ways of operating during the event are likely to be similar to the ways participants operate at work. Staying with what is happening 'here and now' provides very important learning opportunities.

7 We try to get participants to accept that the off-job event is a consulting assignment rather than a standard training course. We then follow our own consulting cycle from initial contact to disengagement while using the skills and intervention styles with the group. To achieve this for all participants, the framework and timetable have to be flexible enough to ensure that everyone's needs are met as far as possible in exactly the same way as we would expect them to operate back at work.

As we highlighted in Chapter 1 we believe that consultants, especially those trying to operate in a client-centred way, need:

- competence in the process of consulting;
- a high level of self-awareness;
- competence in dealing with their own feelings and those of their clients;
- a belief that clients have the ability to solve their own problems with a little help;
- a thorough understanding of the ways in which clients are likely to behave as individuals and in groups;
- a wide range of professional and interpersonal skills;
- sufficient flexibility of style to deal with a wide variety of clients and situations;
- a real understanding of the helping process within the context of their professional discipline.

We believe that the training and the follow-up should attempt to involve as many of these aspects of behaviour as possible.

Change agents often have to work in a large range of situations and therefore need to be able to adopt many different styles. During training we offer opportunities to practise these styles, understand the conditions under which each is likely to be appropriate and develop clear ideas about the risks involved for both client and consultant.

Where do we start?

As in any consulting assignment we start by dealing with the problems and difficulties in making initial contact and gaining entry with the client group which has just assembled.

This is followed by contracting – finding out what everyone wants as individuals, what are the expectations of the seminar consultants by the group and vice versa. Intervention styles are covered in the following way:

Stage 1 Participants share their pre-work to clarify their understanding of the style and agree ways of operating when using it to help a client.

Stage 2 Each person has an opportunity to practise the style with another participant as a client. Then then receive feedback on the effectiveness of the intervention.

Participants are encouraged to present real, current and live issues. We do not use role plays as the element of realism introduced by real problems is extremely helpful to the learning of both client and consultant.

Stage 3 A period of individual reflection to enable people to record their insights from the practices.

Stage 4 Participants come together with the seminar consultants to clear up any outstanding concerns or difficulties and look at opportunities for using the style at work.

Dealing with these concerns or difficulties in a larger group provides opportunities for everyone – not only the seminar consultants – to be consultants to each other, to work with another consultant and get feedback on their performance.

Collecting data

Throughout the whole event participants are helped with their data collection from individuals and groups, using their observation skills and improving their listening. They are also helped to understand and use some of the data-collection and feedback instruments illustrated in Chapter 10. This data is constantly fed back to the participants and used to effect improvements during the event.

Planning for improvement

Towards the end of the seminar participants receive feedback from their colleagues on their consulting skills as they have experienced them during the seminar. From this and their own assessment they are able to develop an action plan to discuss with their manager, in order to effect a continuous improvement back at work.

Implementation

Towards the end of the seminar participants have two opportunities to carry out complete consultations during which they work through all the phases of the consulting cycle. In the first of these each participant has an opportunity to be a consultant to a small group, using a theory or model to help the group make sense of the way they have operated throughout the seminar and decide how they might be more effective.

In the second opportunity everyone is a consultant to a colleague, using either a significant work-related problem which is causing concern or working on the difficulties that might be encountered back at work while trying to implement what has been learned.

In all situations participants are free to make a contract with their client and then apply the strategy and intervention styles that seem most appropriate in helping the client to solve his or her problems.

Disengagement

As has been said earlier in this book, disengagement is important for both client and consultant and if, during the assignment, you have built a strong relationship it can sometimes be very difficult. Saying 'goodbye' is often very hard. We try to make it as painless as possible and see it as a celebration, an opportunity to share commitment to action, thank people for their help and arrange possible follow-up.

It is also a good opportunity to remain within your own model and ask for feedback on your performance. If you have managed to establish a culture which has provided constant, ongoing feedback you shouldn't get any surprises. Nevertheless, sometimes we do!

> Our final plea to you as a training and development consultant is this: If you are there to help other consultants become more client-centred you will have to work that way with them yourself. Whether you are doing the diagnosis, delivering the training, facilitating its transfer back to work or all three, stay firmly client-centred. They may not like it, they may try to pressurize you out of it, but it will work. You will leave the problem where it belongs – with the clients – while you work hard to help them solve it.

And finally, it seems appropriate to end this book by recounting a conversation we were party to several years ago. It concerned a young operational research officer who was about to leave the department to work in personnel. She was discussing the move with her boss who was saying what a valuable member of the department she had been and how much she would be missed. The young OR officer listened and said it was nice to be appreciated but, to be honest, the department was full of people who were much more qualified, more technically competent and more experienced than she was. Maybe, she suggested, the department would get along without her. 'Yes', replied the manager, 'it's true that I have lots of technically competent and well-qualified people, but what I haven't got is many like you whom clients ask back into their departments time and time again'.

We hope that in some way the ideas in this book will help you to be the kind of consultant whom clients welcome into their departments not just a second time, but over and over again.

Summary

- When developing client-centred change agents it is important to take a holistic approach. Client-centred change agents need:
  - an understanding of the issues involved in organizational change initiatives;
  - ability to manage the consultant client relationship using the consulting cycle;
  - a facility with all four consulting skills;
  - a range of interpersonal skills;
  - a high level of self awareness and self-esteem;
  - competence in their technical or professional discipline;
  - a commitment from their organization and management team to the principles of client-centredness.
- When working with consulting departments or management teams to help their people to work in different ways always remember to incorporate all three phases of training:
  - *Getting it right* – making a good diagnosis;
  - *Doing it well* – delivering effective training;
  - *Making it stick* – ensuring carry over back to work.
- When contracting with the manager of the consulting department it is important that he or she retains responsibility for the overall project.

  The trainer's primary contract is with the manager rather than members of the department. The trainer will be responsible for helping the manager agree a contract with group members about how they should work in future, how the training will help and how individuals and groups will be supported and helped to work in a client-centred way in the future.
- Training people to acquire client-centred skills requires:
  - preparation and a clear briefing beforehand;
  - as much practical hands-on experience as possible;

- the application of Kolb's learning cycle;
- attention to all three domains of learning – the knowledge level; the behavioural level; the feeling level;
- attention given to developing skills for dealing with human process issues;
- the creation of opportunities to practise consulting skills with real clients and real client groups;
- that the training event is managed as a real consulting assignment rather than a traditional course. This means starting with building trust and developing relationships and working through to disengagement.

Bibliography

Adair, J. (1979) *Action-centred Leadership*, Gower Publishing Ltd.

Bennis, W. (1989) *Why Leaders Can't Lead*, Jossey-Bass, San Francisco

Bennis, W. and B. Nanus (1985) *Leaders – The Strategies for Taking Charge*, Harper and Row, New York

Blake, R. R. and J. S. Mouton (1983) *Consultation: A Handbook for Individual and Organization Development*, Addison-Wesley

Block, P. (1983) *Flawless Consulting, Guide for Getting Your Expertise Used*, Learning Concepts, Austin, Texas

Block, P. (1993) *Stewardship*, Berrett-Koehler Publishers, San Francisco

Block, P. (1987) *The Empowered Manager*, Jossey-Bass, San Francisco

Covey, S. R. (1990) *Principle-centred Leadership*, Summit Books, New York

Crum, T. T. (1989) *The Magic of Conflict: Turning a Life of Work into a Work of Art*. Simon & Schuster Inc., New York

Harris, A. B. and T. A. Harris (1985) *Staying OK*, Harper and Row, New York

Harris, T. A. (1973) *I'm OK – You're OK*, Pan Books, London

Honey, P. and A. Mumford (1986) *Manual of Learning Styles*, Peter Honey, Maidenhead

Jones, J. A. G. (1985) Training Intervention Strategies, *Training and Development*, February

Kilmann, R. H. (1984) *Beyond the Quick Fix; Managing Five Tracks to Organizational Success*, Jossey-Bass, San Francisco

Kilmann, R. H. (1989) *Managing Beyond the Quick Fix; A Completely Integrated Program for Creating and Maintaining Organizational Success*, Jossey-Bass, San Francisco

Kolb, D. A. (1985) *Learning Style Inventory*, McBer & Co., Boston

Lewin, K. (1951) *Field Theory in Social Science*, Harper and Row, New York

Maslow, A. H. (1954) *Motivation and Personality*, Harper and Row

McGregor, D. (1960) *The Human Side of Enterprise*, McGraw-Hill, New York

Phillips, K. and P. Shaw (1989) *A Consultancy Approach for Trainers*, Gower Publishing Co., Aldershot

Revans, R. W. (1980) *Action Learning – New Techniques for Managers*, Blond and Briggs, London

Rogers, C. and B. Stevens (1973) *Person to Person*, Souvenir Press Ltd., London

Sargent, P. B. (1979) *A Decision Tree Approach to Case Study Solution*, NEBSM

Stewart, A. M. (1994) *Empowering People*, Pitman Publishing

Stone, B. (1997) *Confronting Company Politics*, Macmillan Press Ltd., Basingstoke

Ward, W. (1994) *Why Your Corporate Culture Change Isn't Working . . . And What to Do About It*, Gower Publishing, Aldershot

Zigarmi, P., K. Blanchard and D. Zigarmi (1988) *Situational Leadership II; Facilitator's Guide*, Blanchard Training and Development Inc.

Index